SOCIETY AS EDUCATOR
IN AN AGE OF TRANSITION

SOCIETY AS EDUCATOR IN AN AGE OF TRANSITION

Eighty-sixth Yearbook of the
National Society for the Study of Education

PART II

By

THE YEARBOOK COMMITTEE
and
ASSOCIATED CONTRIBUTORS

Edited by

KENNETH D. BENNE AND STEVEN TOZER

Editor for the Society

KENNETH J. REHAGE

19 NSSE 87

Distributed by THE UNIVERSITY OF CHICAGO PRESS ● CHICAGO, ILLINOIS

96291

The National Society for the Study of Education

Founded in 1901 as successor to the National Herbart Society, the National Society for the Study of Education has provided a means by which the results of serious study of educational issues could become a basis for informed discussion of those issues. The Society's two-volume yearbooks, now in their eighty-sixth year of publication, reflect the thoughtful attention given to a wide range of educational problems during those years. In 1971 the Society inaugurated a series of substantial publications on Contemporary Educational Issues to supplement the yearbooks. Each year the Society's publications contain contributions to the literature of education from more than a hundred scholars and practitioners who are doing significant work in their respective fields.

An elected Board of Directors selects the subjects with which volumes in the yearbook series are to deal and appoints committees to oversee the preparation of manuscripts. A special committee created by the Board performs similar functions for the series on Contemporary Educational Issues.

The Society's publications are distributed each year without charge to members in the United States, Canada, and elsewhere throughout the world. The Society welcomes as members all individuals who desire to receive its publications. Information about current dues may be found in the back pages of this volume.

This volume, *Society as Educator in an Age of Transition*, is Part II of the Eighty-sixth Yearbook of the Society. Part I, which is published at the same time, is entitled *The Ecology of School Renewal*.

A listing of the Society's publications still available for purchase may be found in the back pages of this volume.

Library of Congress Catalog Number: 86-062431
ISSN: 0077-5762

Published 1987 by
THE NATIONAL SOCIETY FOR THE STUDY OF EDUCATION

5835 Kimbark Avenue, Chicago, Illinois 60637
© 1987 by the National Society for the Study of Education

First Printing, 7,000 Copies

Printed in the United States of America

Editors' Preface

"Schools are, indeed, one important method of the transmission which forms the dispositions of the immature; but it is only one means, and, compared with other agencies, a relatively superficial means. Only as we have grasped the necessity of more fundamental and persistent modes of tuition can we make sure of placing the scholastic methods in their true context."

John Dewey

Though this volume is quite distinctive in its scope and purpose, it is by no means the first yearbook of the National Society for the Study of Education to analyze one or more aspects of the interrelations between education and society.

Since the end of World War II, the NSSE has issued four yearbooks that attempt such analyses. To compare and contrast the present volume with its predecessors will help to clarify and illuminate the distinctive character of the 1987 volume.

The most obvious difference is grounded in the unprecedented changes in American and world cultures during the busy quarter century since the publication of the most recent yearbook to focus explicitly on school and society. The nuclear arms race has accelerated and detente between the USSR and the USA has failed. Liberation movements have thrust subjugated groups (racial or religious minorities, social classes, women, homosexuals, or have-not nations or peoples) into postures of active, often hostile, and sometimes successful protest. Widespread belief in the beneficent powers of science and technology and in the inevitable "progress" that these spawn to rescue us from the pitfalls of our greed and stupidity has dwindled drastically, and rightly so. Alternative arrangements for child-rearing are becoming increasingly common as the two-parent family has become less predominant. Each chapter of this volume will have more to say about the present need for fresh analysis of the interrelations between education and society in the new historical era into which we, educators and others, have blundered, largely unaware of its staggering novelty.

But the differences between this and previous yearbooks have additional bases. Previous volumes have focused on the school as a distinctive institution, whether on its internal functions or on its structure and external relations. And "the school" has been treated as virtually synonymous with education, whatever occasional disclaimers have been stated. We take seriously Dewey's comment in *The Social Frontier* (May 1937) that "school education is but one educational agency out of many, and at the best is in some respects a minor educational force." *The present volume focuses on educative functions that schools share with other institutions of society and culture in the socialization and enculturation of persons.* It seeks to illuminate the socialization effects of changing institutions, ways of life and thought, and artifacts, whether favorable or inimical to human survival and welfare, whether consistent or inconsistent with the patterns of socialization widely assumed as good for human beings and promoted by the schools. It also points to needs for new and different patterns of socialization demanded by novel social and cultural conditions in a democratic society—needs that are not now being well met in schools and out. The identification and propagation of some of these needed patterns might well be undertaken by schools and other educational institutions, and propagation of now irrelevant and inimical patterns discarded or meliorated.

This yearbook, unlike most of its predecessors, assesses the bearings of a number of aspects of current society on broad educational purposes and policies. In this respect, it invites special comparison with the Sixtieth Yearbook (1961), which also took a broad view of current society under the title of *Social Forces Influencing American Education.* As already noted, one might well have changed "education" to "schooling" in the title and context of the 1961 volume, an equivalence which the present volume seeks to avoid.

Another difference is the emphasis of the earlier volume upon the separate academic disciplines through which researches into society and culture are most often conducted. The purpose of that volume was to provide a series of analyses of contemporary American schooling and society, each guided by the conceptual framework and favored methodology of a different social science discipline. In the words of Ralph Tyler, who was the chairman of the Sixtieth Yearbook Committee, "This is what the yearbook provides: a series of eight chapters, each analyzing the contemporary situation of American education by use of a different social-science discipline, thus giving the reader eight views of the scene through eight different lenses." The hope apparently was that each reader would make his or her own synthesis of the eight specialized views and find ways to use this synthesis in diagnosing and planning for his or her own school situation.

The present volume also uses specialist resources. But each specialist has been asked to identify and clarify questions that require public choice and decision concerning socialization and resocialization (education and reeducation) as they arise out of an aspect of contemporary society he or she knows particularly well. Such policy questions do not belong to any particular discipline. Rather they are the concern of "Everyman"—each person—particularly in a democracy, and require a cross-disciplinary solution. Each person requires an understanding of important public questions presented by a changing society and the knowledge, motivation, and skill to participate in finding and confirming viable answers to these questions. Or so we believe.

This cross-disciplinary approach stands consciously in a tradition initiated by Harold Rugg, George S. Counts, William Heard Kilpatrick, and others at Teachers College, Columbia University in the 1930s. These men, together with scholars from a variety of disciplines, sought to develop a critical understanding of social institutions, processes, and ideals to engage teachers, administrators, and other educators in social inquiry and criticism. Their work led directly to the first social foundations programs in institutions of higher learning in this country and to the publication of the first graduate level text, *Readings in the Foundations of Education*. Counts had earlier published a study for the Commission on the Social Studies, *The Social Foundations of Education*. In this comprehensive volume, he noted that his work revealed "no new data" to social scientists, but rather assembled significant social research and analysis for a particular purpose. Counts wrote of his volume:

Everything has been subordinated to the single practical aim of illuminating the educational problem in its larger social relationships. For refusing to prosecute new investigations no apology is offered. The need everywhere today, as former Justice Oliver Wendell Holmes once remarked, is "less inquiry into the abstruse and more thought about the obvious." Certainly in the field of education this is the counsel of wisdom.

The material presented in this volume continues in the direction that Counts indicated. This yearbook is intended to illuminate educational problems in their larger social relationships, in part by providing an occasion for more thought about those dimensions of society which we already recognize, however dimly.

It has become a commonplace that socialization is not complete with the coming of persons to chronological majority in a changing society. Resocialization is often required by persons of all ages. This is most widely and clearly recognized in the area of vocations where the obsolescence of old careers, due largely to altered technology, demands learning of new ways of making a living by adults of various ages. But the demands for resocialization are equally severe in person's lives as citizens and as individual persons in their interpersonal and cosmic relationships—whether in family life, recreation, or worship. Meeting the requirements for vocational resocialization is now less than systematically accomplished by schools and various training programs under other auspices. The nonvocational demands for resocialization are left to the vagaries, ideologically or economically stimulated, of sects, cults, or mass media. This volume does not limit itself, as previous yearbooks have done, to an emphasis on schooling of youngsters but gives attention to the needs for resocialization of adults and oldsters as well.

We are quite certain that we have not chosen for analysis all the important aspects of society that now generate novel policy questions which challenge present and traditional modes of education, in the broad sense of socialization and resocialization. We have not, for example, systematically examined the current status of religious life in our society, although two chapters briefly discuss the rising influence of religion in politics. Nor have we systematically treated the institutionalization of crime and criminality in contemporary life, a development pregnant with social and educational significance. While omissions of some issues must necessarily occur, other issues arise repeatedly in different treatments. Democratic values, for example, are discussed in several economic, social, and political contexts in the volume. Similarly, the changing nature of work life arises in different treatments. We have welcomed such overlaps, for they are in part the tissue that holds together cross-disciplinary treatments of different but related topics. While treatments overlap, they do not always agree, for each author writes from his or her own perspective.

We make no apologies for those features of society we have chosen as representative of the social knowledge and understanding that should be part of the equipment of every contemporary educator. We have included treatments of major social, political, and economic dimensions of contemporary life, including the complex and controverted meanings of the democratic concept; the character and control of the accelerating social and economic effects of high technology; the problems of converting the heterogeneity of national and world populations into a democratic pluralism; changing patterns of man-woman roles and relationships and of family life; the character and distribution of power in contemporary society; and changing hopes and expectations for schools on the part of American adults, especially parents. And, finally, one chapter is devoted to the question, what is the meaning of all of these conditions of life for today's education? The author of this chapter, like the others, makes no attempt to speak for others, but to speak from his own perspective and area of expertise.

How we learn or fail to learn to answer the unsolved questions about education and reeducation generated by these and related social and cultural conditions has much to do with whether or not mankind has a future on earth.

KENNETH D. BENNE
STEVEN TOZER

Acknowledgments

This volume began with Harry S. Broudy, who initiated discussion of the need for a yearbook on the social foundations of education during his recent tenure on the Board of Directors of the National Society for the Study of Education. We are grateful to the NSSE Board for its support of the idea. The editorial committee provided us with important guidance in the planning of the yearbook. The Educational Policy Studies Department of the University of Illinois at Champaign-Urbana has made its resources available to us throughout the writing of the book. Many others have contributed to the conception and execution of the yearbook. We would like to make special mention of the help given us by Ralph Page, Paul Blackwood, and Marcia May.

Finally, Kenneth J. Rehage has been a consistent source of sound advice for the editors and the authors of the volume. We thank him for his energy, insight, and thoroughness.

KENNETH D. BENNE
STEVEN TOZER

The contributors to this volume have performed an important service by directing attention to significant developments in contemporary society that can have profound implications for education. Writing from the perspective of their respective disciplines, the authors focus attention upon issues that deserve the thoughtful consideration of all educators, regardless of their areas of specialization, who reflect seriously and continuously upon the complex relationships between school and society.

The National Society for the Study of Education is greatly indebted to the committee that planned this yearbook, to the several authors who have responded so thoughtfully to the invitation to prepare manuscripts, and most especially to Professors Kenneth D. Benne and Steven Tozer, editors of the volume, whose extraordinary diligence and skill at every stage have made possible the completion of the volume on schedule.

KENNETH J. REHAGE
Editor for the Society

Table of Contents

Part One
Technology and Democratic Society

Part Two
Social Heterogeneity and Power

Part One
TECHNOLOGY AND
DEMOCRATIC SOCIETY

CHAPTER I

The Meanings of Democracy
in a Collective World

KENNETH D. BENNE

Though often repudiated in practice by both the individual and the mass and though but vaguely defined and understood by the average citizen, democracy remains today a vital and powerful force in American life—one of the major necessities to be reckoned with in every venture in statecraft or education. Here is the basic ethical reality in the history of the nation.

George S. Counts
The Social Foundations of Education

I submit that an overwhelming majority of Americans believe that *it is only fair* that those who have a stake in the collective action should have a voice in shaping it. This belief colors our consciousness from the first game of hide-and-seek or scrub baseball. The consensus for this principle is based not only on rational grounds; it is part of the common moral intuition. It may be called our fundamental moral reflex.

Harry S. Broudy
"Education in a Pluralistic Society"

Why Assess the Meanings of Democracy
in a Work on Education?

That the United States of America as a nation is the exemplar and principal defender of democracy in today's world is the professed belief of a vast majority of Americans. And that educational

1

opportunity for all people, if necessary at public expense, is a manifestation and a bulwark of democracy is still believed by a majority of Americans, although the belief may be less firmly entrenched than it was a generation ago. The early American democratic idea of developing an enlightened citizenry and, later, the idea of equality of educational opportunity for each person to develop his or her capacities, were two democratic ideals that contributed to the extension of schooling throughout the nineteenth and early twentieth centuries in America.

It can be argued that, in a society that professes allegiance to democratic processes, the very idea of education cannot be understood adequately without attention to the meaning of democracy. This is to say more than to agree with Thomas Jefferson that political democracy depends for its effective operation upon an educated populace. The point is rather that, in a society like that of the United States, the idea of public education depends for its normative meaning upon the meaning attributed to democracy. If this is true, better and richer understandings of democracy contribute to better and richer understandings of education. To understand barriers to the actualization of democracy is to understand barriers to the actualization of an adequate education for ourselves and our fellow citizens.

In what sense is this linkage true? It has become a commonplace to recognize that education always takes place in relation to a particular social context. What it means "to be educated" in any particular culture depends on the demands and expectations that culture places upon its members. The meaning of "being educated" as a Plains Indian in the eighteenth century is distinctively different from the meaning of "being educated" as a citizen in twentieth-century United States. This is because the social institutions, norms, and ideals of the two cultures are distinctively different. "Literacy" in the two cultures has different meanings. Shooting accurately with bow and arrows, dancing, tracking animals, and fighting human enemies were probably elements in the "literacy" of a developing Plains Indian, a brave at least. Reading, writing, and computing are elements of "literacy" for a twentieth-century American.

In addition to instrumental "literacy," developing young people are shaped to understand and internalize values, ideals, and beliefs considered important in the culture in which they are gaining membership. For the Plains Indian, tribal loyalty, respect for animals, and a feeling of oneness with "nature" may have been such values. In twentieth-century America, acceptance of many values and beliefs is expected of bona fide members of American society, though these expectations vary from group to group in our heterogeneous society. But few if any of these are so fundamental to the characterization and justification of our social order as a belief in "democracy." We are brought up to believe in it, however imperfectly it may be understood by most members of society.

Ours is a society, as Abraham Lincoln said at Gettysburg, "conceived in liberty and dedicated to the proposition that all men are created equal." In 1934, George Counts declared that democracy is our "basic ethical reality."[1] In 1980, Harry Broudy argued that the democratic process is our "fundamental moral reflex."[2] If these observers are correct, then democracy has such a central place in our culture that the culture cannot be adequately understood without an understanding of the meaning(s) of democracy itself. And if educational practice is meaningful only in relation to its cultural context, then understanding of the meaning(s) of democracy in our culture is necessary to an adequate understanding and evaluation of educational practice in that same culture. We learn to read and to write; and we learn to make judgments in accord with certain ideals, democracy among them. We know fairly clearly what we mean by reading and writing, but we know less clearly what we mean by "democracy."

None of these observers of American society would have claimed that our social institutions and practices adequately embody democratic ideals. Nor, indeed, would they probably have agreed completely on what these ideals are or ought to be. Yet all, like many other students of American society, have evoked democratic values as normative criteria by which social, economic, and educational arrangements can be evaluated.

In later chapters, an assessment will be made of the educative effects of several contemporary institutions and developments in contemporary American society. As we evaluate these educative effects, we must attend to their consistency or inconsistency with democratic ideals. One of the reasons for including this chapter on democracy is to make explicit the dimensions of democracy that are useful in such an evaluation.

There is still another linkage between democracy and education which students of American education should keep in mind. This has to do with the educational benefits to individual persons who participate in the processes of democracy. It is common to argue for education as instrumental to effective democratic participation. Carole Pateman, however, has argued for the converse of this proposition: We should value democracy because we value education.[3] Citing John Stuart Mill, Jean Jacques Rousseau, and others, Pateman points to the proposition that, in principle, a democratic system of community life, more than any alternative, provides opportunities for individual persons to take responsibility for their own relations with others and thus to develop the capacities necessary to conduct those relations effectively and freely. Pateman argues, in effect, that a fundamental aim of democracy is to educate its participants through their participation in self-management of their chosen enterprises. Looked at in this way, the relationship between democracy and education is ideally of mutual benefit, one to the other.

The Minimal Meanings of Democracy

We have noted Counts's observation that for average Americans the meaning of democracy "is but vaguely defined and understood." Such vague understandings probably becomes evident when questions are raised that take the answers beyond the minimal meanings of democracy which "everyone" is willing to grant. Most often these minimal meanings hold that democracy is a form of rule (by the people, by representation) and that it is an embodiment of freedoms (religious or political, for example).

DEMOCRACY AS A FORM OF RULE

Traditionally, "democracy" has referred to a form of government. The etymology of the word (Greek - *demos*, people, + *kratein*, to rule) underlines this meaning. That democracy is "rule by the people" is one of the first definitions school children typically learn. The people rule themselves by debating and voting on controverted questions and, in most forms of democracy, the *majority* determines the policy that is taken as established. (In Quaker circles, as well as for other devotees of democracy, a consensus is required for legitimation of a decision.)

Participation by all in forming, discussing, and deciding upon policies becomes difficult, if not impossible, where large masses of people are involved, as in our modern nation-states as opposed to the small city-states in classical Greece. In such cases, direct democracy yields to representative democracy. People elect their representatives after campaigns in which various views of current issues are aired and discussed. People can attempt to influence these representatives in office, fail to reelect them if dissatisfied with their records, or, in extreme cases, recall them before their terms of office have expired.

Rule by the people, majority rule, and rule by representation are three variations on the democratic theme of government by the consent of the governed, which attends to rulership in democratic society. All represent a view of democracy that is serviceable at the level of a thumbnail sketch or a slogan but which fails to reveal deeper meanings of the democratic ideal.

DEMOCRACY AS THE EMBODIMENT OF FREEDOMS

For many Americans, the claim that "we are a democratic society" is synonymous with "we are a free society." A democracy embodies and protects for citizens a variety of freedoms, such as political, religious, or intellectual freedom, and democratic forms of governance should seek to protect citizens in the exercise of those freedoms. Majority rule, for example, is not adequately democratic if it does not effectively protect the freedoms of minorities; hence John Stuart Mills's fear of "the tyranny of majorities." Democracy understood as a form of rule, then, is part of a larger, commonly held view that attends to the freedoms democracy ideally seeks to embody. These dimensions of freedom commonly associated with democratic life are civil, political, and economic.

The distinction between civil liberty and political liberty was made by Aristotle in his *Politics*, and it is reflected in American thinking about democracy.[4] For Aristotle, civil liberty is the freedom to live as one pleases—to pursue the good life as one understands it. Aristotle explains political freedom as the freedom to participate in making the laws—"ruling and being ruled"—that protect the interests of individuals. Since individuals are the best judges of their own interests, he reasons, they must have the opportunity to structure the social order to protect those interests. The importance of that action of political freedom, which we might think of as political participation, is illustrated in Mills's criticism of the "benevolent despot." Such a despot, who could perhaps effectively protect civil liberties, would be antidemocratic in that he alone, rather than the people themselves, is free to determine the laws that govern people's lives.

The popular equation of democracy with "free enterprise" and "the free market system" is evidence of the "economic freedom" dimension of democratic ideals. Democratic life, it is believed, embodies the freedom to become as rich or as poor as one's talents and efforts allow, without the regulating influence of government. This notion of economic freedom as a democratic ideal is a product of the Enlightenment effort to free individuals from oppressive feudal or mercantilist political economies and it has become a central dimension of what most Americans consider the democratic ideal to represent.

These three dimensions of freedom, then, are as much a part of the minimal meanings of democracy as are rule by the people, majority rule, and rule by representation. They operate together to form popular conceptions of democracy that attend both to forms of rule and dimensions of freedom.

Majority rule, it is believed, must not be allowed to interfere with continuing attempts by dissident persons, groups, and minorities to defend their interests and to work for changes in governing policies. So the civil liberties of persons are guaranteed, as in the Bill of Rights of our federal constitution—freedom of speech, assembly, petition, and so on, and the disestablishment of any and all religious denominations. One function of government is to guarantee the civil liberties of all citizens, especially of minority persons and groups. The Bill of Rights also prohibits the establishment of any one religion and offers protection to persons in worshiping or not worshiping in the manner of their choice.

Another function of government is to maintain a fair and orderly mechanism for balancing conflicting interests against one another, and the Constitution of the United States is a classic effort to structure that balance via political participation in a representative democracy—one that embodies, to one degree or another, Aristotle's ideal of political freedom.

Finally, government is popularly thought to protect economic freedom. Regardless of how elaborately government agencies seek to regulate economic life today, the American public clings to its high regard for the "free enterprise system," and too rigorous efforts to regulate that system in the interests of economic equality and consumer protection are publicly denounced as "socialistic." Of course, socialism may be understood and practiced as democratic in some societies. But the popular allegiance to economic freedom in the United States continues to serve as an obstacle to overtly socialist policies in health care, for example, or in job security.

Our representation of the "minimal meanings" of democracy in contemporary United States society, then, focuses on both personal and civic aspects of democracy. The personal aspects are dimensions of freedom. The civic aspects sketch a form of governance. Probably few "average Americans" would grow restless or incoherent if questioners concerning the meaning of democracy stayed within the boundaries of such minimal meanings. But the course of history has seen, in America and elsewhere too, a widening and deepening of the meanings of democracy. And, in this widening and deepening, controversies have appeared within the public, and established practices and customs have been challenged and changed in the name of democracy. Conflicts have appeared among those who profess "democracy" as well as between proponents of democracy and proponents of other forms of rule and other conceptions of legitimate freedom.

Broadening and Deepening of the Meaning of Democracy

There are numerous areas in which the meaning of "democracy" has been broadened and deepened since the time of Thomas Jefferson, six of which have been chosen for treatment here. Some of these have resulted from applying the concepts of democracy to areas of human living where other forms of control have operated traditionally. Others have been articulated in response to changing conditions of life or to the challenge of nondemocratic modes, traditional or novel, of organizing and controlling human enterprises. Most of them evoke controversy, even among proponents of democracy.

DEMOCRACY AS A FORM OF RULE VERSUS DEMOCRACY AS A WAY OF LIFE

In modern societies, politics has been isolated from other aspects of society, unlike the integration of politics with other phases of life which prevailed in the Greek *polis*. "Government" has been separated from "industry," "business," "family," "religion," "entertainment," "the arts," and many forms of "mass communication."[5]

Some of these aspects of life have traditionally operated or have come to operate under a form of control and management that is undemocratic or antidemocratic in character. Industry may be taken as an example. Under the assumed "inalienable" rights of private property, owners of industry, especially as units of industry have grown in size, have instated authoritarian forms of rule and management. Workers who had once partially controlled the conditions of their labor came to have little or no voice in making or enforcing the policies and practices that prevailed in their work places.

Families, schools, hospitals, and other institutions have often operated and still operate with similar authoritarian forms of rule.

Proponents of democracy have long criticized the inconsistency of these arrangements with the freedom to live or work as one chooses and to participate in the decisions that affect one's interests. They have further noted the contradictions to democracy in the educational effects of various authoritarian institutions of our society and have sought to extend the notions of democratic life beyond the area of "politics" to other aspects of our common life, first in idea and then in practice—industrial democracy, democracy in schools and classrooms, democracy in family relations, and so on. In industries, for example, unions of workers developed power through organization to gain a collaborative voice in decisions affecting their lives—most often in such limited areas of policymaking as wages and working conditions. Like some turn-of-the-century workers who resisted collective bargaining with respect to wages because it condoned an autocratic work place in favor of limited concessions by owners, theorists of industrial democracy envisioned a wider range of collaborative (democratic) policymaking and participative management in all areas of industrial life.

In actual practice, the extension of democracy into the areas of power traditionally exercised by ownership and management has been resisted, and conflict rather than collaboration has tended to result. Of late, collaboration between management, labor, and public representatives in operating and managing industrial and business enterprises has made greater headway in theory and to a lesser extent in practice. Such management goals as enhanced productivity and more effective learning about and readier acceptance of changed technology and changed ways of working have probably been more powerful than devotion to democratic values in motivating such extended democratic collaboration. But the effect is to bring democracy into operation, however inchoately, in an area of social control where it was until recently resisted and denied.

The most succinct way of describing the extension of democracy from politics to other aspects of society is to contrast democracy as a "political form" to democracy as an "ethical way of life," applicable to all interpersonal, intergroup, and organizational relationships. John Dewey made a strong case for democracy as a way of life in its educational bearings. If persons in our society are to learn that a regard for democratic life is more than a regard for rules of voting and representative government, democracy must come to be seen as an ethos, applicable to political relationships between leaders and other citizens but equally applicable to workers and managers in industry, to school boards, administration, teachers, and students in formal education, and so on. Dewey argued that democracy was not limited in its meaning to forms and procedures in government, but that democracy has a moral significance rooted in what we value in human social life. He commented in *Reconstruction in Philosophy*:

> Government, business, art, religion, all social institutions have a meaning, a purpose. That purpose is to set free and to develop the capacities of human individuals without respect to race, sex, class or economic status. And this is all one with saying that the test of their value is the extent to which they educate every individual into the full stature of his possibility. Democracy has many meanings, but if it has a moral meaning, it is found in resolving that the supreme test of all political institutions and industrial arrangements shall be the contribution they make to the all-around growth of every member of society.[6]

CIVIL RIGHTS AS WELL AS CIVIL LIBERTIES

Civil liberties have been recognized and, in most part, accepted as essential aspects of political democracy in the United States since the addition of the Bill of Rights to the federal constitution in 1791. These generally take the form of limitations upon government (and other agencies) against depriving persons and minority groups of guaranteed freedoms of speech, assembly, freedom from unreasonable searches of one's residence and person, imprisonment without trial, and so on. But civil liberties throughout history have been unevenly distributed among our people. They were denied to black slaves until emancipation in 1863 and afterward to most black citizens by various devices until the civil rights protests of the 1950s and 1960s led to the outlawing of the Jim Crow laws of Southern states. Women were denied their rights as property holders, as public speakers, as voters, and as independent citizens with recourse to due process until well into the twentieth century. Both blacks and women are still victims of discrimination, though less flagrantly than before.

After the Second World War, liberation movements powered by organized minorities flourished and sought the extension of legal guarantees of various civil rights as well as the traditional civil liberties. Instead of civil liberties conceived as "freedom from any interference of government" (Aristotle), government was appealed to for the establishment and protection of civil rights. Civil rights as over against civil liberties tended to take the form of entitlements and negation of discriminatory practices rather than exemption from limitations upon specified personal and small-group freedoms. Blacks, Hispanics, Orientals, women, homosexuals, and handicapped persons were among the minorities who mounted liberation movements directed toward abolition of discrimination against them in employment, in access to public accommodations, housing, and education. In general, the target of liberation movements has been the abolition of second-class citizenship for all persons, whether because of race, ethnicity, sexual preference, gender, or disability. Their goal was to extend democratic rights and equal protection under the law to groups and persons who within our socially heterogeneous society had been denied these rights, whether because of unexamined traditional practices and attitudes or because of conscious prejudices and prejudicial actions.

The struggle for extension of rights has by no means been fully won for and by these groups. For example, differential rewards for men and women doing the same work still prevail. The right to a job for those who wish to work and the right to merited promotions are still aspirations for those devoted to the addition of civil rights to our traditional civil liberties. A later chapter will explore more fully problems connected with social heterogeneity and the unfinished task of creating a democratic pluralism.

But the liberation movements of the 1950s and 1960s have had a tremendous educational effect within our citizenry. Many more people are now conscious of the unfinished tasks of achieving democracy than before minorities organized to publicize their democratic demands. Increased consciousness has led to more open conflict among those who view differently the desirability of complete equality of various minorities before the law. One example of this is found in the ongoing struggle to establish an Equal Rights Amendment to the Constitution which would confirm women's equal status with men in our most fundamental law. This and other efforts to legislate equality where it does not exist have caused many to argue that equality as a value should not be pressed to the point of jeopardizing traditional commitments to liberty.

Proponents of democracy who are individualistic in their view of persons and societies tend to stress liberty as the heart of democracy. They often find an impossible gulf between liberty and equality. This alleged incompatibility arises in part from a confusion of equality with identity and sameness. People, it is argued, are not the same: they are naturally uniquely different. Only an "unnatural" regime can impose equality upon the members of a society and such imposition is an affront to their freedoms. As John Randolph is alleged to have said before the Virginia Legislature in the eighteenth century: "I am a democrat. I hate equality; I love liberty."

On the other hand, equality is perhaps best seen not as identity but as equal access to the resources required by each person for his or her unique development. On this view, the inconsistency between equality and liberty is relieved. And, if freedom is conceived as including opportunity and power to actualize one's choices, along with the absence of legal barriers to choosing and acting as one wills, equality in this sense of ready and equitable access to resources becomes a necessary condition of freedom, rather than an opponent to it.

In a money economy, access to resources is, of course, related to command of wealth in the case of many resources. So equality is jeopardized by large discrepancies in wealth between members of the same society. The widening gap in incomes among groups of citizens of the United States is one of the principal barriers to democracy. And measures undertaken by government to narrow the gaps in income are necessary, it appears, to preserve and advance democracy in our society. The Lockean conception that the government is best that governs least is a remnant of the individualistic tradition that has become a foe both of democracy and of individuality in our collective society.

Finally, in our heterogeneous society, though gains have been made in reducing discrimination against nonwhites, women, and homosexuals in employment, vocational advancement, and distribution of economic rewards, prejudice is still rampant, even though it is widely denied. Sexism and racism remain deep within our culture and stand athwart the development of the fraternity that is necessary to sustain fully the liberty and equality which democracy requires.

POLITICAL REPRESENTATION, PARTICIPATORY DEMOCRACY, EXPERT MANAGEMENT AND PLANNING

It is not often remarked that the Constitution of the United States originally provided that only one-half of one of the three main branches of the federal government would be elected by popular ballot. The others were to be elected by designated electors or appointed. Since that time the role of the federal government in the lives of citizens has grown, and the President, Vice President, and Senators are, essentially, popularly elected. At the same time, appointive regulatory commissions and governing agencies have multiplied manyfold since the eighteenth century.

While leaving national governance in the hands of a relatively elite selection of citizens, the authors of the Constitution envisioned a society in which citizens governed their local affairs democratically, both by popular assembly and by local representative government. If casting a vote for a representative or for a local official is taken as evidence of democracy, then the United States can offer such evidence, for local and national officeholders are elected by the people, although often by a small minority of eligible voters. Yet voting for representatives is at best a minimal requirement for democracy, for such voting takes place in totalitarian societies as well. In those cases, Americans are likely to deny the democracy of voting procedures on the grounds that no real choice is offered, that only one party is represented, and so on. For Aristotle, democracies allowed citizens to govern and be governed in turn, an arrangement which representative government allows. The aim of representative government, it may be argued, is for citizens to participate effectively in their own governance. It is relatively clear that, in the United States today, most citizens do not effectively participate in their own governance, either in national affairs or in local institutions such as the workplace and the schools.

In part, these conditions arise from the overwhelming influence of the "scientific management" movements in industry, in the professional regulation of national and local government and of the schools, that took root in the urbanizing, industrializing society of the early twentieth century. The belief that management of institutions by experts would be most efficient and beneficial to all seemed to justify the decreased participation by common citizens in the decisions that affected their lives. A burgeoning management profession appropriated planning and decision making from workers (often in spite of bitter struggles), from local ward representatives, and from neighborhood school boards. This is part of the allegedly more "efficient" but less democratic legacy of the movement toward professionalization and the power of specialized expertise. Decision making and planning became ever more centralized in the hands of experts whose professional training appeared to qualify them to make policy decisions on behalf of all. Today, broad foreign and domestic policy planning at the national level fall to appointed officials who are expertly trained in those areas; city planners and city managers make plans for local communities; and school policy is planned by curriculum specialists and a central office.

It is somewhat ironic, then, that many people fear collective social planning as a way of meeting the future because they connect it with totalitarian regimes and imposed plans that are centrally formed and enforced. In Dewey's words planning by "a class of experts" has been upon us for some time, however unrecognized this may be. Indeed, planning has, in recent years, been advocated and practiced more assiduously by totalitarian regimes than by political democracies. But there is no necessary linkage between dictatorships and planning as a substitute for improvisation and historical drift in finding direction toward our ambiguous and conflicted future. And democracy, in its fuller meaning as an ethos, should save planning from dictatorial imposition or domination by experts if we can find ways of infusing its spirit and practice into our processes of planning from locality to nation and world.

One way of doing this is never to forget the character of human systems which Kenneth Boulding has noted:

One thing we can say about man's future with a great deal of confidence is that it will be more or less surprising. This phenomenon of surprise is not something which arises merely out of man's ignorance, though ignorance can contribute to what might be called unnecessary surprises. There is, however, something fundamental in the nature of our evolutionary system which makes exact foreknowledge about it impossible, and as social systems are in a large measure evolutionary in character, they participate in the property of containing inescapable surprises.[7]

Plans should be subject to ready alteration in light of developing evaluation of experiences with them, including surprises and unforeseen consequences. And all affected by the plan should be involved in evaluating and criticizing plans and policies in need of attention.

Planning should be from the bottom up, not from the top down. In order to save its economy from the imposition of centrally contrived plans as in the Soviet Union, Yugoslavia provided for planning to begin in each local factory and business, in which workers decide on their next year's plan by joint planning by workers and experts. Local plans are combined and reconciled centrally and differences negotiated. Such an arrangement provides for participation in planning by each person affected by the plan. There is no

impossible barrier to decentralization of planning in the development
of national or even transnational plans.

The extension of participation by workers in making decisions on
problems arising within a factory or other place of business has
already been briefly discussed. But the nonideological factors that
have reinforced this extension of democracy have only been
mentioned. A problem encountered in all industrialized nations that
have introduced mass production methods has been the building and
maintenance of a will to work, to maintain quality of product or
service, and to achieve and maintain a high morale among workers.

In general, it has been found that these motivations cannot be
bought from workers either by increased pay or attractive working
conditions. Workers must come to feel a sense of psychological
ownership toward their work and workplace before they will work to
their fullest capacity, work to maintain high quality in their product,
or accept willingly the changes in jobs and relationships which a
changing technology thrusts upon all industries and businesses today.
Carole Pateman identified this sense of ownership as one of the
fundamental aims and benefits of participatory democracy as found,
for example, in the writings of Mill and Rousseau. A feeling of
psychological ownership can best be generated by participation of
workers in making decisions about production goals, and about the
quality of their work and working conditions. "Democracy" is thus
not an obstacle, but a means to greater productivity, as it enhances
morale and promotes more adequate quality control.

Two able students of organizational behavior were so convinced
of the necessity of workplace democracy for optimal productivity and
product quality as to argue recently that "democracy is inevitable."[8]
No doubt they were much too sanguine in asserting this inevitability.
The question whether a feeling of psychological ownership in their
work can be attained or maintained by workers without the
establishment of common legal ownership remains unanswered. As
already noted, a later chapter will deal more fully with this
manifestation of extended democracy.

Cooperative decision making is in some ways not compatible with
the tradition of competition that still pervades the American economy.
Merle Curti once called John Locke the philosopher of America.
Certainly, his conception of the human being as an atomic individual,
motivated primarily, if not exclusively, by self-interest, normally

related to others competitively, and joining with others only to serve his or her self-interest or protect his or her security is still strong in American thinking about human affairs. Competition is seen as the prime motivator of individuals toward achievement. This view has been strong traditionally in the life of schools where cooperation among students in school work is frequently seen as cheating, and ranking of students is seen as a desirable prod toward good work. How those who fail in the ranking race are motivated by competition is typically left unexplained.

Teamwork is encouraged in play and games, not in work. And teamwork in games is typically instrumental to success in competition with other teams.

Such a view of persons was not a serious distortion of economic reality in a time of many small enterprises in fabrication, business, and commerce. Competition may well have served as a way of sorting out individuals on a scale of productivity and efficiency and in eliminating the inefficient. The free competitive market may well have served to regulate the distribution of effort and investment and the allocation of rewards effectively.

But conditions have changed radically since the time of Adam Smith. Large corporations dominate the economic landscape. The small entrepreneur succeeds only against great odds. Corporations grow ever larger in size and fewer in number. Most people live and work within the framework of a collective world in work and in the provision of health, welfare, and educational services as well. In reality, cooperation has become a virtue in a collective world. Yet our individualistic mentality still attributes virtue to competition in the rhetoric and practice of resistance to public control of enterprises by government.

Ideally, democracy makes a virtue of cooperation. This, of course, does not mean that *conflict*, as over against deliberately engendered competition, has no place within a democratic system. It is precisely because of conflicts in interests among persons and groups that a way of settling the conflicts in a manner satisfactory to all parties is required. And democracy provides for the participation of all parties, along with those who represent the public not involved directly in the conflict, in a process of what Max Otto once called "creative bargaining" to attain a novel resolution of the conflict more satisfactory to all parties than the resolutions initially favored by the conflicting parties.

To understand democracy, the process of creation that comes out of the confrontation of conflicting viewpoints and out of the dialogic search for a common view needs to be emphasized. To the individualist, compromise is the best that can be hoped for out of the settlement of conflicting interests. To the democrat, learning by persons, one from the other, makes dialogue and discussion a creative process, engendering new and better social arrangements.

This involves a view of the human person different from that of the atomic individual. The view is of human persons as inherently social, with internalized social relations as well as the conventional external relations which Locke posited as the only relations between atomic persons. This is not to deny that each person is also unique as well as socialized. It is this uniqueness that lends support to the idea of participation by all persons affected by a decision in forming that decision, in the interest of a maximum induction from various experiences in the solution. Persons have the capacity to take the role of other persons, however different in outlook, and to communicate differences in the interest of creating new solutions to perplexing differences. But this capacity needs to be learned through use.

We live in a collective world. It is also a conflicted world. Creative cooperation is needed as never before in the history of mankind. The excitement of competition should be available to people in games and other experiences governed *by rules cooperatively made and agreed upon.* But the capacity for democratic cooperation must be a prime goal for education in a collective and conflicted world, if humankind is to survive. The minimalist notion of economic freedom that values competition and that disparages cooperative control results in contemporary economic arrangements that serve the interests of some at great expense to others. The "economic freedom" of the poor is not experienced as freedom but instead as an oppressive burden, one that requires bringing collective efforts to bear.

INTELLECTUAL FREEDOM VERSUS DEMOCRATIC EDUCATION

One dimension of freedom embedded in the classical liberal conception of civil liberty is intellectual freedom. This was expressed in the First Amendment of the Constitution in terms of freedom of speech and assembly, and it was fundamental to the colonial and early national regard for freedom of worship—particularly as expressed, for example, in Jefferson's Bill for Religious Freedom in Virginia. In his *Notes on Virginia*, Jefferson argued for a free marketplace of ideas in which the truth of beliefs, religious and scientific, could be allowed to stand by themselves without the support of government.

[T]he Newtonian principle of gravitation is now more firmly established, on the basis of reason, than it would be were the government to step in and to make it an article of necessary faith. Reason and experiment have been indulged, and error has fled before them. It is error alone which needs the support of government. Truth can stand by itself. . . . Reason and persuasion are the only practiceable instruments. To make way for these, free inquiry must be indulged.[9]

This faith in the free marketplace of ideas, and in the ability of an informed citizenry to judge wisely, supported Jefferson's famous dictum: "Were it left to me to decide whether we should have a government without newspapers, or newspapers without a government, I should not hesitate a moment to prefer the latter."[10]

This Jeffersonian optimism in the ability of an informed public to identify and protect its interests stems in part from a classical liberal faith in the inevitability of progress—a faith represented in Adam Smith's invisible hand and much earlier in Bacon's *New Atlantis*. By the late nineteenth century, however, that faith had been shaken in the United States by a devastating war, depressions, and pervasive labor troubles. In Edward Bellamy's influential and enormously popular *Looking Backward*, the twentieth-century citizen proclaims to his nineteenth-century audience that "the idea of indefinite progress in a right line was a chimera of the imagination, with no analogue in nature."[11] Intellectual freedom was not enough, warned Bellamy. The free marketplace of ideas was as likely to produce chaos as truth, and only a society based on planning, cooperation, and expert intelligence could meet the demands of the future.

In practice, such thinking emphasized expertise rather than democratic processes, and the rule by experts that Bellamy envisioned has become one obstacle to democracy in twentieth-century American society, as already noted. We are reminded of the Athenian mistrust of specialized expertise as constituting uneven power among citizens, and of Harold Laski's oft-repeated warning concerning the limitations of the narrow expert. In modern life, the concentration of specialized power in the hands of experts who form social policy, as well as write specialized textbooks, serves effectively to exclude most citizens from policy debate and influence. While we have "intellectual freedom" to an important degree, that freedom bears only a weak connection to the generic problems of democratic governance in contemporary society.

Other limitations on the value of "intellectual freedom" as a measure of democratic life are the control of mass media by a relatively few figures who must rely in turn upon the government for the great bulk of their information about domestic and international affairs, and the role of profit-motivated advertising in shaping the tastes and values of citizens. Both of these will be addressed in a later chapter. The point to be made here is that in "the free marketplace of ideas" a few powerful groups do most of the selling, and significantly divergent points of view are not readily available to the public. Jefferson had assumed that dissenting voices would be heard if censorship by government were prevented, but he did not envision a narrowing of public debate by more subtle and yet more powerful means.

Jefferson, however, recognized that free debate through the newspapers was no guarantee of an informed citizenry. He qualified his rhetorical preference for government by newspapers by adding: "But I should mean that every man should receive those papers and be capable of reading them." He was prepared, as most of his colleagues in the Virginia legislature were not, to establish a public school system to provide the literacy necessary to democratic life. Today we are beset not just with rampant illiteracy of the traditional kind, but of another kind as well: that which some scholars have called "critical illiteracy." If the "intellectual freedom" we now have does not provide an effective critical perspective to the citizenry, then that intellectual freedom falls short of the democratic ideal.

John Dewey argued for something akin to critical intelligence in *Democracy and Education* by proposing an education in a humanized scientific method for all youth in schools so that common people would be able rationally to judge for themselves the worth of social and industrial arrangements. Boyd Bode later argued that "the school is, par excellence, the institution to which a democratic society is entitled to look for a clarification of the meaning of democracy."[12] Both Dewey and Bode recognized that one looks in vain to capitalist institutions for a sustained democratic critique of contemporary society. Only the schools, they believed, were potentially equipped to develop such critical understandings among the populace. But neither Bode nor Dewey adequately foresaw the pervasive ideological grip that antidemocratic commitments would come to have, not only on industry and advertising, for example, but on the powerful medium of television, on government, and even on schools themselves. An effective education appropriate to today's conditions cannot settle for "intellectual freedom" conceived only as prohibitions against government censorship. It must seek out some means of equipping people of all ages to see critically and to resist the hegemony of expertise, the power of advertising, the profit-bound commitments of the government, and other antidemocratic forces in American life.

Another foe to the intellectual freedom that democracy requires is dogmatic belief in ideas and principles which those who espouse them hold as absolutes. To regard ideas and principles in this way is to exempt them from criticism and from confrontation with ideas and evidence that challenge their adequacy. Such devotion to formal ideas and beliefs is found often among devotees of a religious creed that is allegedly based on supernatural revelation. Absolutists in religion regard those who question their dogmas as enemies and, in extreme cases, as evil enemies. They are often tempted to impose their moral absolutes through the power of government, or public opinion, on others who do not share them. They also resent educational efforts to expose their absolutes to critical examination, when necessary, along with the cherished beliefs of others. This undercuts the critical dialogue upon which democratic policymaking depends, whether the issue be the legalization of abortion or elimination of discrimination against homosexuals in employment or any other controversial issue.

Absolutism in beliefs is, of course, not limited to religious believers. Extreme nationalists hold their patriotic slogans with a fervor akin to those religionists who find all truth in the Bible or some interpretation of it. Such absolutism makes free and critical dialogue concerning such questions as the strengthening of international rule and the consequent weakening of national sovereignty or the compromising of our national interests with those of another nation in the interest of peace very difficult to achieve, even where a vast majority of people will it.

THE FUTURE OF INDIVIDUALITY AND DEMOCRACY

We live in a collective world. And we live also in a continually changing world. Through research and the application of its results in a radically changing technology, we have created a world in which traditional ways of managing and directing human affairs can no longer attain or maintain a livable order. We must, as responsible human beings, use our communal intelligence to guide our way into the future. We have used a part of our ingenuity and intelligence in creating a high technology world. It is necessary to use all of our social intelligence to maintain and improve a human way of life in a world possessed of the power for good or ill inherent in that technology.

We can no longer depend on finding direction by following uncritically our own familiar traditions. Finding direction for the future by projecting the forms and values of our traditional culture upon the future has been further undermined by the ever-present fact of intercultural contact and confrontation within nations and between nations. The development of vast networks of interdependence, the spread of mass media of communication, and reduced security in spatial and political boundaries between cultures, due to space-destroying means of transportation, have brought about uneasy contact and confrontation between traditionally segregated nations, classes, races, and subcultures. As we seek new bases for an interdependent future across these cleavages in culture by projecting the traditions of any one culture upon the future, the futility of this way of defining the future for purposes of policymaking becomes more and more apparent. If there is to be a common future, it must be constructed by men and women from aspects of various cultures in a way to lead beyond the present maze of conflicting traditions. Men must plan and create the framework for cooperative planning by their own continuing dialogue on a hundred fronts.

Does this undercutting of tradition-direction mean an end to the cultivation and honoring of individuality in persons which have been part of our democratic tradition at its best? The answer is "No!" We must invent a future that inescapably will be novel in many respects. We will need original, inventive, and creative ideas as never before. And the source of creative novelty will, as in the past, be the minds of individual persons who, out of their uniqueness, see the world differently from the prevailing commonsense view. Actually, the liberation of thought and action from direction by a dominant tradition should free persons to trust their powers of creative imagination more than before and should free others to give a hearing to heterodox opinions and ideas as providing possible mind-holds on a desirable future. The ideas of atomic individualism that were once joined with the democratic view of man and society are no longer viable. The alternative idea of persons emerging out of dialogue between human beings, and of considering and testing the novel ideas which continuing dialogue between persons who differ always engenders, gives individuality a valued basis in the minds of all persons, especially perhaps of those concerned with education. Traditional individualism is no longer the friend of individuality. But individuality is, of necessity, to be valued as never before.

Does the weakening of tradition-dependence undercut reliance upon the democratic tradition in guiding men and women in planning their desirable direction into the future and inventing ways of moving toward it? It does mean that democratic traditions must be criticized, like all other traditions, and not followed blindly. And it does mean that forms and institutions of democracy as they have developed in America and acquired a distinctively American shape and flavor cannot be successfully imposed on other cultures.

But the central meanings of democracy seem still to offer the best chance of incorporating the most desirable values out of different cultures in an emerging outlook toward a *human* future, since that requires the critical and responsible participation of persons from all cultures in its formation and continuing revision. And the recent reemergence of political democracy to supplant dictatorial regimes in country after country—Argentina, Brazil, Uruguay, the Philippines—may indicate agreement with this view on the part of widely divergent peoples.

I once attempted to formulate the basic arts of democratic citizenship, shorn of their distinctive American accretions. These arts promise effectiveness when learned and used by persons and groups engaged in planning for the human future:

1. The art of effective criticism as well as veneration of our traditions.

2. The art of listening to opinions and expressed attitudes and practices different from our own and answering these in light of the full human meaning of what we hear.

3. The art of dealing with conflicts creatively and integratively.

4. The art of evaluating the virtues and limitations of experts and of expert opinion and knowledge, and of using expertise not subserviently but wisely.

5. The art of evaluating openly and intersubjectively the results in practice of decisions formed in the passionate heat of controversy and conflict.[13]

These arts of democratic citizenship follow Dewey in their portrayal of democracy as a way of living rather than merely as a mechanism of voting or as freedom from government interference. These arts require of citizens that they be educated to understand the deeper meanings of democracy and that they care enough about those deeper meanings to measure against them the quality of their participation in such institutions as government at all levels, the workplace, the churches, temples, and mosques, and the schools. Further, these democratic arts engage people in processes that are educational in themselves. The art of evaluating the virtues and limitations of experts, or the art of intersubjectively evaluating social decisions and practices, requires that one continually learn new information and understand conflicting points of view in order to participate effectively. These arts demonstrate the point made earlier in this chapter that in its deepest meanings, democracy not only requires an educated populace but it serves to educate that populace. Dewey's moral meaning of democracy, that "the test of all political institutions . . . [is] the contribution they make to the all-around growth of every member of society,"[14] becomes a standard much more useful for measuring contemporary life than such a minimal meaning of democracy as, for example, "representative government."

The above arts of democracy, like Dewey's moral meaning, suggest criteria for the measure of our schools as well. Do they equip our citizens to exercise those arts? Or do they equip our citizens, by and large, to accept without critical examination self-congratulatory rhetoric about contemporary America as the world's exemplar of the free enterprise system and as the "last, best hope of democracy?"

Each of the subsequent chapters of this volume describes some significant facet of contemporary life and work in the United States. Understanding the educative or miseducative value of each requires that the reader understand democracy not only in its minimal meanings, but in its deeper and richer meanings as well.

FOOTNOTES

1. George S. Counts, *The Social Foundations of Education*, Report of the Commission on the Social Studies, American Historical Association, Part IX (New York: Charles Scribner's Sons, 1934), p. 11.

2. Harry S. Broudy, "Education in a Pluralistic Society," in *Critical Issues in Educational Policy*, ed. Louis Rubin (Boston: Allyn and Bacon, 1980), p. 20.

3. Carole Pateman, *Participation and Democratic Theory* (Cambridge, Eng.: Cambridge University Press, 1970).

4. Aristotle, *The Politics*, with introduction, notes, and appendices by Ernest Barker (Oxford: Clarendon Press, 1946), p. 258.

5. Totalitarian societies are a relatively recent exception to this separation of the state and government from other aspects of social life. They may be thought of as attempts to reunify these scattered aspects of life, usually using amplified powers of the central government as a means of reunification.

6. John Dewey, *Reconstruction in Philosophy* (Boston: Beacon Press, 1948), p. 186.

7. Kenneth E. Boulding, "Expecting the Unexpected: The Uncertain Future of Knowledge and Technology," in *Prospective Changes in Society by 1980*, ed. Edgar L.

Morphet and Charles O. Ryan (Denver: Designing Education for the Future: An Eight-Year Project, 1966).

8. Philip E. Slater and Warren G. Bennis, "Democracy Is Inevitable," *Harvard Business Review* 42 (March 1964): 51-59.

9. Thomas Jefferson, quoted in *Crusade Against Ignorance*, ed. Gordon C. Lee (New York: Teachers College Press, 1964), p. 64.

10. Ibid., p. 65.

11. Edward Bellamy, *Looking Backward* (New York: New American Library, 1960), p. 31.

12. Boyd Bode, *Democracy as a Way of Life* (New York: Macmillan, 1937).

13. Kenneth D. Benne, "The Arts of Democratic Citizenship," in *Education for Tragedy* (Lexington, Ky.: University of Kentucky Press, 1967), pp. 192-96.

14. Dewey, *Reconstruction in Philosophy*, p. 186.

CHAPTER II

Learning from Technology

LEONARD WAKS AND RUSTUM ROY

Introduction

What can educators learn from the study of contemporary technology? The stated goals of education in modern democratic societies remain constant: the development of each person as (a) a worker, (b) a citizen, and (c) an individual. Basic democratic education thus has a vocational, a political, and a personal dimension. However, as the technological context changes, the specific interpretations of these goals and the means for attaining them must be reassessed. We begin by noting some familiar questions raised by recent technological developments.[1]

THE VOCATIONAL DIMENSION

The development of the individual as a worker is a central aim. Increasingly, women as well as men are expected to leave the home for work in the labor market; the once standard household with a husband working outside the home and a wife handling the responsibilities of the home has gradually disappeared. The basis of livelihood is expected to be self-chosen and independent of the state dole. Such a goal is central to democratic theory, which conceives of individuals as shaping their lives independently of the state, with the state serving sharply limited functions. To limit its responsibilities later on, the state mandates that all young people obtain knowledge, skills, and attitudes through education, to prepare them for self-supporting work. This goal appears in key statements of American educational policy, and in many education-related court cases, such as *Wisconsin v. Yoder*.[2]

It is frequently assumed that the young must be prepared for the American "middle-class" work-styles of the twentieth century, standard "jobs" and "careers." On this assumption modern technology appears to pose a harsh challenge; many commentators

24

warn that new technologies are reducing the ratio of standard jobs per capita, destroying the economic value of many skills, and forcing the average person to adjust not merely to one "career," but as many as four or five, requiring new knowledge and skills, over the course of a lifetime. Further, middle-class, high consumption, life-styles (as these have evolved in Western nations in our century) may no longer be appropriate goals for all workers as technology spreads around the globe, bringing about a gradual equalization in the standard of living. If the educational system continues to attempt to train all people during their early years for standard jobs and careers, promising a high standard of material living, then it will breed frustration, for regardless of knowledge and skill attainment, standard jobs and unidirectional career paths will simply not be available for all who desire them.[3]

Work may be organized in fundamentally different ways in the future, but regardless of how it is organized, we believe that work as an economic activity will remain central for most people. We all want to feel that we are productive and contributing members of society, and that what we do connects us with and matters to others. "Working for a living" satisfies these desires. Few would want their livelihood and social standing to depend upon chance or the tolerance of a beneficent state.

The questions raised here are: what opportunities for meaningful and remunerative work will emerge in our increasingly technological society, and what educational provisions will best prepare people to take full advantage of these opportunities?

THE POLITICAL DIMENSION

Citizenship is universally seen as a second goal of democratic education. However, there have been conflicting interpretations of this goal and of the means appropriate for its achievement. What is the meaning of citizenship in our time, and how are we to achieve it?

For many political theorists from the ancient Greeks through Locke and Rousseau, citizenship was conceived as a special "office" in the state; liberty implied a political institution within which free men in their citizen "office" reflected, debated, decided, and acted for the common good. As Jeffersonians, we also conceive of citizenship as a special office, and ideally we want all educational arrangements to promote the knowledge, skills, and attitudes necessary to prepare the masses of people for this office.

We acknowledge that even in the best circumstances (a) not every person will have equal talent for this demanding office, and (b) not every person will be equally attracted to its duties. Realistically speaking, not every person will "take" to citizenship in the modern state. But a large critical mass from all social and economic groups must be recruited and trained for this office or democracy withers away, and "government by the people" becomes an empty phrase.

Once again, modern technology confronts education with a new challenge. Paradoxically, in our technology-dominated world, fewer and fewer people are compelled by occupational requirements really to understand contemporary technology (compare our age with the age of the farmer and craftsperson, who were close to the cutting edge of technical knowledge). But without such an understanding, how can people enter actively and securely into discourses and decision making regarding public policy about, for example, whether to restrict gene-splicing technologies, or how to control the flow of computerized data, or whether to erect a strategic defense in space?

This problem of technological knowledge in the modern state has generated major new, antiparticipatory trends in democratic theory. In these the scientific and technological ignorance of the masses of people is taken as a given. Unprepared for changing circumstances, the masses must be expected to react blindly and emotionally to change, sweeping demagogues and hucksters into office. Elites are seen on this view as potentially more knowledgeable, rational, and capable of planning, hence as more capable of sustaining democratic rule; democracy demands that governing elites be protected from the people.

Such "protectionist" theories fail to consider the developmental potential of political participation. Where people become really active and involved and accept responsibility, they can recognize and remediate their deficiencies in knowledge and skill. They "learn by doing." While powerless people have no motive to learn the technical details, those who feel capable can take the first step, and each step they take shows them what they need to learn in order to proceed effectively. This sort of bootstrapping is central to such modern advocates of participatory democracy as John Stuart Mill and G.D.H. Cole.[4]

The questions raised are: what are the necessary standards of technological literacy for participatory democracy in our technological society, and what educational arrangements will effectively promote their attainment?

THE PERSONAL DIMENSION

The third universally acknowledged goal of democratic education is the development of individuality. An "individual" in this sense is a person who has achieved a high degree of self-determined personality integration, who has succeeded in organizing all significant activities of life around self-determined goals and self-expressive activities involved in their pursuit. Each component of life has meaning in the context of a "wholeness" which it promotes. Individuality in this sense implies autonomy (self-direction) and hence personal responsibility.

Individuality is not a given, but rather a rare achievement. The individual is the person who has transcended merely biological and social conditioning, directing his or her energies toward goals freely chosen on the basis of their inner meaning and value. Goals grounded in self-knowledge are the driving force, and the various life activities are coordinated as unique action patterns that work together to serve those goals. A person who has freely chosen his or her goals, and has organized a life for their effective pursuit, is pursuing "happiness" in the relevant democratic sense (contrast this with "happiness" generated by the state dole and the circus).

In democratic theory it is the function of the state to promote the individuating process, but only indirectly. The state provides the masses of people with such tools as public schools and public libraries, guarantees freedom of inquiry, freedom of speech, freedom of the press, and the free practice of religion, and protects these rights of the individual from interference even by the majority of the people. However, in democratic theory individuality is conceived as being logically prior to and independent of the democratic state, not a product of mandatory, state-controlled treatments. The public schools can promote individuality indirectly. They provide important means, but the ends of development are freely chosen by each person.

Once again, technology poses a basic challenge. The deployment of industrial age technologies such as assembly lines, industrial management routines, and bureaucratic controls tends to standardize roles, on grounds of productive efficiency or bureaucratic accountability. The modernization process is usually taken to include both greater regularity and routine, and the greater diffusion of rational attitudes and knowledge. Rationalization and routinization affect every person in every role from worker and citizen to artist and inventor—and even sexual lover. Technology determines our choices of ends and our available techniques, and thus may shape our lives.

The questions raised are: what place remains for individuality in our technological society, and what educational arrangements promote it?

In probing more deeply into the implications of technology for education it would be desirable to start with an accurate, normatively neutral account of the changing technological milieu, but providing such an account is no simple matter. As David Noble has quipped, the more we find technology at our fingertips, the less we are able to put our finger on just what technology is.[5] Within the past century, science has moved from the assured positivism of Newtonian mechanics to the great openness of quantum mechanics and chaos theory, and even to the near mystical quality of charmed quarks, leptons, hadrons, and antimatter. Technology has likewise changed from the assured march of steel, autos, and electrical machinery dominated by Western nations to the nimbleness of the liberated electron and now the photon, which like will-o'-the-wisps alight here and there to ignite new enterprises and industries. Increasingly these "high technologies" are within the reach of all nations from Saudi Arabia to South Korea. (See table 1 for a schematic representation comparing modern science and technology.)

Several perspectives on this elusive phenomenon are available. Each, like a lens, provides a sharp focus for some aspects of technology while blurring others. As there is no way to grasp a complex phenomenon "directly," without some conceptual scheme(s), in this chapter we will review six important perspectives, and add some further organizing ideas of our own. Finally, we will consider what educators can learn from these perspectives on technology.

Six Perspectives on Technology

Each of the following perspectives contains a view about what technology is and how it develops, and hence implies what it is to "understand technology." The first two define technology in isolation from its broad social context. The other four view technology as inherently social, and they form the background for our emerging field of study and integrative education, "Science, Technology, and Society" or STS.

TABLE 1

SCHEMATIC REPRESENTATION COMPARING SELECTED FEATURES OF
MODERN SCIENCE AND MODERN TECHNOLOGY

MODERN SCIENCE tends toward	MODERN TECHNOLOGY tends toward
Universality	Significance that is strongly influenced by local environment
Precision	Fuzziness
Simple truths, equations, concepts	*Complex* aggregates of complex information
The transfer of *all* content at *speed of light*, to all parts of the world	A transfer that takes *years*, to pointed, targeted audiences
Relatively *easy* transfer	Very *complex* transfer
Enabling a *single individual* to understand and utilize new advances	Requiring an *entire system* (of culture) to utilize advances
Science is *inherently* reductionist (i.e., it isolates the portion of the universe selected for study) and can be done in complete isolation with *no feedback loops.*	Technology is always part of a nature + human + artifact system with manifold feedback.

THE ARTIFACT PERSPECTIVE

The first perspective derives from a "first glance" at technology, identifying it with devices and instruments. Toasters, microwave ovens, televisions, computers, and machine guns—these are all technology. Understanding technology means understanding how these devices work and how to work them. Technological literacy means obtaining a rudimentary understanding of the basic science underlying these devices, and learning to use these devices in at least a rudimentary way. An example would be "computer literacy," learning a few basics about computer science and having some hands-on experience with computers.

On this view technology develops as the underlying scientific laws are discovered and applied in the mass production of these devices. Key artifacts punctuate this development. The railroad age gave way to the automotive age, which was followed by the aeronautic age, which in turn gave place to the television age and most recently the computer age.

This perspective focuses on new gadgets, and hence on the "magic" of technology and its underlying science ("gee whiz" science), rather than on the human contexts of either technology or science.

THE ENGINEERING PERSPECTIVE

On this perspective technology results when quantitative analysis is applied to the adjustment of means to ends, so that various means may be precisely evaluated in order for ends to be produced most efficiently.

Consider the manufacture of automobiles. In the early years skilled craftsmen from the bicycle and carriage trades made each car by hand. This system was replaced by an efficient system designed by industrial engineers. The resulting assembly line permitted unskilled workers relegated to specific tasks to produce cars more efficiently than skilled workers. More was done with less; hence the assembly line on this perspective represents a technological advance over the handicraft method.

On this perspective, technology develops as engineering approaches are applied in more areas of life, increasing the yield of ends per expenditure of means. The relationship of technology to devices is derivative; artifacts are technologies only to the extent that they play a role in the efficient production of ends. Complicated gadgetry which serves no purpose would not be technology, and technology may exist without such devices. Systems for managing workers, training the retarded, and rehabilitating criminals, designed by behavioral engineers, are also technology; the systems improve the yield of determinate and measurable ends per unit of input. Here "technology" stands for a rational method or system, not a device.

While scientific laws may play an important role in any given technology, the relationship between science and technology on this view is also derivative. In the electrical, chemical, and electronic industries, basic scientific research played an essential role. In some other industries, engineers improved means on the basis of empirical knowledge and craft experience, with pure scientific research playing only a minor role.

From an engineering perspective, understanding technology is understanding the rational principles underlying the adjustment of means to ends, including quantitative analysis and precise measurement; understanding technology is understanding engineering.

The engineering perspective dominated thought about technology during the early years of the scientific-technological revolution, when technological advances in industry, based on the application of scientific laws, prompted the applications of technical approaches in a wide range of fields. In the United States, this perspective was dominant during the progressive era, when a fascination for "efficiency" spilled over from industry to politics, education, and other aspects of social life,[6] giving rise to a technological "mystique." Intellectuals such as Thorstein Veblen sought to transform the entire society in accordance with engineering principles.

With the growing complexity of social life in the technological society, however, the engineering perspective has been reassessed. In using technical means to achieve isolated technical ends, this linear approach is seen as oversimplifying complex problems and as neglecting hidden costs, systems interrelations, unanticipated side effects, trade-offs, and other problems. As Waddington states, "If things go unexpectedly wrong once or twice, that is, one might say rather paradoxically, only to be expected; but recently they have been going wrong so often and in so many contexts, that many people are beginning to feel they must be thinking in some wrong way about how the world works."[7] Waddington finds this error in the attempt to understand techniques in terms of simple causal sequences, *a* causing *b* which in turn causes *c*. This way of thinking is benign when *a* causes *b* and very little else, and when each cause in the sequence is relatively feeble. He notes that our new means are so powerful that it is no longer "adequate to concentrate on the primary effects and neglect all secondary influences." He adds:

The scale of very many of the impacts of mankind on the world surrounding him is now so great that they go right below the surface of things. At the deeper level, we find that most aspects of life and its interaction with its surroundings are connected into complexes. . . . We need nowadays to be able to think not just about simple processes but about complex systems.[8]

Various perspectives, which are being integrated in the field of Science, Technology, and Society, are now used to interpret technologies in terms of complex social systems, rather than to sustain the technological "mystique," and to reinterpret or reshape society within a technical framework.

Marxian socialism, the first social perspective we explore, views technology in the context of relations between socioeconomic classes in the productive processes of society. Under capitalism, the essence of technology resides within the relations between two opposed social classes in production, the working class and the capitalist class, and in the political, legal, and cultural institutions that are erected in support of the accumulation of capital. The essence of capitalist technology is neither science nor rationality, but rather the progressive wresting of control over production by the capitalist class.

The assembly line is a good example. It has no basis in scientific discovery; its underlying principles are primitive. It is not efficient; it does not increase the satisfaction of human ends per unit of means utilized. On the contrary, it satisfies the capitalist's desires for increased profits and control while frustrating all basic ends of the masses of people. The products created are largely irrelevant to the basic purposes of life. The most basic ends of the masses of people for self-development, meaningful and creative work, deep and lasting human relations are thwarted by the assembly line. Through industrial engineering the assembly line strips the working class of its productive knowledge, and hence strengthens the capitalist, who works to gain complete control over productive life. Subject to this control, the workers as a group cannot collectively determine either the processes or products of their labor. These processes are particularly important, because by day-to-day reiteration, they have a most important "product"—the workers themselves. These processes determine what the workers do, what they learn, and how they relate to one another, hence what they become. It is only when this "product" is ignored that we can think of a process which turns out more and more television sets, for example, while destroying the intelligence of the workers (who may be dark-skinned, working for subhuman wages, and conveniently hidden in assembly plants overseas) as more "efficient."

And all those television sets themselves cannot be considered simply as means to human ends either. On the one hand, workers diminished by repetitive labor may become addicted to empty amusements such as TV game shows or professional football, or unable to seek more growth-oriented avocational pursuits; on the other hand, television only makes them further subject to propaganda and consumption controls.

The socialist paradigm of technical development brings into focus the socio-technical systems of production (along with the economic, legal, and political institutions regulating the relationships between social classes) that are specific to each major socioeconomic epoch—feudalism, capitalism, and socialism—each further analysed in substages. This kind of analysis shifts our attention away from gadgets and rational design principles to groups of people in relationship. Indeed, from this perspective we cannot even talk about the relationships between technology and human beings, because technology is conceived as inherently political, legal, and social, and hence inherently human. As Herbert Marcuse notes:

We do not ask for the influence . . . of technology on the human individuals. For they are themselves an integral part and factor in technology, not only as the men who invent and tend to the machinery, but also as to the social groups which direct its applications. . . . Technology, as a mode of production, . . . is thus at the same time a mode of organizing and perpetuating social relationships, . . . an instrument for control and domination.[9]

Capitalist technology is divided into the stages of market capitalism, corporate capitalism, and advanced capitalism. In the first, the capitalist established the overall context of work, after breaking the social and legal bounds of feudalism, but productive knowledge and skill remained in the hands of the workers. In the second, the capitalists utilized new economic and legal forms to gain control over the productive process and create national markets. In the third, multinational corporations have expanded beyond national borders, utilizing a global work force (shifting productive processes or laborers from one place to another to take advantage of cost differentials in labor or resources) and selling to an integrated global market. It is in such contexts that we are to understand the development of new technological means, from the railroad and automobiles to computers and telecommunications satellites.

From the socialist perspective, the key to understanding technology is found in class antagonisms in productive processes. Technological literacy is possessing a basic understanding of how existing and emerging technologies reflect these conflicts, and obtaining the basic historical, economic, and political knowledge and skill needed to join in the struggle of the masses of working people of the world for freedom, dignity, and justice.

Technological education in its larger dimension includes the acquisition of both political and technical knowledge and skill. The socialist retains the ideal of a community of workers, each at the cutting edge of technical knowledge, collectively shaping work processes and products for the common good. As Braverman expresses this,

The worker can regain mastery over collective and socialized production only by assuming the scientific, design, and operational prerogatives of modern engineering; short of this there is no mastery over the labor process. The extension of the time of education which modern capitalism has brought about for its own reasons provides the framework; the number of years spent in school has become generally adequate for the provision of a comprehensive polytechnical education for the workers in most industries.[10]

Braverman concludes:

Such education can engage the interest and attention of workers only when they become the masters of industry in the true sense, which is to say when the antagonisms in the labor process between controllers and workers . . . are overthrown, and when the labor process is united in the collective body which conducts it.[11]

The socialist perspective alerts us to *hidden costs*. Emerging "ideologies" (or patterns of thinking and speaking) reflect the interests of powerful groups, and veil the costs of techniques, making it easier to shift them off to the least powerful individuals at home or overseas in developing nations.

THE ECOLOGICAL PERSPECTIVE

The ecological view places technical means and the ends they promote in the context of population dynamics, available resources, undesired side effects, and "whole systems," with subtle multivariable interactions, feedback, and self-regulation.

Typically ecological theorists divide technologies into three stages, the preindustrial, the industrial, and the emerging postindustrial stage. The preindustrial stage was marked by the utilization of limited and local means, primarily renewable resources such as wood and other plant and animal products. Simple tools, requiring the skilled hand and the expert eye, dominated productive activities. Human and animal power was the major motive force in production technologies. The industrial age was marked by the substitution of mechanical devices for human skill and ingenuity, the replacement of human and animal power with inanimate power from nonrenewable sources such as coal and petroleum, and consequently the intensive extraction of these and other nonrenewable resources such as iron ores and other mineral products. "Modern" technology and the engineering profession rose to dominance in this epoch.

Recent decades have witnessed the emergence of a postindustrial society. In the early years (1960-75) there was a prevailing sense of global overpopulation and resource scarcity. The nonrenewable resources were widely perceived as approaching depletion. Toxic by-products of widely utilized technologies were seen as accumulating rapidly, disturbing subtle balances in nature. Utilization of scarce resources was feared to be expanding at a geometric rate, and efforts to promote conservation appeared doomed to failure. Rachel Carson's *Silent Spring* set the stage, and Paul Ehrlich's *The Population Bomb*, Buckminster Fuller's *Utopia or Oblivion*, the Club of Rome's *Limits to Growth*, Ernst Schumacher's *Small is Beautiful*, and Robert Heilbroner's *An Inquiry into the Human Prospect* sustained and advanced the argument.[12]

Our high energy budget life-styles were reevaluated by many. In the mainstream, this led to a "Global 2000" worldview which took seriously the interdependencies of nations and the need to conserve nonrenewable resources. At the margins, alternative, low-resource technologies ranging from Indian teepees to bicycles and woodstoves, appeared in the *Whole Earth Catalogue* and were widely adopted in communes and on the edges of university campuses. The attention of these populations shifted from Vietnam to organic gardening and spiritual values.

The last decade has seen the development of effective conservation and the beginnings of resource substitution, due to which the power of OPEC has been reduced, and commodity prices, after a decade of inflation, have declined sharply. Recent technological advances (bioengineering and silicon technology) do not draw upon scarce resources. An account of recent technology from this perspective is provided by Bruce Nussbaum, who notes that every epoch has "two or three dominant technologies that define it." These technologies determine "what work people do, and where they do it, the number of children they have, the clothes they wear, and the house they live in."[13]

During the past 110 years of the industrial era, roughly from 1860 to 1970, electrical machines, chemicals, and steel formed the core technologies of our lives. Combined with the assembly line of production, these technologies gave us automobiles, plastics, textiles, tanks, and napalm.[14]

These technologies were developed in a period of "cheap labor, cheap raw materials, and above all, cheap energy." All were necessary for the dominance of heavy industry. But these factors no longer obtain, and these technologies of the industrial era are "obsolete." In the early days of the postindustrial era, futuristic books describing "fantastic new wonders" (for example, space colonies) abounded, but none of these visions was realistic, for they were not grounded in present day requirements. For any technology to dominate in the new era, it must have these three characteristics: (a) it must be an energy sipper that not only uses less energy but also makes new things which use less energy; (b) it must have an immediate and pervasive impact on our lives, affecting us where we work and where we live; and (c) it must increase productivity and efficiency by using less labor and fewer raw materials, both of which are high priced items in the world of the 1980s. Only three of the many new technologies, Nussbaum claims, have all three: robotics, bioengineering, and telecommunications. Two are part of the evolution away from labor-intensive, "smoke stack" industries toward computers. The other is part of an economic change from petroleum-based chemistry to genetically based biology. By 1990 these three technologies "will have transformed the entire world we live in."

A similar, if somewhat more upbeat, view is expressed by Paul Hawken, who notes that two economies currently exist side by side in the Western world, an economy of mass production and consumption of material goods, and an emerging "informative" economy that "reduces the amount of materials consumed by industry and individuals by raising and enhancing the information contained within goods and services." The mass economy, he continues, is the economy of the industrial era, "the period from 1880 until today, a time during which oil, the internal combustion engine, and the widespread generation and distribution of electrical power transformed nations into complex industrialized, consumer oriented societies." The word "mass" is apt, Hawken states, because the dominant economic force was "the substitution of fossil fuels for human energy in order to produce mass (physical goods) for the masses (consumers)."[15]

The "informative" economy, on the other hand, is characterized by people producing and consuming smaller numbers of goods that contain more information.

What is this information? It is design, utility, craft, durability, and knowledge added to mass. It is the quality and intelligence that make a product more useful and more functional, longer lasting, easier to repair, lighter, stronger, and less consumptive of energy.[16]

In Hawken's view, the shift from the mass economy to the informative economy began in 1973, when energy and capital costs rose in relation to the cost of labor.

From the ecological perspective, understanding technology means understanding how specific human ends and technical means are shaped by the ecological context, by such factors as population and resources. Understanding industrial technology is understanding the population expansion, the shift to nonrenewable resources and the impact of their use on further population growth, migration, urbanization, cultural evolution, and so on. Understanding the decline of industrial technologies and the emergence of new postindustrial technologies is understanding resource scarcities and side effects of industrial means. Technological literacy is understanding the connection between technology and these basic ecological factors, and adopting appropriate values and attitudes such as favoring technologies that conserve energy and the environment, are information-based, and enhance the development of people.

The ecological perspective alerts us to complex relations between technical means and other aspects of the "system," pointing out that technological benefits will involve trade-offs, that there is "no free lunch," and that large-scale means will have large and now unpredictable impacts upon our natural and social environments.

THE INSTITUTIONAL PERSPECTIVE

The institutional perspective is distinguished by its focus on the domination of life by professional elites and the educational system which authorizes and certifies them. It has been most forcefully developed in a series of essays by our colleague Ivan Illich.[17] Illich analyses the "industrially generated professions" and their "industrial tools," the technologies of the industrial era. While initiated in capitalist economies, the industrial mode of production has been adapted in the socialist nations without any alteration of its basic forms or remediation of its defects. Hence socialist perspectives, in his view, cannot "provide the necessary framework for analysing the crisis in the industrial mode of production itself."

As industrial society evolved, workers became concentrated in cities, and traditional social norms of village and town, which conveyed common productive and living skills and ways of thinking, eroded. Individuals lost control over production of clothing, cultivation of fruits and vegetables, processing of raw foodstuffs, baking of bread, building and repairing shelter, and so forth. With work organized away from the home, various services organized under professional control, including child rearing, emotional counseling, and care of the sick and aged, replaced familiar means of human care.

The division of life in industrial society into its productive sphere and its coordinated system of social organization under professional control allows us to divide the "industrially generated professionals" into two groups, the *production professionals* (inventors, scientists and engineers in corporate research and development, industrial managers, industrial psychologists, corporate lawyers and accountants, and the like) and *human service professionals* (including residential planners, transportation managers, clinical psychologists, social workers, criminologists, physicians and allied health professionals, teachers and professors). The first group is in charge of industrial production, the second in command during an ever increasing share of nonproductive time (time largely devoted to "shadow-work"—onerous nonproductive work such as professional retraining, rush hour driving, or emotional counseling to enable a "positive adjustment" to school or work, all disguised as consumption).

These professional elites owe their position to schooling. With the knowledge and skills and also the attitudes and commitments, which result from school attainments, they derive status, freedom from nasty labor, and command of industrially generated human services and industrially produced consumer goods.

As services, professional endeavors respond to some felt needs of clients. But the service enterprises also create, sustain, and intensify the relative power of the professional elites. The need to learn and discover becomes translated as the need for "an education," which in turn comes to mean schooling under professional control. The need to be healed is translated into "health care," as medical budgets expand to keep sick and dying people alive and dependent upon ever increasing and sophisticated "health technologies."

For Illich, this process passes through two "watersheds."[18] Prior to the first, activities are neither rationalized nor subject to professional domination. People take care of their own needs, with skills shaped by traditional cultural norms. There are few professionals, and their training is less standardized, their arena of action modest, and their range of treatments limited by traditions and taboos.

Within any given sphere, there are some widely recognized problems that resist solutions along traditional lines. Such problems are neither created nor defined by professional cadres, but by common observation and consent, for example, the cholera epidemic of 1832. At the first watershed effective new knowledge is developed by professionals to deal with such problems, and "scientific measuring sticks" are applied to "account for the new efficiency." The first watershed is reached when the marginal utility of additional professionalization is greatest. Professionals do not define the problem, but they develop a scale against which to measure the effectiveness of treatment. Otherwise they could not establish a scientific basis to validate their professional techniques. The first watershed is the "era of the scientific verification of results."[19]

Between the first and second watersheds, the professional cadres extend their knowledge and control to an ever increasing range of problems. Their successes create a rationale for taking control of the sphere of activity they serve, driving out the competition and shifting the balance from lay to professional control. As the second watershed approaches, the "marginal utility of further professionalization declines."[20] For example, as professional health care techniques expand, the benefits of each additional unit decline; the more treatment-resistant diseases will be conquered less readily, so scientific research and new technologies will produce less value per unit cost.

At the second watershed the professional enterprise "frustrates the end for which it was originally designed." Past this point, the total utility *declines* as professionalization increases.[21] At the second watershed in medicine, the general health declines as medical technology advances. At the second watershed in law, rights are increasingly trampled as litigation ties more and more of social life in knots. At the second watershed in education, the general level of adaptation to life decreases as the number of years of compulsory school treatments is extended. At the second watershed in transport, it is more time-consuming and expensive to move around as rush hour congestion slows traffic to a halt.

After the second watershed the ends of life must be redefined by the professional elites so that they may retain authority and control. Professionals continue to make technological "breakthroughs," which are now defined in terms of new landmarks they set for themselves and then achieve, not in terms of clear and widely recognized ends such as those against which the value of professional help was established at the first watershed. Physicians perform "exotic repair jobs" to "keep sick life alive and medically dependent." Educators produce scientifically measurable "behavioral competencies" and call these "excellence." Meanwhile, we get progressively less healthy, less adapted, less protected, and less able to move about conveniently as medicine, education, law, and transport professionals make their new "breakthroughs." A "ritual of service" takes the place of something we value; there is an inversion of ends and means, with professional techniques (the means) becoming ends in themselves. Health care now *means* treatment by a physician (not attentive care which promotes health), education *means* schooling, not development of capacities for life activities.

The institutional perspective alerts us to the divorce of technology from the basic ends of life and the control of the people it serves.

AUTONOMOUS TECHNOLOGY

This perspective has been developed most thoroughly by Jacques Ellul,[22] who characterizes the emerging society as a tightly interlocked global technological system that is no longer subject even to the control of professional elites. "Technique" as an autonomous force reigns supreme. Humanity has "capitulated" to and been "absorbed" by it, existing only as "sensory equipment" and "recording devices." Human goals have been isolated from the context of community life, and redefined as measurable technical objectives. Means for achieving these goals have then been replaced, regardless of their personal meaning, experienced value, or connections with the rest of social life, by the most "efficient" means—those that maximize the attainment of the technical objectives per unit of cost.

In this process of technological transformation each step, considered in isolation, appears to be an improvement, yet the value of life as a whole has sharply declined. Freedom and self-determination have given way to a technological concentration camp, and regardless of our hopes and dreams everything gets done in the most efficient manner because four units of some technical objective, instead of just three, are produced. This analysis of technical rationality leads Ellul to a probing account of the characteristics of modern technology. Among these are the automatism of choice, self-augmentation, monism, universalism, and autonomy.[23]

Automatism. The choice of means becomes automatic when "everything has been measured and calculated mathematically" for then humanity is no longer an agent of choice, but merely a measuring and recording device. In the process a person may abandon tools he regards as excellent, and make "a choice which a calculating machine can also make." This form of rational analysis expands as technique encroaches upon previously nontechnical domains.[24]

Self-augmentation. Technological rationality engenders itself and expands "geometrically and irreversibly"[25] as more people become trained in technical forms of thinking, working away at improvements in all areas of life, isolating ends as technical objectives, devising efficient means, and in the process destroying traditional means and limits. Each advance engenders advances in related areas; an improvement in the automobile engine immediately impacts upon the tractor, with untold implications for the agricultural community.[26] Each advance has unanticipated side effects, which themselves necessitate new technical means.[27] For example, new techniques are needed to clean up after an unpredicted nuclear accident.

Monism. The technical phenomenon, "embracing all the separate techniques, forms a whole,"[28] so that "it is impossible to amputate a part of the system or modify it in any way without modifying the whole."[29]

Universalism. Both geographically and qualitatively, modern technology expands to encompass everything. Traditional cultures collapse on contact with it, for to assimilate any modern techniques traditional cultures must be broken up and reintegrated (monism). They have pressing needs and the new technical means are clearly superior when judged by technical standards (automatism). They are ill-equipped to respond to the culture-shattering side effects of technological transfer, and demand imported techniques of social control (self-augmentation), so that "in all areas, technique is producing the rapid collapse of all other civilizations."[30]

Technological rationality also spreads from the inorganic to the human sphere, with techniques of guidance, persuasion, propaganda, and the like. Ethical concepts of freedom and individuality collapse, and we progress toward a universal civilization which is "by and for technique" and which "ultimately *is* technique,"[31] as the substance of humanity is absorbed and only technique remains.

Autonomy. At this point technology becomes autonomous, for instead of serving human ends it shapes humanity and all ends to its own requirements. Goods are no longer a reflection of human values, adjusted to organic reactions of taste, smell, and touch. There are no longer "any specifically organic reactions," and the bread we "choose," for example, is that most readily produced by technological processes.

There is nothing which unaided humanity can *do* about technique on this perspective, for humanity has been "absorbed" by technique. Any change must come from outside, from a transcendent God, without whom "technique can ... destroy everything, lay all to waste." By this Ellul means that only through the biblical revelation can humanity find "the lucidity, courage, and hope to enable us to intervene with technique;"[32] Technical rationality is the dark blind force against which God and his Kingdom stand in dialectical opposition.[33]

The Emerging Technological Climate

What features of the new technological landscape are most relevant for democratic education? Our views, though sometimes surprising and controversial, emerge from the immersion of one of us (Rustum Roy) as an active participant at the cutting edge of technologically relevant basic research, who also stands back as an analyst of the bigger picture of research and development policies that support and are affected by such research.[34]

Our viewpoint hardly resembles the usual catalogue of fifth-generation computers, new lasers, high-speed trains, and the like, as representative of the emerging technological ambience. In selecting changes to consider, we have asked: What changes will affect the actual choices confronting the masses of young individuals in our schools and colleges? Whether a computer is of fourth or fifth generation is likely to be of significance to a very tiny minority. Most of the information and computer "revolutions" will disappear into little black boxes attached to our already familiar appliances—cars, TV's, and so forth. The real novelty of the emerging technological situation will be the growing clash between an uncontrolled (market) technology and one which is subjected to assessment and control by traditional or innovative ethical or religious value frameworks, however heterogeneous.

1. *Life-style changes directly imposed by technology on the masses of people in the developed world are reaching a plateau.* While in the last fifty years many technologies increased their impact factors by several (4 to 8) orders of magnitude, nothing remotely approaching that is likely to happen in the next fifty years. Fifty years ago perhaps 1,000 people could have been killed at one time by the most advanced weapons. Today it is 10^5 or 10^6 times greater than that, and indeed its effects could continue beyond the first batch of victims. But in the next fifty years there can be no change remotely similar. A hundred years ago it took weeks or months for a point to point exchange of information between two remote points on the globe. Today, for a substantial number it is a matter of seconds using direct dial telephone or satellite TV, a speed that can never significantly increase.

Our asymptotic vision of technological saturation is shared by many cutting edge scientists: Victor Weisskopf, former department head of physics at the Massachusetts Institute of Technology, and former Director General of CERN in Geneva; Gunther Stent, professor of biochemistry at the California Institute of Technology; and Steven Kline, professor of mechanical engineering at Stanford University. We are saying that there will be only relatively minor changes in the typical American's life-style in transportation, communication, housing, eating, and in some ways the changes may go *back* toward earlier times (for example, to conservation rather than profligacy).

Another very different reason for the technological saturation is the emerging *human* response ("enough is enough") to many of the latest technological innovations. Thus the issue of life extension by heroic means has clearly met its match in the rapidly expanding movements for dying with dignity, voluntary suicide, and so forth. Frameworks like those of Illich and Ellul have sharpened awareness of the irrationality of such "out of control" medical technologies, and the economic squeeze will now limit them and shift popular values away from them. Technological saturation is also evident in the automobile markets (in size and numbers) and in the entertainment world (television sets can be on no more than twenty-four hours in any given day). Fast food chains and restaurants after all do have a cap to their market—100 percent of all meals eaten!

We do *not* claim that new discoveries will cease; millions of scientific papers will be published, thousands of scientific conferences held. Extensions will be made of known science and technology to new parts of the world. Refinements and elaborations of increasing beauty and decreasing functional relevance are the trend of the high science-related technological future. A baroque era in science is imminent.

2. *Known, useful, cost-effective technologies available to Western nations today will spread widely across the earth.* While this will provide a small extension of markets for a short time for the developed world, it is a major factor in assuring the "globalization of the economy." This factor guarantees a tilt toward equalization of the standards of living worldwide, accepting, of course, a great deal of politically and militarily determined unevenness. The most significant impact of this technological "megatrend" is the necessity of lowered wages and standard of living for the majority of Americans—a major challenge, for many will be learning to live on less and finding new nonmaterial goals and values to give meaning to life.

3. *The information technologies will continue to create a "meta-reality" within which we will live and choose.* The most significant, unheralded postwar development in technology is the enormous increase in the power of propaganda, the molding of plastic minds. Television, newspapers, and magazines create to an extent unimagined previously the "meta-reality" in which most citizens live. Repetition of visual image creates an instant, and often illusory, world of reality in which people live and make choices. Orson Welles illustrated this fact decades ago with a single radio broadcast.

For example, the recent "economic recovery" and the federal deficit has been so stage managed in the media that the vast majority of citizens, unable to handle big numbers like million and billion, see no connection between the scary data and their own economic futures. The media could have shown the relevant facts by showing a family of four borrowing $3200 per year from the children's piggybank and borrowing another $1000 from a dark foreigner, and spending it on VCRs and fancy restaurants. This would have conveyed a more accurate image of irresponsible fiscal behavior to the mass of viewers, but this image of personal and national behavior would not be popular. Indeed, a wealthy citizen produced thirty-second TV "ads" graphically depicting the terrifying implications of the budget deficit, and the three major networks refused to sell him time to air them—the images were too "negative." Thus, even with a "free" press, the new technologies have made the masses of citizens a captive audience for those images which support the interests shared by the administration in power and the Lords of Industry and the Media.

4. *The new technologies create pressures toward a bimodal society of masters and consumers.* As technology and its management become more complex, there are strong pressures toward a bimodal society, where a minority (10 percent) can master and control the technology while the great masses of people remain consumers of (well advertised) real and illusory benefits and victims of hidden (unadvertised) costs. The ideals (never, of course, realized) of a democratic society with roughly equal access to goods, services, and power will be increasingly strained.

5. *Emerging technologies will require cooperation at least as much as competition.* A major cultural handicap our nation will carry into the next century is its emphasis on the virtues of competition. The spirit of entrepreneurship has been very important in the tremendous industrial development of the United States. But the emerging, exceedingly complex, globalized technological system will require collaboration and cooperation from the workbench to the boardroom. At the highest levels this seems to be recognized, but the "meta-reality" that competition alone is sacred will be difficult to dislodge from mass consciousness.

6. *There will be a growing potential for de-linked subcultures emphasizing ethical and religious values.* Interwoven into the main fabric of world technological development is a recurrent American motif: the insulated alternative community. Most of these alternative communities, such as the Mennonites and Amish that have existed for hundreds of years as insulated subcultures, have *placed effective controls on technology.* One cannot conceive of Amish children watching television for seven hours a day. Shorter-lived social experiments such as Oneida and New Harmony also controlled both social and technological climates, though the latter were very positive toward the utilization of technology for social ends.

Some new developments, including the ease of worldwide communications, the availability of transportation, the decentralization of power, water, and other conveniences, will increase the potential for a much wider range of partly de-linked subcultures emphasizing ethical and religious values. The new low-input agriculture promoted by our colleague Robert Rodale could provide a secure economic base for small communities serving metropolitan areas. New "cottage industries" are a likely response to the anticipated endemic unemployment and underemployment. The slowness of response is due to the fact that these educational and religious communities remain technologically "underprivileged" and unaware of what new technologies can do for them rather than *to* them.

Implications for Education

What can educators learn from these perspectives on technology? We suggest the following lessons, which guide our current thinking in STS education.[35]

1. *Social perspectives on technology provide frameworks for a radical reassessment of the system of schools and colleges as an educational technology.* The social perspectives all point beyond the technological "mystique." Once we break our fascination with the "magic" of "revolutionary" technologies and the "gee whiz" science connected with them, we can reassess very familiar everyday means to basic ends as technologies. The system of schools and colleges itself is a modern technology for shaping learning contexts and providing experiences needed for adaptation and growth. It is at the center of technological development (through its research and development, and its graduate training activities) and of the socialization of the young for serving the technological society. It has expanded in the last one hundred years from a little speck on the institutional map to a monolith with a radical monopoly over socially legitimate learning activities. Powerful social groups have shaped this system to serve their ends and to exclude others from obtaining their fair share of material and social goods. A powerful professional elite has worked this system for its own good, obtaining the power to supervise and control every learning activity. Meanwhile many young people, locked into an endless cycle of compulsory programming, have become less skilled and less adapted to life as they become "better educated," and better conditioned to fit the technological system, which both controls and "services" them.

We must reconsider this system in terms of the basic needs of masses of people, not in terms set by the educational system itself, such as years of educational attainment, numbers of dropouts prevented, scores on tests of school achievement. When we consider the system of schools and colleges as a technology in a social context, new questions arise. What are the hidden costs and social inequities in this means for sharing social knowledge and skill? What are the trade-offs and the unanticipated consequences of granting to this system a radical monopoly over socially legitimate learning? Are the ends promoted by the system consistent with the basic needs of the masses of people? Is the system out of control, no longer subject to democratic assessment and reform, producing as its end result little more than its own means, reducing the meaning of education to nothing but submission to compulsory treatments?

Educational reform efforts, such as those stimulated by *A Nation At Risk*, tend to lose the forest for the trees, restricting themselves to changes *within* the system—more hours and days, higher required scores on tests, more years of science and mathematics, while failing to reconsider the system itself. The first lesson the educator has to learn from the study of current perspectives on technology is the need to reassess radically this system that sorts the population into winners and losers, determines the social value and authority of all knowledge and skill, serves as the primary gatekeeper for all forms of meaningful and remunerative work, and establishes increasingly unrealistic and frustrating life-style expectations and aspirations and a normative "meta-reality" for the population. (Our colleague Ivan Illich has of course been forcefully raising these questions since 1971.)

We are *not* saying that there is no need for or value in formal educational experiences. We *are* saying that there is need for a more diverse mix of educational technologies, including both formal and informal education, learning experiences which place young people into meaningful contact with their working elders, and self-determined learning in both in-school and out-of-school contexts. Such a mix cannot be established unless the radical monopoly of the system of education over access to work and other arenas of social life is broken.

2. *Technology in its social context is an ideal integrative field of study for democratic education at all levels.* Within the school curriculum, technology in the broad sense of means to human ends can serve as an ideal organizing and integrating theme for education at all levels. The study of technology in its social context permits the integration of science and values, art and craft, the quantitative and the qualitative. The technological issues of any community are an ideal way of introducing themes in its work life and political processes. Active engagement in the study of such issues, joined with responsible citizen action, empowers citizens to take their responsibilities seriously and to seek once again to bring technology under citizen control for the common good. (This was a main theme in the educational theory of John Dewey.)[36]

When we advocate a technology-centered curriculum, we do not, of course, mean a curriculum dominated by the "magic" of the "revolutionary new technologies" and "gee whiz" science, which students will come to "appreciate" even if not to "understand." Rather, the curriculum should be organized around a balanced assessment of means to community ends, including training in the political, organizational, and rhetorical skills needed for effective and responsible democratic citizenship. "Technological literacy" for us is not inert knowledge of new technologies—computers, robots, satellites; we include in this term the skills for assessing the social benefits and costs of these technologies, and for taking effective action in the political arena, in legislative action, in the courts, in labor unions, and elsewhere to bring them under community control. To become technologically literate, in this sense, is not to acquire isolated knowledge or skills, but rather to integrate all of one's knowledge and skills: to be able to synthesize multiple perspectives, to become sensitive to subtle relationships and interconnections in nature and the man-made world, to become increasingly aware of one's own developing point of view and to become skilled at expressing it, communicating it to others, and negotiating positive solutions to common problems.

All this implies a diminished role for disciplinary instruction, subject matter coverage, and standardized evaluation. It implies a revitalization of the "liberal arts" tradition, with an enlivened trivium and a new quadrivium which includes whole earth ecology and technology. It points toward an augmented role for individual and group learner-directed projects, conducted both in and out of school, contending with real-world technological issues in their social context.

At the beginning of the 1970s at a few pioneering institutions, including Cornell, SUNY-Stonybrook, and Pennsylvania State University, genuinely interdisciplinary faculty groups including philosophers, engineers, and scientists formed to reflect *upon* (and not merely reflect) our technological society, and began seriously to consider some of the emerging critical insights about the impact of technology. These efforts are now reaching maturity in the academic field known as Science, Technology, and Society (STS). Today scarcely a decade and a half later, perhaps 1,000 colleges teach at least a course or two in the area of STS.

STS involves insights from literally every discipline on campus, and the typical STS faculty is composed of representatives from the same wide spectrum of disciplines. But STS is fundamentally different from a mere collection or cafeteria of disciplinary insights. It is the articulation of insights within what is becoming a clearer, more coordinated, and more comprehensive framework. Some basic "principles" or "precepts" of STS are emerging (for example, the principles of "holism" and "systems," the "trade-offs" or "no free lunch" principles, and the principle of inevitable unanticipated side effects). These are used to elucidate current and future distributions of benefits and costs (including hidden costs) between sectors of society, between regions of the country and the world, and between current and future generations. This intellectual ferment is extending to the traditional disciplines, where exciting new subdisciplines such as environmental ethics are forming, complete with meetings and scholarly journals.

While STS was growing on university campuses, academics maintained their posture of benign neglect toward precollege education. Yet in 1983 a sudden change in national mood thrust science education into the limelight. We were bombarded with terms like "science literacy," "technology literacy," and "computer literacy" from every side.

The National Science Teachers Association (NSTA) endorsed STS in their position paper, "Science-Technology-Society: Science Education for the 1980s." PROJECT SYNTHESIS, a NSF-sponsored effort for identifying appropriate science education also endorsed STS, identifying such goals for science education as "an understanding of the impact of technological developments on society, in order to make reasonable and responsible decisions." In its influential report of September 1983, *Educating Americans for the Twenty-first Century*, the National Science Board Commission on Precollegiate Education stated that "the greater the degree to which all the sciences and technology can be integrated in new curricular approaches, the broader the understanding in these fields will be." It urged educators to take advantage of the "numerous opportunities to demonstrate the interdependence of human knowledge," and recommended an integrated approach to learning about the social, political, economic, and ethical dimensions of science—that is, STS. While there is still active debate about the form in which STS education will be delivered, several different approaches appear promising in different school environments.

3. *Educators must prepare young people for world citizenship.* The spread of technology and the globalization of the economy imply a pressure toward a gradual equalization among nations in the standard of living. This means that developing nations may become more

wealthy while the developed nations adapt to a gradual lowering in their living standards. This poses direct challenges for educators.

First, there is a need to promote understanding of the global economy, so that future workers can react in an effective, reasonable, long-term manner to the changing world of employment and remuneration. Current American workers have reacted to foreign competition as though they had God-given rights to their middle-class jobs and incomes. They regard their overseas competitors as little more than thieves, and demand government protection. Students and workers need a better framework for understanding the globalization of the economy.

Second, this means fostering attitudes of multicultural awareness, tolerance, and appreciation. It means breaking out of the mind-set of international competition and learning new attitudes and skills of international cooperation. This demands the fostering of nonmaterial life goals and values.

4. *Educators must prepare the young to accept some limits to their expectations, and to seek meaning in values other than possessions and domination.* The frontier, the west, new lands, provided outlets for the underclasses looking for the main chance. But where after Alaska? The blueprint for the march of United States science and technology after World War II, prepared for President Roosevelt by a committee headed by Vannevar Bush, was titled "Science: The Endless Frontier." The United States now faces the difficult task of dealing with finitude: of space, of resources, of wealth and incomes, of meaningful jobs, and of technology as the route to comparative economic advantage. The traditional social ambience of Horatio Alger, of "big is best," of "the sky is the limit," of "everyone can be as rich as Rockefeller" and (seen on a Yuppie T-shirt) "the winner of the game is the person who has the most things when he dies," must be replaced with a value framework which is better adjusted to contemporary realities. This cannot be done by politicians campaigning for office. It is the job of education in schools, growth centers, and churches.

5. *Educators must confront technology as "magic," "savior," "hope"— technology as religion.* For the masses of United States citizens, technology (often misnamed "science") is the operational religion. Science/Technology (S/T) is the source of Truth, and all veridical judgments are allegedly based on scientific evidence and proof. Existential hope for deliverance from death, disease, or unemployment is always placed in Technology. S/T fulfills—in the form of endless

pictures of the rings of Saturn, moons of Jupiter or endless treks to distant stars, or journeys into the brain—the human need for the mysterious. Almost by subversion these have become the new ikons, the holy pictures, accompanied by the appropriate music, the liturgies of the new Church of Technology. Of course, they turn out to be wholly inadequate for this task, at best producing a one-dimensional reduction of a nourishing spiritual life.

In the coming decades the educator's task will include the presentation of the "Clash of the Titans" between traditional religions and international technology. How will educators deal with the tremendous pro-S/T tilt of all the other "educative" forces of the "meta-reality" creating machine? Indeed, how many teachers are themselves not now shaped by that same machine into less than critical appraisers of contemporary technology?

6. *Technology for society.* We have spoken above of the new potential for decentralist, alternative communities and worldviews. Educators have the job of exposing the young in a sympathetic and tolerant spirit to such systems, through the study of utopian and dystopian fiction, historical utopian community experiments, contemporary community experiments such as Twin Oaks, Findhorn, and Steven Gaskin's Farm, or urban centers experimenting with food co-ops, "people's" medical centers, or Rodale's "regenerative technologies." Here we find experiments, whether in imagination or reality, with social arrangements and technological means that promote meaningful work, health and vitality, quality of environment, creativity, and full human development. The common thread in all of these experiments is an attitude of "Technology for Society, Not the Other Way 'Round."

* * * *

Education which supports "technology for society" is now in remarkably active ferment. The emergence of STS education, first within the colleges and universities and then within secondary schools, qualifies as well as any recent educational development as a "mega-trend." While the STS education movement points the way to the revision of form, content, and process, it is still in its infancy. It is exposed to the obvious danger of being co-opted by discipline-based higher education; it has no power base in the faculties, and is hardly a "buzz word" among funding agencies.

Yet the movement is remarkably resilient. It has succeeded in integrating many nonacademic thinkers into the educational reform process. These include Ivan Illich and Jacques Ellul—among the most cited scholars writing about technology. Robert Rodale, Chairman of the Board of Rodale Press—who "teaches" some millions of readers every month about health and agriculture issues via the magazines he publishes, is a leading force in a new style of technology education. Governor Richard Lamm of Colorado is likewise doing STS in his books and in the arena of public decision making. In our STS program at Pennsylvania State University we have involved all of these people and others like them (Illich and Rodale as members of our faculty) in our effort to make STS a new paradigm for integrative general education in our technological society.

FOOTNOTES

1. Harry S. Broudy, *The Real World of the Public Schools* (New York: Harcourt Brace Jovanovich, 1972); idem, *Truth and Credibility: The Citizen's Dilemma* (New York: Longman, 1981); Thomas F. Green, *Work, Leisure, and the American School* (New York: Random House, 1968); idem, "The Formation of Conscience in an Age of Technology," John Dewey Lecture (Syracuse, N.Y.: John Dewey Society, 1984).

2. *Wisconsin v. Yoder*, 406 U.S. 205 (1972).

3. Charles Handy, *The Future of Work: A Guide to a Changing Society* (Oxford, Eng.: Basil Blackwell, 1984).

4. George Wood, "Education for Democratic Participation: Democratic Values and the Nuclear Freeze Campaign," *Theory and Research in Social Education* 12 (Winter 1985): 39-56.

5. David Noble, *America by Design: Science, Technology, and the Rise of Corporate Capitalism* (New York: Knopf, 1977).

6. See Raymond E. Callahan, *Education and the Cult of Efficiency* (Chicago: University of Chicago Press, 1962), and Samuel Haber, *Efficiency and Uplift: Scientific Management in the Progressive Era—1890-1920* (Chicago: University of Chicago Press, 1964).

7. C. H. Waddington, *Tools for Thought* (New York: Basic Books, 1977).

8. Ibid., p. 12.

9. Quoted in Noble, *America by Design*, p. xxii.

10. Harry Braverman, *Labor and Monopoly Capital: The Degradation of Work in the Twentieth Century* (New York: Monthly Review, 1974).

11. Ibid., pp. 444-45.

12. Rachel Carson, *Silent Spring* (Boston: Houghton Mifflin, 1962); Paul Ehrlich, *The Population Bomb* (New York: Ballantine, 1968); Richard Buckminster Fuller, *Utopia or Oblivion: The Prospects for Humanity* (New York: Bantam Books, 1969); Donella Meadows et al., *The Limits to Growth: A Report to the Club of Rome's Project on the Predicament of Mankind* (New York: Universe Books, 1972); Ernst F. Schumacher, *Small Is Beautiful: Economics as if People Mattered* (New York: Harpers, 1973); Robert Heilbroner, *An Inquiry into the Human Prospect* (New York: Norton, 1974).

13. Bruce Nussbaum, *The World after Oil: The Shifting Axis of Power and Wealth* (New York: Simon and Schuster, 1983), p. 17.

14. Ibid.

15. Paul Hawken, *The Next Economy* (New York: Holt, Rinehart and Winston, 1983), p. 7.

16. Ibid., p. 8.

17. Ivan Illich, *Deschooling Society* (New York: Harper and Row, 1971); idem, *Medical Nemesis: The Expropriation of Health* (New York: Pantheon, 1976); idem, *Shadow-Work* (Boston: M. Boyars, 1981).

18. Ivan Illich, *Tools for Conviviality* (New York: Harper and Row, 1973).

19. Ibid., p. 6.

20. Ibid.

21. Ibid., p. 7.

22. Jacques Ellul, *The Technological Society* (New York: Knopf, 1964); idem, *The Technological System* (New York: Continuum, 1980). See also, Langdon Winner, *Autonomous Technology: Technics-out-of-Control as a Theme in Political Thought* (Cambridge, Mass.: MIT Press, 1977), and William D. Taylor and Jane B. Johnsen, "Resisting Technological Momentum," in *Microcomputers and Education*, ed. Jack A. Culbertson and Luvern L. Cunningham, Eighty-fifth Yearbook of the National Society for the Study of Education, Part 1 (Chicago: University of Chicago Press, 1986).

23. Ellul, *The Technological Society*.

24. Ibid., pp. 79-80.

25. Ibid., p. 89.

26. Ibid., p. 87.

27. Ibid., p. 92.

28. Ibid.

29. Ibid., p. 116.

30. Ibid., p. 124.

31. Ibid., p. 128.

32. Jacques Ellul, *In Season Out of Season* (San Francisco: Harper and Row, 1982), p. 206.

33. For a more complete account and critique of this perspective, see Leonard J. Waks, "The Oil in the Machine: Jacques Ellul on Human Techniques in the Technological Society," in *Research in Philosophy and Technology*, vol. 9, ed. Carl Mitcham (Greenwich, Conn.: JAI Press, 1986).

34. Deborah Shapley and Rustum Roy, *Lost at the Frontier: U.S. Science and Technology Policy Adrift* (Philadelphia: ISI Press, 1985).

35. Rustum Roy, "The Science/Technology/Society Connection," *Curriculum Review* 24 (January-February 1985): 12-14, 16; Leonard J. Waks and Madhu S. Prakash, "STS Education and Its Step Sisters," *Bulletin of Science, Technology, and Society* 5 (Winter 1985): 105-119.

36. John Dewey, *The School and Society* (New York: McClure Phillips, 1900); idem, *The Child and the Curriculum* (Chicago: University of Chicago Press, 1902); idem, *Democracy and Education* (New York: MacMillan, 1916); idem, *The Public and Its Problems* (New York: Holt, 1927).

CHAPTER III

Contemporary Work and the Quality of Life

ARTHUR G. WIRTH

A democratic political economy must begin and end with the person-in-society, seeing him as both end and means, and combining his reason and his actions in empowered participation.

Kalman H. Silvert
The Reason for Democracy

Few trends could so thoroughly undermine the very foundations of our free society as the acceptance by corporate officials of a social responsibility other than to make as much money as possible. This is a fundamentally subversive doctrine.

Milton Friedman
Capitalism and Freedom

The Background

American society has been moved by these two visions of its destiny: (a) a vision of the democratic ideal of a society of informed free men and women participating in the formation of institutions which honor human dignity and the conservation of the bounties of nature; and (b) an ideal of access to unfettered economic competition in the marketplace, with management's prerogative to secure efficiency to maximize profit. Freedom of economic action is assumed to be the precondition for all other freedoms, and for a boundless increase in the material standard of living.

In the evolution of American experience, both work and schooling have been affected by the tension between these two value orientations. The tension is heightened at present as we confront three momentous global changes: (a) the emergence of a computer/robotics/communications revolution comparable in its social effects to the advent of the railroads and the automobile; (b) the thrust of the United States into a competitive world market; and (c) threats to ecological well-being due to unprecedented economic and population growth.

After sketching some dimensions of the changes in work now under way, I shall examine two fundamental value choices we confront about the design of work—choices with profound consequences for what we shall become as a people as we enter the next century. I shall note briefly consequences for life in schools. Finally, I end with a perspective from *WorldWatch Report 1985*, which points to issues mainly neglected in current debates about work and schools.

We are at the beginning of a third major change in American work life. At the time of the founding, after breaking with feudal restrictions, we were overwhelmingly self-employed—in farming, the trades, and small commercial enterprises. Agriculture dominated, with four-fifths of nonslave Americans working on farms. By 1900 that figure had been halved to 41 percent, and by 1985 to 3 to 4 percent.[1]

At the end of the nineteenth and throughout most of the twentieth century the corporate industrial revolution created a radically different work life. By 1985 the shift from self-employment to wage employment and from employment in small to employment in large enterprises had been affected. Over 90 percent of Americans now work for corporations, government agencies, and other organizations that hire their labor. Corporate bureaucracies with top-down managerial directives have become the American way at work. It was an approach that combined the free market ideology of Adam Smith with the scientific management controls of Frederick Taylor. Democratic process was ruled irrelevant in daily work because competitive reality decreed unquestioned managerial authority. Democracy belonged in the *political* realm with the opportunity to vote periodically. As the twentieth century unfolded, work became more complex but remained hierarchical and fragmented. A pyramidal arrangement placed a few people, representing various levels of management, at the top; a somewhat larger number of technicians and supervisory personnel in the middle; and a large number of relatively low-paid workers at the bottom.

With the goal of cutting costs and centralizing control, labor was routinized and deskilled at the bottom and increasingly at middle levels. Only those at the top retained comprehension of the overall process of production. There was room for vertical advancement for a few. For most, wages and salaries, which provided access to consumption of goods and services, became the primary motivation for work. For some, with access to capital, there were openings to the zest of entrepreneurship. American corporate capitalism worked, when combined with the power of science and technology. It brought longer life, and a material standard of living that was the envy of the world.[2]

It also exacted its price. The fundamental democratic value of the dignity of the person has not fared well under authoritarian and fragmented work conditions, nor has the democratic aspiration to participate in decisions affecting one's life. Ties with community, based on the principle that people need each other, have been weakened under the emphasis of self-centered individualism.

We have created a society of powerful means and material plenty but with ambiguity about ends. Should we give clear priority to the individual pursuit of gain, on the assumption that all other goods flow from it? Or, should that pursuit of gain be made subordinate to the values of a more humane community?

Sources of Changes at Work: The Global Market and High Technology

For a quarter of a century after World War II American industry was the dominant giant on the world scene. While we complacently took for granted our position of eminence, new forces of underlying change were at work. American enterprise was to be challenged not only at the international level but in the huge home market as well.

In *The Next American Frontier*, Robert Reich caught the essence of one major challenge to complacency.[3] He pointed out that at the opening of the century we had been economic pioneers. We had perfected mass production techniques which could use ill-educated, rural, or immigrant labor guided by Taylorist scientific management. Nonunion labor, deskilled by assembly-line technology, provided low-cost production. But our preeminence was not guaranteed by history. Twenty-five years after "unconditional surrender" by Japan in 1945, our enemies as well as our wounded allies had marshalled their own productive forces. They were joined by third-world countries using our own type of mass production, and energized by modern equipment and drastically lower labor costs. After the oil crisis and the higher dollar we suddenly found ourselves on the waves of the one global market with everyone else. We were under stress both at home and abroad. We were, in fact, confronted by what Reich had labelled "the next American frontier." According to Reich we had to learn to pioneer again, but this time in a work world of high technology marked by rapid and unpredictable change. The classical scientific management style, said Reich, was cutting us off from a major source of strength: our massive, better educated work force (75 percent having completed secondary education or beyond). The need to meet the challenges of complex change with flexible, intelligent responses by people at work was wasted by the technical control mode of management. We could, Reich said, be confidently competitive in the global market only if we found a formula to bring together rapidly advancing technology with a committed, engaged work force.

The gist of Reich's argument can be seen more clearly as we look at the impact of high technology on work.

Changes in the Structure and Nature of Work

We are in the midst of a historic shift in the structure and nature of work in America. Computer technology is the engine driving change. It forces us to confront both the fact of new kinds of work, and the need to choose which values will guide its design.

FROM MANUFACTURING TO SERVICE INDUSTRIES

The much heralded shift from smokestack industries to the service sector is demonstrated by a few illustrative statistics. A *New York Times* report of November 1985 stated that American manufacturing now employs only 19 percent of the work force. The sprawling services-producing sector (including such disparate elements as communications, government agencies, insurance, wholesale and retail trade, foods, health) produced 68 percent of the 1984 gross national product, compared to 32 percent for the goods producing sector.[4] "Information workers" alone—managers, clerks, sales, technical, and professional people—comprise 53 percent of the labor force.[5]

A few additional figures illustrate the direction of change in manufacturing. While there were a half million production workers in the steel industry in 1970, by 1983 there were 258,000. In textiles the drop was from 855,000 to 641,000, and in chemicals from 804,000 to 580,000.[6] Two million manufacturing jobs have disappeared since 1980. Nearly all of the seven million jobs created since 1981 have been in service industries and construction.[7]

In addition to structural changes of such staggering proportions, the microelectronics revolution is leading to dramatic changes in the way work is done, whether in manufacturing or the services. Indirect changes ripple out to affect the entire culture.

CHANGES IN THE NATURE OF WORK

An example of the rate of change is exemplified in the use of robotics. In 1970 there were only about two hundred robots in all of America's factories, with the leader being General Motors. By 1980 General Motors alone had installed three hundred robots, and the robots carried a message far beyond their numbers. Between 1970 and 1980 the wage bill at General Motors soared by 240 percent, while the cost of operating a robot had stabilized at $5 or $6 an hour. The result: 5,000 robots operating in General Motors plants by 1985, with plans to buy an additional 15,000 or more by 1990.

The greatest advance in the use of robots is shifting now to the electronics industry itself. For example, about nine-tenths of Apple's MacIntosh computer is assembled automatically. Some electronics manufacturers in Japan claim to have automated one-half to three-fourths of assembly operations.

Meanwhile, not too far from Silicon Valley in California, 40,000 migrant workers a year used to be hired to pick the tomato crop. After starting to use a robot picker named Tomato Harvester in the early 1980s, only eight thousand laborers now pick a crop three times as large. (The tomato itself has changed also. It takes a sharp knife to get through the toughened skin to the fruit.)

Within buffeted manufacturing itself a still more ambitious concept is emerging: "computer integrated manufacturing" that can fuse product design, manufacture, and marketing into a single stream of information. For example, at McDonnell Douglas Corporation, the sales people can send an order for a part directly to a computer-aided design system. This dispenses with the services of the old-fashioned draftsmen. An engineer can now make a freehand sketch on a cathode ray tube linked to a computer that automatically transforms it into an electronic blueprint that can be revised endlessly. The part can be made "automatically" by computer-controlled machine tools similar, in essence, to robots. Other computers update the inventory and keep sales records. Meanwhile, upper management has access to whatever information it wants.[8]

We can get another glimpse of the impact of computers on work by turning to the service sector. Since nearly half of Americans work in offices, a look at the insurance industry is instructive. It is on the cutting edge of exploiting the capabilities of computers and information technologies. The Institute for Research on Educational Finance and Governance at Stanford University made a study of a representative group of insurance companies which showed that, on the one hand, routine clerical jobs such as keyboarding, typing, and filing, often held by minorities, are fast disappearing. On the other hand, new jobs for skilled clerical workers now contain tasks that formerly were the work of lower-level professionals. Many aspects of underwriting and claims estimation have been automated. In sum, the study concluded that

Office automation wiped out thousands of jobs for low-skilled clerical workers, created new jobs for skilled clerical workers and eliminated many professional jobs that comprised the middle of the career ladder by which clerical workers move into better paying, more highly skilled and prestigious jobs. . . . Both the bottom and the middle of the occupational distribution are shrinking in the insurance industry.[9]

At the same time the requisite skill level for upper managerial and professional jobs is rising. A college degree is an entry requirement for such positions where the work is challenging and financial remunerations are proportionately higher.

What are we to make of such dramatic changes? What overall consequences are in store for American workers and education? Will high technology raise the skill level of work, or extend the deskilling of work into middle-level technical and managerial levels? Will it create more jobs than are lost? The safest generalization is that we do not really know. It will do some of all of the above. We are confronted with turbulent change, that is, change that is rapid and unpredictable. Who could have projected the ramifications for American life when Henry Ford got the gleam in his eye for a mass-produced horseless carriage? Nevertheless projections are being made and have affected the national reports on education. They bear a closer look.

For example, two widespread beliefs are that as low-skilled manufacturing jobs are eliminated, they will be replaced by high technology jobs requiring greater technical or professional skills such as computer programmers and engineers, and that high technology will upgrade existing jobs.

National reports on education have reflected the general belief that high technology will require workers with more sophisticated job skills. A report from the Education Commission of the States (1982) says, for example:

Occupational growth throughout the 1980s is projected to expand most rapidly in the higher-skilled, technical occupations. Tomorrow's workers will likely need improved skills in the selection and communication of information. Many of today's skills considered to be of a "higher" level are the potential basic skills of tomorrow.[10]

Studies of the real world of work, however, point to a more complex and less rosy picture. The Institute for Research on Educational Finance and Governance has made detailed studies of the impact of high technology on work. They find that while many higher-skill jobs are, in fact, being created, most new jobs will not be in high technology occupations.

For example, Bureau of Labor Statistics (BLS) projections for 1978-1990 show that three of the fastest growing occupations are for machine mechanics, computer operators, and systems analysts—jobs which do indeed deal with high technology products. Such jobs are projected to increase by over 100 percent.

But these percentage figures are misleading. The BLS estimates that high technology occupations, as a group, will account for only 7 percent of new jobs between 1980 and 1990. Job growth, moreover, is restrained by rapidly growing productivity due to upgraded technology. Data Resources, Inc., estimates that the number of new high technology jobs created between 1983 and 1993 will be between 730,000 and 1 million. This is less than half the jobs that were lost in manufacturing between 1979 and 1982.

Slower-growing occupations with a large employment base will contribute markedly more new jobs. In fact, of the twenty occupations the BLS expects to provide most jobs, not one is related to high technology. The five occupations predicted to produce the most new jobs are all in low-skilled areas: janitors, nurse's aides, sales clerks, cashiers, waiters, and waitresses. Only three or four of the "top 20" require education beyond the secondary level, and only two (teaching and nursing) require a college degree.

The picture becomes more vivid when we note that for the 1978-90 period, 150,000 jobs were predicted for computer programmers while 800,000 new jobs were expected for fast food workers and kitchen helpers.[11] As technology becomes more sophisticated it will be able to perform more complex mental functions, which will affect technical and professional jobs as we saw in the case of the insurance industry.

Thus, while the prospect of a high technology society clearly contains exciting aspects, it also has more somber possibilities.

PROSPECTS FOR A DUAL ECONOMY

One of these is a drift toward a dual economy, both within the society at large and within specific industries. At one end, many at the technical/professional/managerial levels will find satisfying challenges, ample financial rewards, and perhaps more leisure, while at the other end, there is the disturbing possibility of a growing underclass. It will often be composed of people of color who have been squeezed out of both blue-collar and service-sector jobs, and who failed to respond to the press for academic performance in the schools. It is fair to ask what will be the social costs if we let their destiny be decided by the simple law of supply and demand. There also are signs of dualism within the work world itself. In places like Silicon Valley in California, we find engineers and other highly trained personnel in computer industries who work in interdisciplinary collaborative task-forces, while minority women who produce the silicon chips work in low-wage, monotonous, unhealthy work conditions.

In the face of this actual and potential dualism, national reports on education urge all students to prepare themselves with higher academic studies, especially science and mathematics. Higher preparation brings higher expectations. But studies of the Institute for Research on Educational Finance and Governance conclude that growth in high technology and in managerial and professional occupations will not expand sufficiently to meet higher student aspirations.[12] If we relinquish the romantic faith that expansion of computer technology contains automatic solutions to employment problems, we see that we are confronted with both practical and moral problems.

The Congressional Office of Technology Assessment (OTA) describes a fundamental policy choice we face in the design of technology-worker relations—a choice that could increase or decrease dualism in American work.[13] The OTA says that the combination of microelectronic robotics and telecommunications technology provides an opportunity to revitalize the competitiveness of American industry. But benefits will not come automatically. One option is to maximize profits by turning to cheap third-world, off-shore labor for much industrial production. Then with domestic, nonunion workers disciplined by fear of unemployment, management may design technology to deskill work to maximize efficiency. It may "work" but it increases the gap between technical-managerial elites and a growing body of deskilled workers. It also produces high levels of unemployment, and wholesale abandonment of some communities. The second option is to use electronic technology to redesign production toward an economy of high technology, high-skilled, high-wage industries. This choice is based on the assumption that flexibility of response by both technical components and a committed work force with high morale are indispensable for survival in a computerized, competitive era.

OTA studies show that the integration of programmable, automated processes from marketing to work design, to shipment, and to customer service can produce continuing advantage in international markets. But technology alone will not produce competitive advantage. It must be accompanied by changes in the organizational structure and uses of the work force.

The Value Choices

The core question is: What values will corporate and union leadership use to guide the design of work in the emerging electronics era? Hackman and Oldham found deep division among corporate leaders regarding philosophies of management.[14] This led them to project two scenarios for the near future of work in the United States.

In Scenario I the emphasis is on "fitting people to jobs" by technological and behavioral engineering. It is a sophisticated extension of scientific management in the Frederick Taylor tradition. In this scenario, techniques for engineering tasks into minute trainable steps will create more and more "people proof" jobs. External controls will be used to shape desired behaviors with financial rewards for correcting performance. Psychological tests will facilitate a closer fit between people and work tasks. Integrated circuit microprocessors will facilitate gathering performance data that presently defy cost-efficient measurements. Worker productivity will be supervised by micro-second electronic monitoring. Experts who *think* about the design of production will be separated sharply from people who *do* the work. In this scenario, in spite of generous material rewards for desired behavior, self-esteem levels will tend to drop and symptoms of alienation will increase. Statements will be heard like, "The harder I work, the more pay and praise I get and the more headaches I get." To counter the problems of alcohol and drug abuse, absenteeism and apathy, management may introduce drug and alcohol abuse programs for those who "slip into bad habits," and "counseling" for the depressed and resentful. Such firms may publicly congratulate themselves for their progressive employee maintenance programs.

We continue to move strongly toward Scenario I. We know how to operate it. Workers and managers have internalized its ways and are uncomfortable with change.

But there are doubts. In 1980 a General Motors Vice-President in charge of new plant design told me:

In our history we designed work so that every task on the line could be learned in fifteen minutes or less—so simple that any idiot could do it. When trouble occurred we stepped up supervision. We have finally concluded, however, that increased control by supervisors of a reluctant work force that produces shabby products is not viable for survival.

Counterforces have developed from a sense that the costs of Scenario I are too high—that it is dysfunctional for survival.

For several decades there have been stirrings for reform, from rather superficial efforts like flex-time and job enrichment to a more thorough conceptualizing of an alternative theory of work. First we sketch a Scenario II as set forth by Hackman and Oldham; then we take a more detailed look at the emerging theory of democratic socio-technical work design.

In this Scenario II the aim is "to fit jobs to people." As often as possible, responsibility for ways of planning and executing work will be located at the level where the work is done. Those who do the work will have a voice in the technical design; they will be included in problem solving, and in quality control of their efforts. As more initiative is shifted to persons at the work site, organizations will be leaner with fewer hierarchical levels of management. Information required to do the work will be given directly to the people at work. Deliberate efforts will be made to break with the Taylorist tradition which separated thinking from execution. The question will be: How can work be organized so as to treat people as adults and responsible members of the workplace community? There will be a relinquishing of the assumption that there are single expert-designed answers for getting work done. Initiatives, when possible, will be shifted to individuals or to autonomous work groups. Organizations will be designed to be places where people can learn and grow because it is necessary for adaptation to turbulent change, and because the need to continue to learn is strong in many or most people.

Democratic sociotechnical work theory is a term that captures the idea behind Scenario II. The clarification of this philosophy of work has been an international process. Ideas have come from people like Einar Thorsrud and P. G. Herbst of Norway, Fred Emery of Australia, Eric Trist and Michael Maccoby of the United States, and thinkers at the Tavistock Institute of Human Relations in England. Much of the underlying theory and practice came out of the work of Leland Bradford, Kenneth Benne and Ronald Lippitt at the National Training Laboratories in Bethel, Maine.[15] In the United States an early place of implementation was the Harman Auto Mirror plant at Bolivar, Tennessee. Sidney Harman, President of Harman International Industries, and Irving Bluestone, United Auto Workers Vice-President, demonstrated the union-management collaboration necessary for such an effort. With variations, some of which contradict genuine democratic work theory, the idea of "participative management" has been spreading to selected plants of major corporations. At General Motors, for example, features of the idea are being integrated with computer-controlled production of the new Saturn car in what could be a major step toward sociotechnical work design.

The basic criticism of scientific management by sociotechnical theorists is that it is guilty of the "technological fix" error, that is, the assumption that all problems will yield to expert-designed technical solutions.[16] The reality of human work, they say, is "socio" as well as "technical." "Socio" refers to the purposive, collaborative, idea-generating aspects of human beings.

The mainline efficiency model is out of touch with the "socio" dimension. The system falters because it fails to engage the commitment and personal enthusiasm of people, and their capacity for learning and problem solving.

At a more basic level the new concern for the quality of life is not merely an aberrant wish of impractical humanitarians. The old production model is fundamentally out of touch with "postindustrial" aspects of reality. It worked, P. G. Herbst says, when man's fundamental relation to the world was the physical environment. In the industrial stage, life is seen as man fighting against the physical environment—an environment conceptualized as an aggregate of elements that can be manipulated for human gain. This was the model—atomistic, mechanistic, and deterministic—on which classical science built its theory of universal laws. It was also the orientation that provided the conceptual framework for the creation of bureaucratic organizations based on the principle of replaceable parts. When "fixing" is necessary one turns to the engineering expert who provides the thinking "to restore efficiency." The pathology emerges when humans begin to treat other humans as parts of the physical environment.

In emerging postindustrialism the physicalist model is called into question. The fundamental problem becomes how to cope with turbulent change that is the product of human thought and action. Efforts to solve turbulent-type problems with procedures based on principles of the mechanistic, aggregate model increasingly break down. The social ecologies that have come into being do not conform to the universal principles of classical science. The capacity to deal successfully with the reality of turbulent change depends on building a learning, value-choosing capacity into the system itself.

The shift from the old to a new model of effective productivity requires also a shift in our image of human nature. In *The Structure of Evil*, Ernest Becker caught the underlying issue. It involves, he said, a shift from La Mettrie's eighteenth-century rationalist image of the human as *l'homme machine* to the image of *homo poeta*—the human as meaning maker. We create "structures of evil," says Becker, whenever we design institutions that prevent people from "staging the world so that they can act in it creatively."[17]

Hardheaded men of management and labor are unlikely to be convinced by such poetic abstractions. The truth is, however, that there is undeniable movement in the direction of "horizontal-participative" management. There is convincing empirical evidence that it works.

The Institute for Research on Educational Finance and Governance reports studies showing that more educated workers place a higher priority on having a challenging job than on financial rewards; that workers with education exceeding the requirements of the job tend to be more dissatisfied than those where there is a match between job and skills. In fact, data from twenty-two regional Bell system companies showed that each year of underutilization of education was associated with a loss of over 8 percent or almost $5 billion in 1981.

Studies over the last ten years of a wide variety of worker participation arrangements, from "shop floor democracy" to worker-owned and managed firms, clearly show a positive relation between the extent of worker participation and the productivity of the firm. As an example, Zilog, Inc., a major manufacturer of silicon chips, introduced a study of productivity and quality control. It found that a plant organized by work teams making decisions by consensus reduced the cost of "rework" and raised yields by 25 percent compared to traditionally managed plants.[18]

Finally, there is the plan for producing Saturn, "the car of the future," by General Motors. Behind the public relations rhetoric there is a goal to lay the groundwork for combining robotics with a new style of human relations. (This from the company with the 1972 Lordstown experience of worker revolt against assembly line speed-up.) The proof, of course, will be in the doing. But the agreements worked out with the United Automobile Workers (U.A.W.) change the status of assembly-line workers from hourly laborers to salaried employees. Union workers are to be involved in decision-making processes that formerly were the sole prerogative of management. Workers in production work units of six to fifteen persons are to have responsibilities for relevant work place decisions and quality control. This work style is to be combined with "computer integrated manufacturing."[19]

The skeptics are many and may prove to be right: Is it another ploy by management to undermine unions? (Some corporations have used it to forestall unionization or to weaken the union allegiance of workers.) Can there be any legitimate incorporation of democratic values within corporate capitalism? Can union and management leaders change ingrained habits of adversarial relations at the work place?

With all of the difficulties, those of us who welcome alternatives to the "thingification" of human beings find much to welcome in these tendencies. The trend seems to fit the sentiment in Hazel Henderson's statement, "For the first time in history it is pragmatic to be ethical."[20]

It appears to be an occasion for enjoyment, so why do doubts persist? Perhaps because there is such a rush to seize on the pragmatic payoff aspects. There is, for example, a difference between much American corporate talk about "person-centered" workplaces and Scandinavian talk about "democratic" workplaces. Locus of control is at issue. For example, Norway and the United States share long democratic traditions. We find, however, Norwegian work theorists much more inclined to combine language about democratic values and ideas about work than do American corporate leaders. The Norwegians, for instance, acknowledged a specific need to democratize work because the authoritarian "efficiency" type of management they had borrowed from the United States was in conflict with democratic processes they valued in their community life. Corporate management in the United States has been less comfortable with the language of democracy, which seems at odds with managerial prerogatives of control. Nevertheless it has entered discussion as part of the critical review of the American style of management.

Irving Bluestone, a U.A.W. vice-president, spoke bluntly to a group of General Motors executives. The bedrock issue, he said, is whether the democratic values of American society will be taken seriously in corporate life. Bluestone accepted that most corporations are a long way from accepting the larger implications of democratic worker involvement. There is little sentiment, for example, to follow the Europeans in providing union representation on Boards of Directors. "But," he added, "we know that decisions relative to where the product will be produced, even your accounting procedures, your marketing analysis, all have an impact on worker security. At some point down the road, you may as well face it, workers are going to be saying, 'Look, those decisions are important to us and, therefore, we want to have input. . . .' I think at some point in time, the wisdom of seeing to it that this mutuality of concern is shared with the worker will be recognized." And Bluestone added, "Let me say that improving the quality of life is not a sometime thing. It is not a concept which lives only in periods of recession or depression or uncertainty, but it should be embraced simply because it is the right thing to do. It is the moral, human way to treat people. It proves to be of advantage to everybody."[21]

And D. L. Landen, General Motors Vice-President for Research and Development, said:

I don't believe our authoritarian corporations can continue to coexist with democratic institutions in a democratic society, and the reverse is true, too. In Poland, I can't imagine that a free labor movement will continue to exist in their authoritarian society. . . . Either the Polish government will change as their labor movement becomes more democratic, or the unions will be crushed. In this country, we must democratize our corporations.[22]

In the mid 1980s the issue of which route American industry will travel is moot. Our habits push us toward Scenario I. On the other hand, there are those who see that our deeper self-interest lies with Scenario II. It is likely that we have entered a period of prolonged irresolution—with the issue very much in doubt.

Since the dominant institution of "a business civilization" is business, the schools cannot avoid being affected. In the past decade and a half they have been strongly influenced by systems-efficiency ideology. When corporate philosophy begins to be of two minds they will be influenced by that, too. There is evidence that that is already happening.

Policy Issues for Schools

VALUE TENSIONS AND EDUCATIONAL POLICIES

Cultural tensions between "technical efficiency" and "democracy and education" are deeply embedded in the twentieth-century history of American education.

In the opening decades, as a loose parallel to the push for scientific management in industry, one set of school policies centered around the work of Edward L. Thorndike and the aim to bring science to learning through scientific measurement. Thus began the tradition that "that learning counts that can be counted." Related was the social efficiency philosophy of the pioneers of vocational education. It called for specific skill training and teaching of the work ethic to "hand-minded" youngsters to meet the needs of industry: a functional efficiency ideal.

A different ideology and set of practices centered around John Dewey and his call for education for democracy via inquiry-oriented learning. Dewey made a plea for democracy with a *moral* meaning: "The supreme test of all political institutions and industrial arrangement shall be the contribution they make to the all around growth of every member of society."[23] In school practice, however, Dewey's criticism of "inert subject matter" was trivialized by some of his followers into slogans like "I teach children, not subject matter."

Readers of this volume will recall the pendulum swings of these two orientations as the century wore on. In the 1970s and 1980s a curious development took place. While venturesome leaders in industry were exploring the relevance of participatory involvement at work, school policymakers moved strongly toward the scientific measurement-technical efficiency tradition.

In the 1970s falling test scores and fear of foreign competition coincided. Schools were called on to tighten their performance with the business efficiency model as guide. A language was introduced that fitted a view of learning as a production function: inputs/outputs, competency-based learning, performance-based instruction, accountability for results. Schools and teachers were to be evaluated in cost-benefit terms. Arthur Wise spoke of this trend as the "hyper-rationalization of learning and the bureaucratization of the classroom."[24] The assumptions were clear: effectiveness of teaching can be measured in terms of test scores. If teachers are given clear measurable objectives, the objectives *will be met.* The goal was to secure the educational equivalent of "more bang for the buck."

That other tradition, while in a minority position, was not completely silent. You could hear echoes of Dewey's perspective in the misgivings of some. Thus C. A. Bowers:

The application of systems theory to the teaching process . . . is likely to transform teaching and learning into a mechanical positivistically oriented process. . . . (Its) language is not concerned with the truth claim of statements, the adequacy of values people live by, or the discrepancy between the energy demands of our culture and the carrying capacity of the ecosystems. In effect, it creates an encapsulated technological universe where only technological and management problems are real.[25]

The relentless efficiency emphasis also seemed at odds with earlier strands of educational ideals that had shaped conceptions of humane learning for a society of free people. The classical scholar C. M. Bowra reminds us of the Greek ideal:

Man serves a purpose in the scheme of things and realizes his full nature in it. This is to develop his *areté*, or inborn capacities as far as he can. . . . In the fifth century . . . *areté* was found in the full development of the individual within the social frame.[26]

To be fair, however, pressures for schooling with pragmatic payoff comes not only from the business community. An international observer like Torsten Husén of Sweden notes that when unemployment stays at 7+ percent, competition for jobs increasingly revolves around school test scores, grades, and degrees. Learning becomes a competitive win/lose affair with middle-class parents turning to coaching in test taking to gain advantage.[27] As Adam Curle put it, schools expend enormous energies so students "can learn to compete for right answers so they can advance within the system."[28]

In short, there is no doubt about the powerful influence on schools of the efficiency model in Scenario I. By the mid 1980s, however, it could not be denied that the "democratic workplace" idea in Scenario II was beginning to assert its own influence on educational thinking. To illustrate we note first developments in vocational education, and secondly, recommendations for general education from the Committee for Economic Development.

ALTERNATIVE PHILOSOPHIES OF WORK AND VOCATIONAL EDUCATION

Frank Pratzner, senior researcher at the National Center for Research in Vocational Education at Ohio State University, argued in 1985 that the time was ripe for "a new paradigm in vocational education."[29] The impetus for change, he said, was the combination of high technology and quality of work life development to improve the international competitiveness of American industry. He compared features of the current model with the paradigm needed to replace it. The established model, with roots in the early 1900s, assumes that the content of vocational studies should be derived from analysis of the needs of industry. Training aims to provide entry-level skills for specialized jobs. Performance-based curricula, norm-referenced testing and grading, individualized instruction, and involvement of business and labor in planning, operating, and evaluating programs are common features.

The alternative paradigm, he said, instead of stressing the learning of specialized occupational skills should focus on development of *sociotechnical literacy*. Sociotechnical literacy emphasizes a balanced concern for the social-human aspects of work, as well as the technological dimensions, and an appreciation of their interactions. It includes development of basic skills, but also (a) higher-order transferable skills such as interpersonal and group-process skills, problem solving, decision making, planning, and communication, and (b) skills in the organization and management of production such as skills in business economics, business operation, and statistical quality control. It also includes an understanding of the philosophical underpinnings and consequences of the shift from a mechanistic, technological, scientific management perspective of work to a high worker involvement, participative management perspective.

Evidence that this is not a private dream of Pratzner may be found in Public Law 98-524 enacted October 19, 1984.[30] It states that the purpose of vocational studies is to develop higher quality workers (a) who are responsible and flexible enough to take an active role in the design and productivity of their work places, and (b) who will develop entrepreneurial skills useful in reviving and maintaining the overall development of their communities.

States are required to establish that their programs contain provisions like the following:

1. to provide study and training in a vocational setting in order to give students an understanding of all aspects of the industry they plan to enter. For example, a student involved in a housing rehabilitation project is required to learn not just carpentry, but all about the business, from planning, to financing, to labor and community relationships;

2. to enhance basic and problem-solving transferable skills to cope with technological change;

3. to expand vocational-agriculture type projects in which students, for example, plan for a crop and deal with unpredictable problems that occur from its planting to marketing.

The law commends student involvement in economic needs assessments that foster school-community ties projects in which students use social studies concepts to identify community needs and economically viable responses. It cites commendable examples ranging from day-care centers, to a town newspaper, to a woodfinishing business, to swine production.

These references to current forces at work in vocational education establish that Scenario II work changes are advanced enough so that they cannot be ignored. This does not mean that the issue in work has been settled in favor of participative management patterns. There is, in fact, a serious challenge for vocational educators who confront a world of industry divided by two different images of the effective workplace. Evidence that the nature of the two images is being clarified is provided in Table I—Current and Emerging Paradigms of Vocational Education.

Vocational educators must be attuned to events in industry. They do not pioneer in new educational directions unless something is going on to warrant it. Pratzner's 1985 statement was followed in that same year by *Investing in Our Children: Business and the Public Schools*— a policy statement by the Research and Policy Section of the Committee for Economic Development (CED).[31] This statement was

TABLE 1

CURRENT AND EMERGING PARADIGM OF VOCATIONAL EDUCATION

COMPONENTS OF A PARADIGM	VOCATIONAL EDUCATION	
	CURRENT PARADIGM	EMERGING, ALTERNATIVE PARADIGM
An Image of the Subject Matter	• Entry-level skill development for specialized jobs • Content/subject area • Serves the interests of employers/jobs/society	• Alternative instructional approach to learning • Process • Serves education and development needs of students
Beliefs in Particular Theories and Models	• Job analysis • Scientific method • Behavior modification • Teachers impart knowledge • Learning as product/emphasis on content • Acquiring "right" information once and for all	• Cooperative learning • Socratic questioning • Learning how to learn • What is "known" may change • Encourages autonomy • Supports general education development of learner
Values	• Job placement/earnings • Employer satisfaction • Inculcate specialized skills for specific roles • Alternative track for academically less-able/less-willing	• Individual performance in terms of potential • Egalitarian/democratic • Students assume responsibility for own learning • Achievement plus enjoyment • Alternative approach to learning for all students
Methods and Instruments	• Lockstep progress • Norm-referenced grading/testing • Rigid, prescribed curricula • Traditional occupation service areas • Business/industry involvement	• Criterion-referenced grading/testing • Cooperative/group learning • Divergent thinking encouraged • Electives • Focus on transferable skills
Exemplars	• Most secondary and postsecondary programs, to varying degrees	• Some graduate-level programs • Some industrial arts/career education programs • Some career guidance programs
Social Matrices	• AVA divisions, convention, journal; student vocational clubs; federal legislation; state department of vocational education	• Informal networks; *Paideia Proposal*; Society for Humanistic Education; AERA SIGS on School Effectiveness and Holistic Education

Source: Frank C. Pratzner, "The Vocational Education Paradigm: Adjustment, Replacement, or Extinction," *Journal of Industrial Teacher Education* 22 (Winter 1985): 5.

directed not at vocational education but at the reform of general education in the public schools. The motivation, once again, grew out of industry's concern about what is needed to survive and prosper in global market competition.

The co-directors of this report, Denis P. Doyle and Marsha Levine of the conservative American Enterprise Institute, expect it to have wide influence.[32] The 200 members of the Institute are drawn from the highest ranks of the business community and academia. Individuals listed on various committees are people like Owen Butler, Chairman of Proctor and Gamble; Ralph Lazarus, head of Federated Department Stores; William Woodside, Chairman of American Can Co.; Robert Davenport, head of Sheridan Broadcasting Co.; Roger Smith, Chairman of General Motors; and Thomas Vanderslice, President of Apollo Computer, Inc. From education there are well-known figures like Harold Howe, former U.S. Commissioner of Education; Albert Shanker, President, American Federation of Teachers; J. Myron Atkin, Dean, School of Education, Stanford University; and John Brademas, President, New York University. The project on education followed a major CED study of American economic productivity, which came to the conclusion that "economic productivity and the quality of education cannot be separated. Particularly in the modern world, education and economic performance are inseparable." Their studies of Asian and European competitors demonstrated to the CED "that human resources are more important than physical ones. And a well-educated work force, with habits of collaboration and cooperation as well as competition, is the most important asset a nation can possess."[33]

The study provides an opportunity to see how American schools are viewed when seen through the lenses of top corporate leaders. The influence of Scenario II type thinking is clearly evident, but the perspective of the older business tradition is far from absent. We must settle here for a limited sampling of the perspective from "the top of the top."

The endorsers of this report are corporate leaders of industries being transformed by the rush of computerized technologies. They are forthright in declaring that a work force educated simply by "old school basics" will not be equipped for meeting challenges of turbulent change.

The report presents the case of Proctor and Gamble as a prototype of how significantly the nature of work is changing in America. In the past, workers joined Proctor and Gamble to enter low-skilled tasks in narrowly defined jobs that changed little during a person's work life. The strong trend now is toward participative work systems. Employees perform a broad range of tasks including operating and maintaining equipment and performing their own quality controls. They participate in activities such as goal setting and budgeting, formerly reserved strictly for management. Increasingly work is centered around self-directed teams where problem solving and decision making are important parts of the job. The company provides retraining in the higher-level skills needed to meet the flow of change. Training is effective only if employees have strong literacy and number skills, and above all the ability to learn.[34]

With this view of work in America the report turns to what is needed in the schools. We pass over their recommendations for greater involvement of business in seeking more funding and ways to raise standards. We focus on how their call for "nothing less than a revolution in the role of the teacher and the management of schools"[35] reflects their sense of the needs of new work places.

High technology firms, they say, are not served well by old organizational forms. Centralized rigid bureaucracies, in schools or industry, are hostile to needed creativity. They stifle it because their goal is to keep control in the hands of centralized authority. The essential obligation of organizations in the new era is "to nurture creativity." Schools, and previous national reports on schools, have neglected this fact. School policymakers must learn the lesson of industry—to decentralize decision making to the lowest possible level: "solve the problem where it exists." Give employees a stake in the system by letting them exercise their own creativity and energy in the work at hand.[36]

More specifically, the report recommends a "bottom-up" policy for school reform. Focus is on the individual school as the key place for meaningful improvements in quality and productivity. The role of the states, they say, is to set clear goals and high standards, then give the schools the maximum freedom to implement them.[37]

The interaction of teachers, students, and administrators in individual schools becomes the key arena for action. The report assumes that the able, sensitive, highly professional school people now needed will not choose teaching, nor choose to remain in it, if they are stifled by present bureaucratic regimentation, or shackled with "teacher-proof" materials.

Teachers as creative actors will respond only if their professional roles are enhanced by maximizing opportunities to exercise judgment, make decisions, and reshape their own working environment. Furthermore, teachers may be surprised, the report says, that contrary to narrow "back to basics" emphases of recent years, the CED calls for liberal education for all: for higher-order learning—to think critically and analytically, to cooperate and communicate as well as to compete, to solve problems, to assume responsibility, and to learn how to learn. They advocate strengthening "teacher centers" where peers can exchange ideas on strategies for advancing learning, and for changing "the culture of the school."

Where teacher evaluation is concerned they shy away from "merit plans" which often undermine collegial relations. Teachers working in a largely competitive environment, they say, will be less inclined to support the feeling of community that is essential for effective schools. They advocate experiments with two-tier systems of evaluation: one for decisions on contract renewal, tenure, or dismissals; and a second for encouraging professional growth and development, with teachers having an active role in establishing the criteria and the method of use.[38]

This hasty sketch simply illustrates that these major corporate leaders now assume that Scenario II is the way of the future. These corporate managers, in growing up and living in American society, experienced the democratic cultural values as well as the technical efficiency traditions of industry. Clearly, however, it is too much to expect a sudden reversal of older, deep-seated personal and institutional habits and perspectives. There is in the report a kind of bland, upbeat image of American life that glosses over unpalatable features such as race and class differences and social conflicts.

There is, for instance, their approach to the embarrassment of poverty in the United States. Under the heading of "Choosing Wise Educational Investment" the following sentence appears: "Some 46 per cent of all black and 38 per cent of all Hispanic children lived in poverty (1984), compared to 22 per cent for children of all races."[39] Such youngsters, we learn, tend to have the highest rate of school failure.

One might expect shock at the raw reality of such figures in the world's leading free market economy. Instead we find the co-directors responding with statements such as: "to let large segments of its population fail" is a practice "both wasteful and dangerous"; "all young people need higher-order cognitive skills in addition to work habits of self-discipline and initiative"; "in tomorrow's workplace, success will go to those who are flexible and adaptable"—for a person who "can expect multiple careers over his or her productive lifetime."

One senses relief when they find that research has uncovered a remedy for laggards in the poverty sector. It is successful preschool intervention of "children at risk" (that is, poor children). It offers the cost-effective strategy "for better chances for success in later life." We are told that "the trustees responded to this finding as they would to a business proposition. They concluded that it costs society more *not* to intervene than it costs to do so."[40]

As they look out on America from their corporate towers they nowhere acknowledge that children from the bombed-out streets of the ghettos have life spaces significantly different from children they know. There is the tendency to assume that poverty in America will lend itself to school-fix solutions: beefed up preschool education, teaching the work ethic and "higher-order learning," and job corps for the dropouts. It seems that work settings such as those at Proctor and Gamble beckon for all who prove worthy. Such visions leave minds untroubled by the reports of the Institute for Research on Educational Finance and Governance on the kinds of work actually available, and of the uncomfortable possibility of a permanent underclass in the electronic age that may not yield to free market solutions.

Even within the sections on decentralizing one still finds the tendency to approach school learning with "the production function" image. Various corporate divisions and units within divisions, they say, are given a great deal of autonomy on how they organize themselves as long as they meet corporate directives—"decentralization works because the results can be measured." While verbalizing that schools are not the same as industry, they insist that outcomes of schooling can and must be measured. States should look to output measures rather than to process requirements to hold schools accountable.[41]

The problem with such statements is not that they are devoid of good intentions, but that they slip into the mistaken idea that the productivity of measurable units of production in industry is analogous to measurable units of learning in schools. They ignore the fact, as John Goodlad put it, that there simply does not exist a science of education sufficient to give credence to the "scientism" necessary for these quantifiable accountability models.[42] We do not get such a "science" by simply saying we must have one. The complexities of human learning are not the same as or even analogous to the complexities of industrial production.

To ignore that is to miss the warning of George Madaus, Director of Boston College's Center for the Study of Testing, Evaluation, and Educational Policy, that multiple-choice tests are inappropriately being used "to make automatic policy decisions about such things as high school graduation, grade-to-grade promotion, teacher certification, and merit pay. The preeminent peril latent in the new technologies is that they can further strengthen the illusion that test results are totally significant, absolutely rational, objective, definitive, and right."[43]

By supporting reductionist approaches to learning, those more humane qualities the authors seek in decentralization may be vitiated.

There is another feature of the report that warrants a second look. The report repeatedly asks for higher-level learnings such as problem solving, reasoning, learning how to learn, and how to adapt to change. These words, in the holiest of holy category of educators' vocabulary, would appear to deserve a salaam. But the substance of what should be "problem solved" remains vague. The leaning is toward rational thinking skills that would be useful for solving technical problems at the work site, supplemented by communications skills to improve teamwork. These are laudable goals and on the face of it represent important advances beyond Taylorism. But as the media remind us, the quality of life in America is affected by business activity unmentioned in the report. To be blunt, corporate behavior, as *Time* put it, is leading to the poisoning of America—to the dumping in third-world countries of products judged unsafe for United States citizens, and to the abrupt closing of plants that decimate factory communities.

There are, indeed, differences between technical problems and quality of life problems. Comments by E. F. Schumacher in *Small is Beautiful: Economics as if People Mattered* are useful in clarifying the differences.[44] There are, in his account, *convergent* type problems that lend themselves to solutions by abstract logical reasoning. These are the well-structured problems usually found in critical-thinking programs in schools, or in courses in mathematics, physics, and chemistry. Such skills are enormously useful for solution of technical/scientific problems. The CED report clearly supports strengthening their place in school curricula.

But there is a dearth of reference to the other category Schumacher identifies as *divergent* problems: the type which do not lend themselves to neat solutions of logical thought. Divergent problems are the type that divide people in politics, economics, education, and family life. They involve the imprecise requirements for weighing conflicts of values, and how to reconcile opposites. For example, weighing the pros and cons of smallness vs. bigness, or struggling to find a tensional balance between the claims of freedom and authority. Divergent problems require *lived* answers that come from the struggle of involved persons. They might include a questioning of taken-for-granted corporate policies regarding locus of power and societal consequences of production. We heard Irving Bluestone of the United Automobile Workers address such an issue when he told General Motors management that corporate areas now reserved for management were eventually going to be challenged by American unions.

We cannot be serious about quality of life issues if we avoid thorny problems concerning value choices and power shifts, yet the CED report largely ignores them.

Work and Education for a Sustainable Planet

The argument that it is urgent to include thinking about quality of life choices in work and schools is forcefully made in the WorldWatch Institute's *Report on Progress Toward a Sustainable Society: State of the World 1985*. Its summary conclusion is that both natural and human life-systems are under increasingly severe ecological stress. The source of stress comes from several extraordinary areas of growth:

1. Population growth: the world's population, increasing by 81 million in 1984, now approaches 5 billion. (This compares with 1 billion 600 million in 1900, and 2 billion 500 million in 1950).

2. Economic growth: since 1950 the world's output of goods and services has nearly quadrupled to an annual $12 trillion.[45]

These levels of growth are a testimony to human energy and achievement. But we are just beginning to perceive the damage accruing to interconnected life systems.

The crisis is most apparent in Africa where desertification, mass malnutrition, and starvation are far advanced. But disruptive strains are felt across the globe. In order to conserve land, authorities in China are encouraging cremation instead of traditional burial mound interment. In Europe, West Germans may have to choose between reducing auto use or sacrificing their forests to acid rain. Cities in India and the United States live with fear of toxic leaks from operations of multinational chemical corporations.

WorldWatch maintains that the years ahead are likely to be traumatic, and could be catastrophic. Nothing less is required than whole new orientations to the way economic and social policies relate to deteriorating life systems.

While pessimism is understandable, the Report holds that we have knowledge and insight to move toward sustainable living. But political processes are required to reverse deterioration. The key is broad-based political and educational processes that involve people from all walks of life. Actions of technical elites of themselves cannot coerce uninformed and uninvolved populations. What is required is inventive grass roots leadership at local levels together with enlightened leadership at national and global levels.

This cannot be secured without engaging people in personally involved learning. Narrow information accumulation that still prevails in the world's classrooms and in passive deskilled work situations will not do. What is needed is contextual learning—learning that assists people in seeing the interconnectedness of events and policies. In John Dewey's terms, this is learning that helps people reconstruct their experiences so that they see new meanings about themselves and their world. It is learning that helps people examine social and institutional practices in terms of whether they are destructive or conserving of life systems. It requires inclusion of reflective ethical judgments.

This kind of learning cannot be left to formal education alone. It must be incorporated into the world of work itself. No one should underestimate the level of difficulty involved.

Weighing the impact of technology on global problems in *The Uncertain Promise*, Denis Goulet says that we need to face the fact that the exclusion of "quality of life" values has simply been built into the profit-maximizing, efficiency calculations of the Western socioeconomic system. According to Goulet, a fundamental question for life in a high technology era is what concept of *efficiency* we will choose: Western "engineering-type efficiency," or a new type of "integral efficiency." Engineering-type efficiency is the kind employed in closed-circuit mechanical systems in which work done is compared to energy supplied to the system. Efficiency is determined by quantifiable measures of inputs and outputs. "Quality of life" dimensions fall outside the system of calculations as "externalities."

This type of efficiency has become dysfunctional in terms of human well-being. It is so deeply ingrained in Western thought, however, that it will be extremely difficult to change. The urgent need now, says Goulet, is to create "new modes of operating efficiently, simultaneously solving problems in the conventional style and optimizing social values hitherto externalized but now needing to be internalized. . . . Managers and designers of technology will need to explore ways of becoming *integrally efficient*, that is, of *producing efficiently while optimizing social and human values*. This they must do with as much passion, singlemindedness, and practical sense as they now devote to making profits or creating new products."[46]

From the perspective of WorldWatch and Denis Goulet it is clear that the appearance of a democratic sociotechnical philosophy of work is arriving at a propitious time. When people have an opportunity to raise questions about the quality of their life at work it helps them become aware of their power to act to change things. It introduces the habit of raising questions about quality as well as quantity. But to limit such questions to the workplace is clearly inadequate. As Eric Trist and Fred Emery argue in *Towards a Social Ecology*, democratic work design must be seen as only a first step—a "leading edge" toward the principle that *productive development* in an interdependent world depends on policies that promote the well-being of all in the system.[47] Increasingly the significant system is seen to be global, as witnessed by economists who view the international market as the one of primary significance. In addition to becoming able to compete, we eventually will need to see that an international economy in which per capita income ranges from $280 per annum in some southern hemisphere countries to $11,000 in some northern countries has an inherent instability that endangers the welfare of the whole. The point becomes even clearer when we note that in 1984 $647 billion went for worldwide military expenditures and only $39 billion for worldwide development assistance.[48]

How to cope with the complexity of such dysfunctional features of contemporary life is, of course, no simple matter. There is a paramount need for theorists and statesmen who can articulate the case for seeing global interconnectedness. But we cannot neglect the other warning of WorldWatch that there must be deep and widespread participation across the population. This will require widening the range of issues considered by people at work. Involvement of unions, for example, in corporate policies which Irving Bluestone says until now have been put on hold.

Even more basic than the question of "how to work" is the question of "what work to do." The barest beginnings have been made in raising questions about "what will be produced."

Under fear of economic survival both labor and management have shied away from the troublesome question of whether they are engaged in socially useful or harmful work. An exception was the action of the Combine Shop Stewards Committee of Lucas Aerospace Industries in England. When confronted with layoffs in a technologically advanced corporation the unions raised a new order of questions. They identified the paramount contradiction of our time as the growing gap between what technology could provide for society and what it actually does provide. They demanded that the advanced technology and human skills of Lucas plants be employed to produce a long list of socially useful products which they identified. They asserted that they had the right to be engaged in socially useful work.[49]

We may hope that such isolated actions, combined with the more general awareness of the need for workplace reform, may be beginning steps toward creation of a new business paradigm: a paradigm complete with values and ethics consistent with demands for a just and healthy society. We can already identify companies that are moving to incorporate economic, environmental, and social concerns in corporate decision making. Such an example is Wang Laboratories, Inc., the second largest producer of office automation systems. Wang offers self-improvement programs for employees, provides free day-care, makes substantial donations to cultural and community development in the Boston area, and is an aggressive equal opportunity employer. Wang recently built a $15 million dollar factory in Boston's inner city and takes the lead in locating high technology factories in high-risk economically depressed areas.[50] The groundwork is being laid for creating corporate cultures capable of considering the broader WorldWatch type issues. The basic goal is to return to the early nineteenth-century American tradition that incorporation is a concession of public authority to a private group *in return for* service to the public good. Management then becomes accountable not only for technical competence but for meeting standards of public obligation.[51]

If the goal is a sustainable planet, neither workplaces nor schools can do it alone. Of themselves, schools do not have the power for social reform that the early progressives assumed. In a business civilization they cannot avoid being affected by values of the corporate work culture. Potentially, though, they find themselves in a new situation in which the Taylorist efficiency tradition is challenged within corporate life itself. The role of teachers is not the same as workers in industry but schools are workplaces for the young and adults who do their daily stint there. Educators may want to take a proactive role in exploring the meaning of democratic sociotechnical philosophy for their own workplaces. They can take advantage of support for such ideas as: creating small participative learning communities, either within large school units, or as autonomous entities; creating administrative leadership that "taps the brains" of everyone in educative settings; creating learning strategies that give priority to distinctive human capacities for individual and group inquiry and problem solving, and nurturing personal creativity and enthusiasms (remembering that enthusiasm comes from the Greek *en-theos*—the personal God within).

With regard to the technical dimension, educators can focus on how computer-assisted instruction can be used not only to orient students to an electronic work world, but also how to advance the thwarted goal of equity. The Office of Technology Assessment says that judicious use of computer technology may help secure a more equitable distribution of learning for students with handicaps due to poverty. Research shows that narrow skill information can be learned in one-third less time through computer instruction. This can leave more time for understanding basic concepts, and for individual or collaborative problem solving. The critical issue, however, is what kind of minds and values control the design of software—those committed to supporting effective thinking, or those merely anxious to produce a salable product.[52]

The same issues will apply to the inevitable expansion of recurrent education where responsibilities will fall jointly on industrial training and teaching through formal institutions of learning.

Educators may find support from those "leading edge" sectors of management and labor interested in democratic inquiry forms of learning. But educators also have an obligation to reverse the usual question asked by industry: Are the schools producing students prepared for corporate work? Educators must insist that an equally relevant question is whether American business and labor leaders are designing places of work worthy of students coming from creative, intellectually stimulating learning settings—for those in lower paying as well as those in high paying jobs.

Furthermore, teachers must be prepared to resist rationales of industry, new or old, which interfere with their central educative obligation. Teachers have a primary task that transcends the needs of beleaguered industry. Teachers are carriers of liberal culture—of the liberalizing skills of citizens of a free society; of the skills of verbal and computational literacy; of the skills of critical thinking; of ways of understanding the evolution of values of a democratic culture and the complexities of living in a society of plural and conflicting world views; of ways of weighing policy choices in terms of whether they nurture or are destructive of social well-being; of assessing where we have fulfilled the vision of a just society and where we have failed; of gaining insight into the unique opportunities and dangers in an electronic nuclear era in which humans reach out beyond the planetary home.

To avoid the dualisms in work and education that betray the democratic aspirations of American culture we face a two-fold problem: how to create more work that is personally fulfilling and socially useful and how to educate Americans so that they will struggle to realize such a goal.

The argument in this chapter may be summarized as follows: (a) we face three major challenges affecting work and the quality of life: international competition, the computer revolution in communications, and dangerous ecological imbalances; (b) if we are to take constructive actions to meet these challenges we need to question both top-down technocratic organization of work and laissez-faire economic assumptions devoid of ethical and ecological concerns.

There is little sentiment in America, with its pioneer past and skepticism of central government, to turn toward West European democratic socialism. The question for the near future is whether we can create a third alternative that combines the innovative entrepreneurial drives of a capitalist economy without the amoral destructiveness of an unchecked profit imperative.

We are still torn over what identity we will assume for entering the twenty-first century. At the end of our first decade as a dominant world power, Max Lerner caught nicely the divided soul of the American people: America as the "business civilization" with an overriding commitment to pursue material prosperity and world economic preeminence, and that other America—the libertarian, pluralist, democratic, populist experiment.

It is hard not to feel that while America is still on the rising arc of its world power it is on the descending arc of its inner social and moral origin; that it has allowed itself to be switched off from the main path of its development into the futile dead ends of the fear of ideas and the tenacious cult of property. Toynbee has suggested how frequently a civilization has been weakened by its "pathological insistence upon pushing to extremes its master institution." . . . If the master institution of America is property, there is evidence of the beginning of a pathological insistence in pushing it to extremes. Linked with it is a fear of subversive movements which may threaten or overthrow the institution—a fear that therefore induces a . . . loss of belief in the inherent efficacy of democracy. The result is a negativism of outlook which puts stress on the defense of the master institution rather than upon the affirmation of its linkage with democratic human values. . . .

One may guess that America will lead the world in technology and power for at least several generations to come. But it is one thing to fill a power vacuum in the world with transitional leadership, and quite another to offer to the world the qualities of leadership which it requires, attuned at once to the life of nature and life of the spirit.[53]

Writing these words in 1957, Max Lerner was concerned about the corrosive effect of McCarthyism but could still write that the American people had not yet "suffered decisive defeat in a war, nor the agony of internal revolutionary violence." All of that was to change in the years to follow as we experienced the sobering traumas of the burning of the cities in the Civil Rights struggle, the humiliations of Vietnam and Watergate, the oil crisis of the 1970s and the spectacle of being surpassed economically by a defeated island nation of Asiatics.

It has been difficult to admit that we have lost overwhelming world preeminence and are locked into the mutual interdependencies of the shrunken planet. In neither the stage of preeminence nor the stage of interdependence have we given a clear indication of our capacity to provide "the qualities of leadership . . . attuned at once to the life of nature and the life of the spirit."

The issue that Max Lerner set forth remains unresolved. In the eyes of much of the world, struggling to rise from degrading poverty and repression, America has taken on the image of the conservative defender of property—the ally of entrenched elites opposing aspirations of human dignity for the majority. Time is running out on our chance to demonstrate that we can marshal the qualities of leadership "which a beleaguered humanity requires," a leadership that would demonstrate the possibility of linkage between our economic life and democratic humane values appropriate for a technological era.

FOOTNOTES

1. Martin Carnoy and Henry M. Levin, *Schooling and Work in the Democratic State* (Stanford, Calif.: Stanford University Press, 1985), pp. 53, 167.

2. Ibid., pp. 53-56.

3. Robert Reich, *The Next American Frontier* (New York: New York Times Books, 1983).

4. Eileen Shanahan, "Measuring the Service Economy," *New York Times*, 27 October 1985, p. F4.

5. Institute for Research on Educational Finance and Governance, "Skills, Schools, and Technology" (Policy notes of the Institute for Research on Educational Research and Governance, Stanford University, Summer, 1985), p. 2.

6. U.S. Bureau of Labor Statistics, "Employment by Industry—National," Bulletin 2217 (Washington, D.C.: U.S. Government Printing Office, June, 1985).

7. David Brody, "The CIO After 50 Years," *Dissent* 32 (Fall 1985): 471-72.

8. Robert Draper, "The Golden Arm," *New York Review* 32 (October 24, 1985): 46-49.

9. Institute for Research on Educational Finance and Governance, "Skills, Schools, and Technology," pp. 2-3.

10. Henry M. Levin and Russell W. Rumberger, "The Educational Implications of High Technology," Project Report No. 83-84 (Stanford, Calif.: Institute for Research on Educational Finance and Governance, Stanford University, February, 1983), p. 2.

11. Ibid., pp. 4-5.

12. Russell W. Rumberger, "The Job Market for College Graduates, 1960-1990." Project Report No. 83-A3 (Stanford, Calif.: Institute for Research on Educational Finance and Governance, Stanford University, February, 1983), p. 20.

13. Office of Technology Assessment, "Technology and the American Economic Transition" (Washington, D.C.: Office of Technology Assessment, 1986).

14. J. Richard Hackman and Greg R. Oldham, *Work Redesign* (Reading, Mass.: Addison-Wesley Publishing Co., 1980), 259-71 et passim.

15. See "Collaboration in Work Settings," *Journal of Applied Behavioral Science* 13, No. 3 (1977): 261-464. A special issue commemorating the thirtieth year of the National Training Laboratories.

16. Arthur G. Wirth, *Productive Work in Industry and Schools* (Lanham, Md.: University Press of America, 1983), chap. 3, "Democratic Socio-Technical Theory."

17. Ernest Becker, *The Structure of Evil* (New York: Free Press, 1978) p. 172.

18. Henry M. Levin, "Improving Productivity through Education and Technology," Report No. 84-825 (Stanford, Calif.: Institute for Research on Educational Finance and Governance, Stanford University, November, 1984), pp. 10-13.

19. See, for example, John Holusha, "Saturn Division Finds a Home in the Heartland," *New York Times*, 4 August 1985, p. E5.

20. Hazel Henderson, "A New Economics," in *Relating Work and Education*, ed. Dyckman W. Vermilye (San Francisco: Jossey-Bass, 1977), p. 235.

21. Wirth, *Productive Work in Industry and Schools*, pp. 59-60.

22. Delmar L. Landen, *Los Angeles Times*, 23 October 1980.

23. John Dewey, *Reconstruction in Philosophy* (New York: American Library, 1950), p. 47.

24. Arthur E. Wise, *Legislated Learning: The Bureaucratization of the American Classroom* (Berkeley, Calif.: University of California Press, 1979), chap. 2, "Hyper-rationalizing the Schools."

25. C. A. Bowers, "Emergent Ideological Characteristics of Educational Policy," *Teachers College Record* 79 (September 1977): 50.

26. C. M. Bowra, *The Greek Experience* (Cleveland: World Publishing Co. 1957), pp. 198-99.

27. Torsten Husén, "The School in the Achievement-Oriented Society: Crisis and Reform," *Phi Delta Kappan* 66 (February 1985): 398-402.

28. Adam Curle, *Education for Liberation* (New York: John Wiley and Sons, 1973). See chap. 1.

29. Frank C. Pratzner, "The Vocational Education Paradigm: Adjustment, Replacement, or Extinction," *Journal of Industrial Teacher Education* 22 (Winter 1985): 6-19.

30. Carl D. Perkins Vocational Education Act, PL 98-524. For discussion, see "Key Provisions in New Law Reforms—Vocational Education" (Washington, D.C.: Center for Law and Education, 1985).

31. Committee for Economic Development, *Investing in Our Children: Business and the Public Schools* (Washington, D.C.: Committee for Economic Development, 1985.

32. Denis P. Doyle and Marsha Levine, "Business and the Public Schools: Observations on the Policy Statement of the Committee for Economic Development," *Phi Delta Kappan* 67 (October 1985): 113-18.

33. Ibid., p. 114.

34. *Investing in Our Children*, p. 16.

35. Ibid., p. 10.

36. Doyle and Levine, "Business and the Public Schools," p. 117.

37. *Investing in Our Children*, p. 7.

38. Ibid., pp. 60-68.

39. Ibid., p. 43.

40. Doyle and Levine, "Business and the Public Schools," p. 118.

41. Ibid., p. 117.

42. John I. Goodlad, "Can Our Schools Get Better?" *Phi Delta Kappan* 60 (January 1979): 342-47.

43. Lynn Olson, "$30 Million Project Will Develop Tests for Next Century," *Education Week*, 6 November 1985, p. 14.

44. E. F. Schumacher, *Small Is Beautiful: Economics as If People Mattered* (New York: Harper Torchbooks, 1973), pp. 89-90.

45. Lester R. Brown and Edward C. Wolf, eds., *State of the World 1985: A WorldWatch Institute Report on Progress toward a Sustainable Society* (New York: W. W. Norton and Co., 1985). See chap. 6, "Getting Back on Track."

46. Denis Goulet, *The Uncertain Promise* (New York: IDOC/North America, 1977), pp. 18-19.

47. Fred E. Emery and Eric L. Trist, *Towards a Social Ecology* (New York: Plenum-Rosetta, 1973).

48. *Rethinking the North-South Relationship*, Report of the Twentieth United Nations of the Next Decade Conference (Muscatine, Iowa: Stanley Foundation, 1985), p. 7.

49. Mike Cooley, *Architect or Bee* (Boston: South End Press, 1981). See also, Wirth, *Productive Work in Industry and Schools*, pp. 232-41.

50. Mark Dowie and Theodore A. Brown, "The Best and Worst of American Business: Taking Stock," *Mother Jones* 10 (June 1985): 20-25.

51. See Robert N. Bellah et al., *Habits of the Heart: Individualism and Commitment in American Life* (Berkeley: University of California Press, 1985), pp. 286-90.

52. Office of Technology Assessment, "Technology and the American Economic Transition."

53. Max Lerner, *America as a Civilization* (New York: Simon and Schuster, 1957), p. 947.

CHAPTER IV

High Technology and Education: An Economist's View

MARTIN CARNOY

The economics of education has focused heavily on the relation between changing labor markets and the amount and the kind of education in which the young and their families invest.[1] The principal assumption of those analyses is that increases in the relative wages paid to higher levels of schooling will increase the amount of education that the young take and that decreases in relative wages will produce a corresponding decrease.[2] In addition, the economics of education literature is concerned with the relationship between schooling and social mobility, and the effect of education on racial, ethnic, and gender discrimination.[3]

How useful are such analyses for understanding the effects of structural changes in the economy on the educational system? We are now in the midst of a high technology revolution. That revolution, originating largely in the United States, has profound implications for the production process, and probably for employment and wages. Innovations in microelectronics and computers have sharply reduced the cost of processing information. They have made possible the automation of a host of services, including banking, insurance, and parts of wholesale and retail trade. Microelectronic innovations have also created commercially viable robotics, and as robots become less expensive, they are expected to replace labor in a number of production tasks.

Computerized information processing and the use of robotics are parts of a vision of technological progress that, in the eyes of many, holds great promise for economic life in American society. In this optimistic view, the "information revolution" will have an impact as great as the industrial revolution of the past. The new prototype of production will not be the smokestack industry of the nineteenth and twentieth centuries, but the high technology industries of the twenty-first. Automation and robotization will make it possible to increase high productivity, eliminate repetitive, low-skill jobs, and virtually eliminate unemployment. The technological work place will place a premium on highly skilled workers, and the schools will respond to that need with increased emphasis on mathematics, science, and technological curricula, with special efforts to implement computer assisted instruction (CAI). Further, CAI will make possible the individualization of instruction so that students will be able to reach their learning potentials regardless of ethnicity or socioeconomic background.

In this vision of a better society through high technology, both the processes of producing and of implementing high technology goods will help solve enduring problems of the economy and the workplace, and schooling will benefit as well. This chapter represents an effort to understand the effect of high technology industries on labor markets,[4] their impact on the division of labor and on the organization of work, and through those impacts, their effect on workers in those industries. We will also note probable future effects on schooling, how the economic value of schooling will change, and how much schooling different social groups are likely to demand and obtain (the distributional consequences of the high technology revolution).

The analysis of the effects on labor markets can be divided into two parts: (a) the characteristics of high technology industry and the implications for labor markets in high technology industry itself; and (b) the implications of high technology information systems, office automation, and robotics for employment and division of labor in other industries.

With the results of that labor market analysis, we can discuss the implications of high technology on the demand for schooling and on the distribution of that demand. Moreover, high technology industry produces inputs that are used in education and promotes certain notions of knowledge production and work ethics and organization on those engaged in education as producers and consumers. As we will see, knowledge production and work ideology are key elements in the whole concept of high technology. Have these notions of knowledge production and of work ethics and organization affected the timing and supply of schooling?

The Characteristics of High Technology Industries

The microelectronic industry—the largest by far of the high technology sectors—developed rapidly after the invention of integrated circuits in 1959. There were several phases in the growth of microelectronics and the related computer industry. In the 1950s, semiconductors were still expensive and computers were large and relatively slow, and the cost of information processing was so high that there were doubts about the commercial viability of computers.[5] But by the early 1970s, these costs had dropped dramatically, opening up tremendous commercial possibilities and the high technology explosion.

In 1954, the cost of a silicon transistor was $23.95; in 1972, it was $0.27. In the last ten years, the cost has fallen even farther. Integrated circuit prices fell from the $17-30 range in 1964 to $1 in 1972.[6] In addition, the "quality" of transistors and integrated circuits has improved greatly. Each of these units could perform a much larger number of tasks in 1972 than it could a decade earlier. So the price decline per unit underestimates the fall in cost per unit of quality.

The principal input in high technology products is highly educated, scientific/engineering human capital. It is this characteristic that distinguishes high technology industry from traditional manufacturing and services. In the latter, the factors governing location are access to raw materials, distance to markets, and availability of low-wage skilled production and clerical workers. But most high technology products neither require inputs with high transportation costs, nor produce outputs that are expensive to ship. The most important inputs are the skilled technicians who can develop new products, lower the production costs of a firm's output by developing new processes, or improve the reliability and quality control of existing products. The new technology is "embodied" in engineers and technicians who move from universities, where government contracts subsidize state-of-the-art research, to industry, where the knowledge they have acquired is turned into profit-making technology. High technology industry in the United States has therefore generally located near universities with strong programs in microelectronics from which well-trained engineers are easily recruited and where industries have ready access to new ideas.

Highly educated labor is primarily involved in research, development, marketing, and sales of high technology products. But there is an important production aspect to high technology. For the most part, assembly lines are not long, and quality control is as important as the actual assembling of the products. Much of the production is subcontracted to other firms, many of them in other countries (for example, the IBM personal computer is fabricated largely in Asia, with the final assembly done in the United States). Assembly of subpieces and final assembly in the United States is carried out primarily by semiskilled, low-paid women workers (many of them from the Third World), who are able to work under exacting conditions doing the repetitive work of placing electronic elements into integrated circuits, assembling final products, and inspecting devices for faults at various stages of assembly.

Production in high technology manufacturing in the industrial countries is increasingly susceptible to automation, as robots and complex (programmable) machines are developed that can assemble circuit boards and final products more rapidly and more accurately than can human beings. The Apple plant that produces the MacIntosh microcomputer in Fremont, California, is a good example of an automated, high technology factory.

At the same time, because of the relatively low percentage of total cost in transporting assembled inputs and final products to markets, the industry is highly mobile horizontally. A number of United States companies have moved their entire production facilities to Asia. Whereas research and development units tend to stay in localities near universities and near other high technology industries, larger companies are not averse to opening new divisions in new locations that have favorable conditions for attracting highly educated labor from other areas.[7] The attractiveness of high technology industry to localities also enables firms to extract considerable concessions from local and state governments in return for locating in a particular place.[8]

Implications of High Technology Expansion for Labor Markets

All these features of high technology industry have shaped the nature of its labor force. The structure of employment in electronics is significantly different from that of traditional manufacturing and from that of commerce and services.[9]

In Santa Clara County, California, 24 percent of the labor force in 1980 was employed in electronics manufacturing, and another 15 percent in defense and traditional manufacturing.[10] Both traditional and defense manufacturing were overwhelmingly male (72 percent and 75 percent, respectively), with the main difference between them being that traditional manufacturing employs a high percentage of Hispanics (18 percent males and 5 percent females) whereas defense has almost no Hispanics (4 percent males and 4 percent females). In electronics manufacturing, however, only 58 percent of the labor force was male (only one in eight Hispanic), and of the 42 percent females, almost one-third were Hispanic and Asian minorities.

The electronics industry is more human capital intensive than traditional manufacturing or the labor force as a whole. In Santa Clara County, where high technology employment is admittedly more human capital intensive than nationally because of the large R&D component in the county, about 34 percent of the labor force in electronics has completed university or attended graduate school, compared to less than 20 percent in traditional manufacturing and about 27 percent in the country's labor force as a whole.

Both men and women employed in electronics are relatively well paid (about the same as in traditional manufacturing for all but the highest levels of education, where Anglo males are paid more in electronics) because they (especially women) tend on the average to work longer hours than workers in other sectors.[11] But the labor force in electronics is highly gender-stratified, much more so than the labor force in the rest of the county or in traditional manufacturing, with Anglo males occupying the professional and managerial positions, and women—Anglos, Hispanics, and Asians—filling the assembly-line and clerical jobs. More than 55 percent of the Anglo females working in electronics versus only 22 percent of Anglo males had completed high school or less in 1980. The figures for all sectors of the county were 50 percent for Anglo females and 38 percent for males, and in traditional manufacturing, 57 percent for females and 50 percent for males. At the other end of the spectrum, 49 percent of the Anglo males in electronics had completed four years of college or more, compared to less than 13 percent of the Anglo females. In the county labor force as a whole, 35 and 22 percent of Anglo males and females had completed university or gone to graduate school, and, in traditional manufacturing, 22 and 18 percent.

Although the small size of the sample of Hispanics employed in electronics manufacturing and software production precluded statistically significant analysis of their earnings by education level, the census data did show a high payoff to completing high school or some college for Hispanics (especially females) employed in all sectors of the county's economy.

Thus, labor in high technology industry is more highly educated but also more gender-stratified than either traditional manufacturing or the labor force as a whole. Even though fewer jobs are available for women in traditional manufacturing than in electronics, those that are

are more equally paid than in electronics, at least in Silicon Valley.[12] In part, this is due to the absence of unions in electronics firms, where attempts to unionize have failed. Many firms attempt to mimic what has come to be called the Hewlett-Packard model (see below), treating their employees to generous benefits and giving them more responsibility.[13]

Depending on how it is defined, high technology industry employed 2.5 million, 5.7 million, or 12.4 million Americans in 1982, out of a total of 92 million employees.[14] Based on the three industry definitions of footnote 4, the projected increase of high technology employment varies from 34 to 36 percent between 1982 and 1995. Employment in all industries is projected to increase in the same period by 28 percent, so new employment in high technology industries will represent anywhere from 3.4 percent to 16.5 percent of all new employment from 1982 to 1995. In the broadest definition of high technology, one of six new jobs will be in high technology industries. If we take high technology occupations (see footnote 4) as the basis of the projection, however, they represented 3.2 percent of all civilian workers in 1982, and even with a 47 percent projected growth rate between 1982 and 1995 (compared with a 25 percent growth for total employment), high technology occupations represent only 6 percent of all new jobs—1.5 million in absolute terms.[15]

The small absolute number of high technology jobs has significant implications for what most Americans will be doing in 1995. Whereas eight out of ten of the most rapidly growing occupations to 1995 in percentage terms are high technology jobs, those eight will only produce 935,000 jobs in the 1982-95 period. The nine fastest-growing jobs in *absolute* terms are all service jobs, such as building custodian, office clerk, or secretary. Those fastest-growing jobs are projected to increase by six million in 1982-1995. Moreover, seven of the nine require completed high school education (12 years) or less, whereas six of the eight fast-growing, high-technology-related jobs require some college or more.[16] And the high absolute growth occupations have mean earnings that are 30 percent lower than the average in the United States, whereas the fast-growing high technology occupations average about 30 percent *higher* than average earnings in the United States.

These figures suggest that high technology industries and high technology occupations will create a significant but not massive number of new jobs over the next decade, certainly not the number implied by proponents of high technology. Even in the most optimistic projection of jobs in high technology industries, it appears that a majority of those jobs will not be in professional work, but rather in production or clerical work. This is consistent with the nature of the job structure in Santa Clara County's electronic industry, where somewhat less than 45 percent of electronics jobs in 1980 were professional-technical or administrative-managerial. And this percentage is observed in a high technology location that is more R&D oriented than most. For the country as a whole, the professional-administrative percentage in electronics tends to be lower.[17]

The growth of the high technology industry itself will therefore have an important impact on certain geographic regions and in the manufacturing sector, but not on employment in the United States as a whole. The labor force will continue to expand largely in trade and services, that expansion will depend primarily on the overall growth rate in the economy, and trade and service jobs will continue to be relatively low skilled and low paying, according to projections by the Bureau of Labor Statistics.[18] Real average weekly earnings in United States declined by about 16 percent in 1973-83, and this wage trend—although it has leveled off in 1983-1985—has not reversed. At the same time, high salaries have risen rapidly since 1982, contributing to an increasing inequality of income distribution in the United States in 1980-84.[19] The Rumberger-Levin data suggest that the future pattern of job growth could exacerbate that trend. If anything, high technology expansion could contribute to that exacerbation because of the polarized nature of the labor force in the industry.

The Effect of High Technology on Labor in Other Industries

Although there is disagreement about the contribution that high technology industry will make to the expansion of employment and about who will get that employment, the more controversial and speculative discussion focuses on the implications of informatics and robotics for employment in other industries.

The optimists contend that high technology will not only create many new jobs as an industry, but that as its products are adopted in other industries, it will raise productivity, therefore raising profits and/or lowering costs, so that new demand will be created and hence new jobs.[20]

The pessimists, on the contrary, argue that high technology jobs will only be a small proportion of jobs for many years to come, and that high technology in the form of office automation and robotics may actually eliminate jobs in other industries more rapidly than higher productivity can create new jobs.[21]

The pessimists' argument that the use of high technology products will produce a leveling off of employment through office automation and robotization is supported neither by the past performance of the United States economy nor by Bureau of Labor Statistics projections to 1995, although these data show certain industries and occupations as being affected negatively.[22] But neither has the argument that high technology will produce more jobs through increases in productivity been supported by any concrete evidence. United States productivity remained flat between 1973 and 1982, even though this was a period of rapid adoption of high technology. Productivity growth in manufacturing industries also slowed down sharply despite increases in capital per worker.[23] Productivity increased in 1983-85, but this increase could be attributed as much to traditional business cycle factors as to new, secular increase. Both the 1973-82 and 1983-85 periods were marked by overall increases in employment.

Productivity growth appears to be as associated with general macroeconomic growth policy as with technology per se, and there is apparently no systematic relationship between rising productivity, which is at least partly attributable to technology, and employment in American industry. "In some cases rising productivity is associated with declining employment, while in others it is associated with rising employment. . . . The inability to determine the net employment impact of technology also makes it difficult to determine the effect of technology on unemployment."[24]

Yet average unemployment in the United States has increased over the last three decades: the unemployment rate averaged 4.5 percent in the 1950s, 4.8 percent in the 1960s, 6.2 percent in the 1970s, 8.2 percent in 1980-85, and no less than 7.2 percent during the height of the 1983-84 recovery. Similarly, unemployment rates in the 1980s in Europe have remained high even with moderate growth rates. All this suggests that it is increasingly more difficult to employ everyone who wants to work. Rumberger shows that in 1960 averages of $11,000 in sales and $8,000 of capital were required in the United States economy to support every job, and in 1980 it took $14,600 (constant dollars) of sales and $12,300 of capital.[25] This trend will continue into the future. If the costs of labor increase, and the costs of capital, especially computers, continue to decrease, capital will continue to be substituted for labor in producing goods. Because of the particularly rapid decline in high technology capital costs, real wages in the United States would have to decline even more rapidly than the 16 percent drop in the 1973-82 period to slow down the capital-labor substitution process. In the future, there may be a slowdown in this present round of decline of (high technology) capital costs, and then, as in the period 1947-73, wage rates could increase again substantially.

The Bureau of Labor Statistics projections of a growth of twenty-five million jobs in 1982-1995 view such substitution as minor compared to the effect of overall economic growth on jobs. But there are some employment projections that disagree substantially with the Bureau's projections: Leontief and Duchin estimate that increased technical innovations and their diffusion throughout the economy will lead to a net reduction in aggregate employment.[26] They argue that rapid diffusion of robots, word processors, and other computer-based technologies throughout the economy could eliminate twenty million jobs by the year 2000, or 11 percent of all the jobs that would exist in the absence of further technological diffusion beyond 1982.

We have mentioned two ways in which high technology industry in industrial countries remains competitive: by moving parts of their production to lower labor cost economies and by robotizing and automating at home. Other manufacturing industries are doing the same, and the effect of robotization on employment is the newest ingredient in this trend. While robots in the United States numbered fewer than 3,000 in 1983, their number could increase to 100,000 by 1990. They will be part of flexible manufacturing systems, where programmed machine tools produce the parts, robots handle the materials, and computers control the entire production system.

These systems allow small quantities of goods to be produced inexpensively and permit rapid changeover to the production of other products. While such factories may keep American manufacturing in the U.S., they are unlikely to produce many new jobs: a showcase Japanese plant employs only one-tenth the workforce of a conventional factory it replaces; a new General Electric plant will produce one locomotive frame a day entirely by machine when it formerly took 70 skilled machine operators 16 days to produce it.[27]

Office automation equipment (microcomputers that perform word processing, financial analysis, and filing functions), automatic tellers in banks, computer-aided design, laser scanners, are all innovations that are drastically labor saving. They also produce the possibilities of new kinds of services, and allegedly increase profits that allow the expansion of existing services and therefore more jobs.

All this suggests that the adoption of new technology itself may not cause a net decline in employment in industrial countries, but that it will tend to put more, not less, pressure on overall economic growth to continue at a rapid rate in order to increase employment. Macroeconomic policy will be an even more crucial factor in the future than in the past in producing growth with increased employment and low inflation.

What will office automation and robotics do to the skills required in industry and the service and trade sectors? In the optimistic view, not only will many new jobs and new kinds of jobs be created by the growth of high technology, but increased skills will be required, there will be less skill polarization, and there will be greater opportunities for developing countries (a) to increase jobs available in industry and services supplying the rapidly growing industrial countries; and (b) to increase the efficiency of other domestic industries. In the pessimistic view, not only will net growth of new jobs be slowed by the new technology, but (a) real wages will have to fall in the industrial countries and remain low in the developing countries in order to combat substitution by falling-cost high technology capital; (b) new technology will result in a general deskilling even as a small percentage of high-skilled jobs grows, and (c) this will lead to an increasing polarization of the labor force, nationally and internationally.

In the case of robotics, studies suggest that semiskilled production jobs—operatives, assemblers, welders, and painters—will be replaced with semiskilled maintenance and clerical jobs—robot technicians, secretaries, and clericals.[28] Thus, robotics will eliminate more jobs than it creates, but will not change the general skill level of those remaining.

In offices, a recent study of the insurance industry suggests that the introduction of high technology eliminates the lowest skilled jobs, upgrades some semiskilled clerical and secretarial jobs connected with the operation of the equipment, and also tends to eliminate many lower- and middle-management jobs.[29] It is precisely those lower- and middle-management jobs that provided upward mobility in the industry for women. One of the effects of office automation, then, may be to upgrade women into dead-end, relatively high-skilled and relatively low-paying clerical and secretarial work.

These data, combined with the overall projections of future job growth we discussed earlier, indicate that the continued growth of the service and trade sectors in the United States will produce many more low-skilled jobs than the number of high-skilled jobs expected to be produced by the growth of high technology. Even the expansion of the high technology industry itself, while much more high-skill intensive than traditional manufacturing or trade and services, will create somewhat more jobs for semiskilled workers than for professionals and technicians.

High Technology, Work Reorganization, and Policy Alternatives

Our prognosis of the impact of high technology on employment is that there is little evidence that it will provide the number or quality of jobs that its most avid proponents claim, and there is some possibility that its impact through automation and robotics in other industries may be negative. Job polarization within the industry is great. Some of the polarization domestically in the United States and other industrial countries may be reduced by shifting the most manual and repetitive production jobs to the Third World and simultaneously robotizing and automating production at home. Neither does it appear that high technology growth and diffusion offset the generally greater increase, in absolute terms, of low-skill, low-income service and commercial jobs both in industrial and developing countries over the next fifteen years.

We conclude that job growth will depend even more in the future, at least in the industrial countries, on general economic growth unless some changes occur in the trend of labor/output ratios and labor/capital ratios. In the 1970s, much of the increase in employment in the United States was achieved by declining real wages combined with economic growth, and little productivity increase. It is difficult in a democratic society to continue to reduce average wages or to keep them from rising, especially during periods of growth, without a political reaction. The newly industrializing countries of Asia have based their increase in growth on exports, using low-wage labor and a high degree of quality control; but if wages rise in those countries, they will have to compete on other grounds. European producers have been particularly constrained historically in lowering wages, particularly the social wage, associated with industrial labor.[30]

Job growth and wage growth can only occur, then, if productivity rises and is accompanied by increased employment and higher wages rather than strictly higher profits (average after-tax profits in the United States rose from 8.1 percent in 1977-80 to 17.8 percent in 1985).[31] Some futurists, such as Alvin Toffler, believe that the "electronic cottage," where workers would become "computer commuters" and self-employed computer service subcontractors, will provide the creative employment of the future.[32] People will stay at home, doing brain work at their terminals and communicating with their supervisors and fellow workers, or with their clients, by electronic mail. The electronic cottage is already a reality for a few. But if it is ever to become a reality for the many, it will have to compete with the computer used by management in automated offices to exact more work from clericals by keeping automatic tabs on performance.[33] In both cases, productivity may rise, but in one case high technology is "an ominous Big Brother to office workers," whereas in the other it is a "liberating force." Which role technology plays depends on how it is used.[34]

Another source of higher productivity is the organization of production. Firms such as Hewlett-Packard have developed a management style that produces intense worker loyalty. Hewlett-Packard features stock options, extensive employee benefits, and personal relationships with employees. It has pioneered flex time, and during the last two recessions, employees as a whole chose to reduce hours rather than lay off some individuals while others worked full time. Many high technology companies have followed this model, both because it is good for productivity and because it helps keep unions out.[35] Yet, even Hewlett-Packard will gradually hire fewer new workers per unit of output as production, clerical, and management processes are automated.

In the next decade almost every country of the world will come to face the domestic economic growth, employment, and wage policy implications of the rapid diffusion of high technology and the increasing integration of the world economy made possible by that technology.

The technology itself will probably not create more jobs. And in one context, the rapid adoption of high technology inputs could also create significant social costs (to labor) as work becomes more disciplined but less stable, with much of it subject to automation, robotization, and even elimination. Enterprises would also be able to utilize a greater possible locational space for their activities and move about that space with less cost to the firm.

Yet the new technology also creates the potential to increase productivity through greater participation in decision making at the level of the enterprise.[36] The miniaturization of the computer, the availability of user-friendly software, and intraenterprise computer communications could make accessible vast amounts of information about firm operations to most employees. With such increased information, employees could understand where efficiency could be improved, would be able to communicate suggestions easily to higher management, and participate intelligently in decision making. Although the Hewlett-Packard model does not yet include this level of employee participation, the model does demonstrate that increased employee involvement in product development and manufacturing reaps high rewards in employee productivity. The new technology can therefore mean more economic democracy, and, with it, new and effective management based on greater worker freedom and even job security. To achieve such objectives, however, firms must emphasize higher labor productivity through more creative management rather than the reduction of wage costs.[37]

The Implications of the High Technology Revolution for Education

Changes in the educational system result not only from shifts in the labor market but also from demands on schools by parents and students, and the interaction of those demands with the school bureaucracy. In the case of the high technology revolution, there is an additional factor: since high technology is much more human capital intensive than other sectors of the economy, and much more reliant on ideas and innovation, the industry as a knowledge producer attempts to influence public education. Moreover, the microcomputer (a product of high technology innovation) is being used as an educational tool, again promoted by the electronic industry itself. High technology therefore influences both the demand for *and* supply of education.

SCHOOLING AND THE EXPANSION OF HIGH TECHNOLOGY JOBS

On the demand side, we have discussed two important aspects of the possible effects of high technology. The first concerns the expansion of high technology manufacturing itself and the structure of demand for educated labor in that industry. The second concerns the impact of robotization and automation (the use of high technology innovations in the production of other goods and services) on skills demands and the implications of that impact on the educational system.

The sum of these effects, we suggest, is increased demand for higher scientific and technical education, especially by Anglo (and Asian-American) males, but much less need for scientifically trained employees in the labor force than the current literature would have us believe.

Recent reports on the "crisis" in American education have stressed the rapid expansion of highly skilled, technical occupations and the corresponding need for upgrading science and mathematics education, computers in the schools, and support for high technology education.[38] But as has already been suggested above on the basis of other recent studies: "Most new jobs will not be in high technology occupations, nor will the application of high technology to existing jobs require a vast upgrading of the skills of the American labor force. To the contrary, the expansion of the lowest skilled jobs in the American economy will vastly outstrip the growth of high technology ones."[39]

So contrary to most expectations, the vast majority of American workers will not require high levels of skill in mathematics and science or specialized training in computer skills. To the contrary, since one of the major objectives of high technology is to simplify work tasks and to reduce the skills required for jobs, most jobs in the future will not require higher skill levels. Moreover, while robotization and automation will create new jobs requiring higher levels of skill and therefore the need for higher levels of schooling, many jobs requiring skills will be eliminated by the same process.

At the same time, there will be a rapid expansion of a relatively small number of very highly skilled jobs requiring university-level technical and scientific training. Our results for the Santa Clara County labor market suggest that the expansion of the high technology (electronics) industry, even though it is expected to slow somewhat in the future, will continue to provide increased demand for highly educated labor that already commands and should continue to receive higher than average salaries. The great majority of these jobs will go to technically trained Anglo males (although many Asian Americans are also entering this part of the labor market). So the push from these groups for the expansion of educational opportunities in higher level technical occupations and engineering will continue.

But the difference in salaries paid in electronics to the higher educated is especially evident in the case of women: college-educated women earn more in electronics because they work more hours per year there than in other sectors. The effect of these higher salaries should provide a particularly great incentive for women to get into the electronics industry, and, in order to increase the probability of obtaining jobs there, to go into technological professions requiring college education. If young women respond to these economic signals, secondary schools will be called upon increasingly to provide college preparatory courses in science and mathematics for women.

The data suggest that more than any other group, Hispanic and black males will be hurt by the rise of high technology manufacturing and the relative decline of traditional manufacturing. It is in traditional manufacturing and construction that these gender/ethnic groups have obtained access to higher incomes. For example, in Santa Clara County, the slow growth of traditional manufacturing could reduce the presently very high return to Hispanic males. On the other hand, the rapid growth of other jobs requiring completion of secondary education, and the high return to taking some years of college education, should keep the value to Hispanics (both males and females) of completing secondary school very high.

If economic incentives mean anything, Hispanics of both sexes in the high technology areas of California should also be pressuring to complete high school, without necessarily going on to college. Yet, the high return for Hispanics to continue on to college (a higher return overall than for Anglo females), should also push Hispanics to demand more college preparatory courses and college counseling. The question is whether California secondary schools are prepared to provide high quality education for Hispanics to take advantage of these high returns to college education or even a completed high school education. It also raises the question of what the school system is doing to convey to Hispanics the value and possibilities of going on to college.

In sum, it appears from our analysis that the greatest relative payoffs to those now in secondary education in the county are for young women in science and mathematics as a preparation for technical fields in college, and for Hispanics to complete their high school education in college preparatory courses as a way to go on to college. Of course, young Hispanics of both genders would do well going into technical fields at the college level, but the difference this would make for young Hispanic women, earnings wise, would probably be greater than that for young men.

Public schools will have to change significantly from the first grade or even kindergarten onward if they are to respond to the labor market payoffs shown in this analysis and if women and Hispanics are to have similar opportunities as Anglo males to obtain the better jobs in the labor market, especially the higher paying engineering and technical jobs. A greater emphasis will have to be placed not just on science and mathematics, as has been suggested by others, but on reaching girls with that science and mathematics. Even more important, there will have to be a shift to preparing (in the case of California) Hispanic boys and girls—the least successful group academically—as early as possible in primary school for college entrance and success.

The greatest danger to the continued integration of United States society that began a new phase after World War II until the mid-1970s (an integration that saw in that period increased incorporation of minorities and women into professional jobs) is the possibility of increased polarization of employment accompanied by a two-tiered educational system, one tier of public and private schools that prepare young people for careers in the innovation and management levels of the information economy, and another tier of public schools (with largely minority clients) that provide the minimum educational requirements for what will be the mass of semiskilled service and production workers in that same economy.

THE IMPLICATIONS OF HIGH TECHNOLOGY
FOR THE SUPPLY OF EDUCATION

A crucial input in the production of high technology is the skill embodied in highly educated labor. Have local educational systems come under special pressures to develop the capabilities, values, and attitudes demanded by high technology firms and by firms using high technology to automate their production of goods and services?

Two studies of the relation between education and high technology already exist, one of Route 128 in Massachusetts[40] and the other of Silicon Valley.[41] They are based on interviews with officials from education, industry, and government and a survey of secondary mathematics and science teachers at high schools on Route 128 (but apparently not in Silicon Valley). Useem shows that there is some cooperation between high technology firms and the schools, but "for the most part, school-industry ties are fragmentary, weak, and of short duration."[42] Many high technology executives, especially in Silicon Valley, hold public schools in contempt as inefficient and inflexible (unionized), at the same time expecting the schools to produce the kinds of skills required by a high technology future. The studies also found that the schools, beset by funding problems, were having difficulty recruiting mathematics and science teachers, especially because of the competition from high technology firms for people with these skills. In both locations, Useem concludes, "the public schools, starved for funds and beset by the conflicting demands of many constituent groups, are moving in a direction opposite to the economic trends in the area."[43]

Useem's results are useful because they show how the values of productive innovation inherent in the expansion of high technology clash with those of a public institution such as education, an institution needed by high technology firms for their long-term expansion. Her discussion also suggests that the industry's short-term-oriented management tends to emphasize immediately attainable goals (such as reducing local property taxes) over longer-term goals such as increasing the quality of public schooling. Yet her results do not tell us much about the directions in which schools *are* being transformed by the presence of high technology industry. In that sense, they give us little insight into what schools influenced by these production organizations would be like when they do change. For example, Useem's analysis does not even begin to discuss the implications for public education of a possible dual culture in the industry.

More popular accounts of the relation between high technology industry and education suggest that schools in high technology areas are under considerable pressure to improve their performance, particularly to provide effective, high quality scientific training to students and much more computer orientation in curriculum and teaching methods.[44] The pressure comes from two sources: (a) the firms themselves, which have a direct interest in the local availability of highly qualified engineers and technicians, and which also rely on the existence of excellent public schools to attract professionals from elsewhere to live in the area; and (b) the highly educated professional parents of children attending schools in high technology areas.

Parent pressure on schools for high quality education, especially in higher income areas of the county, appears to be considerable, and includes demands for a learning environment in the schools that fosters independence and self-motivation.

But the influence of education as a factor in determining position and salaries in high technology should cause even less educated and minority parents in high technology areas to put pressure on their children's schools to improve quality, especially in terms of the percentage of youth graduating from high school and going on to a four-year college. And given the relatively high payoff to young women in technical careers, pressure should be coming from parents of girls as well.

It is not at all clear that parents of either women or minority students are pressuring schools to provide quality scientific and technical training for their children. Thus, it is not necessarily true that the intimate relation between high technology and education reaches all groups working in the industry or in related industries in the same way. To the contrary, the already significant social divisions between professionals and production workers in high technology and related industries may be reflected in an increasingly two-tiered educational system.

It is not surprising that high technology firms should see the solution to educational problems in computer-assisted instruction.[45] Firms such as Apple and IBM have shown considerable interest in the educational market for their hardware. (In 1982, Apple sold one-fourth of its volume to educational institutions.) Computer-assisted instruction and programming courses are part of a more general influence of high technology firms on teaching and management in public schools. Yet, even if CAI were cost-effective—and it is not clear that it is[46]—the access that most children have to microcomputers in the more than 90 percent of American schools that now have them is rather minimal. Teachers are not well trained to employ the computers effectively in teaching even in high technology areas such as Santa Clara County, where the overall environment should make CAI and programming courses particularly easy for teachers to learn.

Do changes in the work process in high technology have an effect on the organization of the teaching-learning process in schools? These new "soft" work styles, intended to increase productivity through a more "human" work atmosphere that relies more on self-discipline and love of job rather than externally imposed discipline and rewards, are an important feature of some high technology firms. Do parents who work in such environments expect schools to provide similar conditions of "work" for their children? Although there have been theoretical suggestions that such "correspondence" exists,[47] and empirical studies of the relation between parents' occupations and the kind of attitudes toward work they instill in their children,[48] there is no systematic empirical analysis of parents' working conditions (the type of firm they work for and their occupation) and the kinds of school conditions they prefer for their children.

Even if all social groups applied equal pressure on the schools for excellent high technology-oriented education, and even if high technology firms put the same kinds of demands and made available the same kinds of computer capabilities to all school districts, we may find that schools and school districts respond differentially to these pressures and availabilities.

First, all school districts in California (and now Massachusetts) have had to contain their spending for the past nine years as a result of Proposition 13, passed in 1976. Nevertheless, those generally higher-income school districts where school populations fell more rapidly in the 1970s and early 1980s were in a better position to maintain high per pupil spending than districts such as San Jose (one of the fastest-growing cities in the country), where school population remained relatively stable but where the student population became increasingly non-Anglo.

Second, the rapid growth of high technology with its need for low-cost, semiskilled labor has attracted a significant immigration of Asians and Hispanics into high technology areas such as Santa Clara County and Orange County. In 1980, for example, children from minority groups made up 43 percent of the under-five age category in Santa Clara County. The county's schools apparently do not have the resources to deal with the many languages that make their way into classrooms. But perhaps more important, traditional educational practices have difficulty responding to learning styles of students not in the upper middle class.

Third, schools as bureaucracies are less likely to view pressure from Asian and Hispanic parents for high quality education in the same way that administrators and teachers do in high-income school districts, where pupils' parents are professionals.[49] Administrators are also less likely to consider that lower-income, minority pupils require the same access to computers and computer literacy as children of professionals.

Finally, the rapid expansion of high technology may itself be to blame for schools' difficulties in providing high quality education in mathematics and science. The availability of high-paying jobs in industry for anyone with mathematical and scientific skills may have created a shortage of mathematics and science teachers, especially in high technology areas.[50]

At this juncture, it is not clear whether the traditional public school—an institution developed well before the advent of high technology—is capable of responding to the demands of parents for high quality mathematics and science education even in the context of a high technology environment. In an institution with a different structure and organization (and different product), what are the conflicts between high technology demands and institutional response? Where pressures are similar from different social groups, do the schools respond similarly? Are schools more "equalitarian" in dealing with such demands than high technology industry is in employment, as Useem implies?

There are many questions left unanswered on the supply side. It is unclear what role microcomputers can play in improving learning or in preparing students for various roles in a computerized society. Is the management of schools moving into the high technology age? Are parents and students as aware of various opportunities as they should be? Schools are not responding to the information as quickly as many think they should or others thought they could. Whether they do so in the future depends in part on how seriously the information revolution is taken and that, in turn, may depend on how many jobs are available that require knowledge of computers or even computer literacy.

Conclusion

If the analysis offered in this chapter is correct, then there is reason to be skeptical of predictions that the high technology revolution will significantly help to solve enduring problems in unemployment, the workplace, and schooling in the United States. The evidence here presented suggests that neither the production of high technology goods (computers and robotics, for example), nor the application of those goods to producing other goods and services in the information age will cure traditional ills associated with economic development in the United States. Further, the benefits of this technology for schooling are also doubtful.

Evidence does not support the claim that the production of high technology equipment nor the use of the equipment in factories and offices is likely to create enough jobs to put a serious dent in unemployment. High technology industries will employ an increasing but relatively small number of people, compared to the faster growing numbers of service and trade jobs being created. Further, the hope that robotics will create more or better jobs than they eliminate appears unfounded. Unemployment rates appear to be more a function of overall economic productivity, and this is contingent as much upon organizational innovation, including the provision of greater decision making by workers in the work place, as upon technological change.

The notion that repetitive, low-skill employment will decline significantly as a result of the technological revolution also appears unsupportable. Some of these low-skill jobs will be exported to developing nations, but many new ones will remain in the United States. Not only will jobs in the service and trade areas outnumber the jobs created by high technology, but in high technology-related industry the lower-skill, lower-status jobs will probably outnumber high-skill, high-status science and technology jobs that high technology production and application require. These two opposing trends are contributing to increasing polarization of the job-market structure, with jobs requiring either highly rewarded scientific and technological training or not requiring much in the way of skills at all. Finally, if present trends continue, the high-skill, high-reward jobs will be filled by Anglo and Asian-American males, with the low-skill jobs being filled primarily by women.

This two-tier employment structure is further exacerbated because the need for scientifically skilled laborers is apparently less than has been predicted. One implication of this is that the need for schools to respond with high quality mathematics and science programs for the majority of their students will not be supported by the employment structure. Schools will be able to help women and minority students break into the upper tier, however, if they find ways to deliver high quality mathematics and science curricula to those traditionally low-income groups, and act to promote their pursuit of academic subjects leading to such careers.

FOOTNOTES

1. For a review of this literature, see Mark Blaug, *An Introduction to the Economics of Education* (London: Alan Lane, Penguin Press, 1970); Martin Carnoy, "Education and Economic Development: The First Generation," *Economic Development and Cultural Change 25*, Supplement (1977): 428-48.

2. For example, see Richard Freeman, *The Overeducated American* (New York: Academic Press, 1976).

3. Carnoy, "Education and Economic Development"; idem, "The Political Economy of Education," in *Encyclopedia of International Education* (London: Pergamon, 1984).

4. The broadest definition of high technology industries includes industries where the proportion of workers employed in high technology occupations (engineers, life and physical scientists, mathematical specialists, engineering and science technicians, and computer specialists) is at least 1.5 times the average for all industries. A narrower definition includes those *manufacturing* industries in which the proportion of workers employed in high technology occupations (those listed above) is equal to or greater than the average for all manufacturing industries. An even narrower definition only includes industries with a ratio of R & D expenditures to net sales at least twice the average for all industries. See Russell Rumberger and Henry M. Levin, "Forecasting the Impact of New Technologies on the Future Job Market," Project Report No. 84-A4 (Stanford, Calif.: Institute for Research on Educational Finance and Governance, Stanford University, 1984). When I refer in this chapter to high technology occupations, I am referring to the list included above.

5. Barbara G. Katz and Almarin Phillips, "Government, Technological Opportunities, and the Emergence of the Computer Industry," in *Emerging Technologies: Consequences for Economic Growth, Structural Change, and Employment*, ed. H. Giersch (Tübingen: J.C.B. Mohr [Paul Siebeck], 1982). The role of the public sector was crucial in the first phase and continues to be crucial in the development of high technology industry in three fundamental ways: (a) by funding basic research, primarily in universities but also in quasi-public companies such as Lockheed and General Dynamics (military contractors) and (prederegulation) "natural" monopolies such as American Telephone and Telegraph (Bell Laboratories); (b) by subsidizing the production of engineers—who embody the new technology—through university research grants, student loans and scholarships, and direct university support (state universities); and (c) by providing a ready market for new high technology products in their early, high priced, noncommercial phase. The Defense Department and federally supported university acquisition programs were the principal buyers of early computers and the Defense Department provided a market for early integrated circuits, thus allowing leading manufacturers like Fairchild Semiconductor and Texas Instruments to learn to produce such circuits more efficiently by manufacturing them in large quantities, which Rosenberg calls "learning by doing." See Nathan Rosenberg, *Inside the Black Box: Technology and Economics* (New York: Cambridge University Press, 1982).

6. Luc Soete, "Electronics," in *Technical Trends and Employment: Electronics* ed. Luc Soete (Brookfield, Vermont: Grower Publishing Co., 1985), Table 1.1.

7. Engineers and technicians tend to be highly mobile. Under the right conditions they can be attracted to where the plants are. Low-cost, upper-middle-income housing, and a pleasant environment (Colorado, for example) factor into location strategy, since these are means to reduce salary costs of the highly educated labor required for research and development units of high technology enterprises.

8. "High Tech Sweepstakes," *High Technology*, January, 1985.

9. Richard Gordon and Linda Kimball, *High Technology, Employment, and the Challenges to Education* (Santa Cruz, Calif.: Silicon Valley Research Group, University of California, 1985); idem, *Small Town High Technology: The Industrialization of Santa Cruz County*, Working Paper No. 1 (Santa Cruz, Calif.: Silicon Valley Research Group, University of California, 1985).

10. Martin Carnoy, "The Santa Clara Labor Market and Its Implications for Education," Project Report No. 85-A8 (New York: Institute for Economic Analysis, 1983).

11. Ibid.

12. Ibid.

13. *Business Week*, 8 July 1985, pp.71-76.

14. Rumberger and Levin, "Forecasting the Impact of New Technologies on the Future Job Market," Table 3.

15. Ibid.

16. Ibid., Table 4.

17. Gordon and Kimball, *High Technology, Employment, and the Challenges to Education.*

18. See Rumberger and Levin, "Forecasting the Impact of New Technologies on the Future Job Market."

19. Martin Carnoy and Manuel Castells, "After the Crisis?" *World Policy Journal* 1 (Spring1984): 495-515.

20. See Robert Lawrence, "The Employment Effect of the New Information Technologies: An Optimistic View," Brookings Institution, September 1984 (mimeographed).

21. Ian Benson and John Lloyd, *New Technology and Industrial Change* (New York: Nichols Publishers, 1983).

22. Russell Rumberger, "High Technology and Job Loss," Project Report No. 84-A12 (Stanford, Calif.: Institute for Research on Educational Finance and Governance, Stanford University, 1984).

23. Martin Carnoy, Russell Rumberger, and Derek Shearer, *A New Social Contract* (New York: Harper and Row, 1983).

24. Rumberger, "High Technology and Job Loss," pp. 6-7.

25. Ibid.

26. Wassily Leontief and Faye Duchin, "The Impacts of Automation on Employment, 1963-2000" (Stanford, Calif.: Institute for Research on Educational Finance and Governance, Stanford University, February, 1983).

27. Rumberger, "High Technology and Job Loss," p. 20. See also, Gene Bylinsky, "The Race to the Automatic Factory," *Fortune* 107 (February 21, 1983): 57, 60.

28. David R. Howell, "The Impact of Robots on Employment: An Input-Output Analysis" (unpublished manuscript, Institute of Economic Analysis, New York University, 1984), cited in Rumberger, "High Technology and Job Loss."

29. Barbara Baran, "Office Automation and Women's Work: The Technological Transformation of the Insurance Industry," in *High Technology, Space, and Society*, ed. Manuel Castells (Beverly Hills, Calif.: Sage Publications, 1985).

30. See the extensive literature on employment problems in Europe (for example, Jean-Pierre Jallade, *Emploi et Chommage en Europe* [Paris: Economica, 1981]) and on the growth of the public sector (for example, Organization for Economic Cooperation and Development, *The Role of the Public Sector*, OECD Economic Studies No. 4 [Paris: Organization for Economic Cooperation and Development, 1985]).

31. Martin Carnoy, "The U.S. Economy and the World Economics Crisis," Stanford University, 1985 (mimeographed).

32. Alvin Toffler, *The Third Wave* (New York: Bantam Books, 1980).

33. Everett Rogers and Judith Larsen, *Silicon Valley Fever* (New York: Basic Books, 1984), p. 256.

34. Ibid., p. 257.

35. Ibid.

36. Benson and Lloyd, *New Technology and Industrial Change.*

37. Carnoy, Rumberger, and Shearer, *A New Social Contract.*

38. Education Commission of the States, "The Information Society: Are High Schools Ready?" (Denver, Colo.: Education Commission of the States, 1982).

39. Henry M. Levin and Russell Rumberger, "The Educational Implications of High Technology" (Stanford, Calif.: Institute for Research on Educational Finance and Governance, Stanford University, 1983).

40. Elizabeth Useem, *Education in a High Technology World: The Case of Route 128* (Boston: Institute for the Interdisciplinary Study of Education, Northeastern University, June, 1982).

41. Elizabeth Useem, "Education and High Technology Industry: The Case of Silicon Valley," *Economics of Education Review* 3, no. 3 (1984): 215-21.

42. Useem, *Education in a High Technology World*, p. 1.

43. Useem, "Education and High Technology Industry," p. 215.

44. See, for example, *Mercury News* (San Jose) 17-24 February 1985, and "High Tech Sweepstakes," *High Technology*, January 1985.

45. Leonard Siegel and John Markoff, *The High Cost of High Tech* (New York: Harper and Row, 1985), chap. 4.

46. Henry M. Levin, Gene V Glass, and Gail Meister, *A Cost-Effectiveness Analysis of Four Educational Interventions*, Project Report 84-A11 (Stanford, Calif.: Institute for Research on Educational Finance and Governance, Stanford University, 1984).

47. Martin Carnoy and Henry M. Levin, *Schooling and Work in the Democratic State* (Stanford, Calif.: Stanford University Press, 1985).

48. Gavin MacKenzie, *The Aristocracy of Labor: The Position of Skilled Craftsmen in the American Class Structure* (London: Oxford University Press, 1973); Melvin Kohn, *Class and Conformity: A Study of Values* (Homewood, Ill.: Dorsey, 1969).

49. Carnoy and Levin, *Schooling and Work in the Democratic State*, chap. 5.

50. Useem, *Education in a High Technology World*; idem, "Education and High Technology Industry."

Part Two
SOCIAL HETEROGENEITY AND POWER

CHAPTER V

Changing Gender Roles in Familial, Occupational, and Civic Settings

ELISE BOULDING

Men, Women, and Community

There are three gender-articulated communities which together foster the social development of the human species: the community of women with women, of men with men, and of women with men. In every society all three of these communities will be found, although the social patternings vary in time and place. The basic position taken here is that social learning and human development, in its fullest sense, including the development of gender identity and gender roles, depends on the health and strength of the bonds within each of these three closely interdependent communities. They provide the prime material out of which society is constructed. Much has been made of the nature of the male bond and its importance to civilization.[1] Much has also been made of the special bonding among women. Jessie Bernard's major study, *The Female World*, explores the gemeinschaft qualities of that world.[2] Books on male-female relationships, while legion, tend to emphasize increasing tensions in the male-female bond, whether in the context of the family or other social settings.

We will examine how socialization and enculturation take place for women and men within each of the three types of communities at this moment of history. Structures handed down from past traditions fit poorly the developmental needs of women and men in these rapidly changing times. By looking first at the historical reality and the straitjacket of stereotypes which has constrained that reality, we get a

112

better sense of the ongoing nature of the struggle in which women and men now find themselves. It is new, but it is also very old. What is new is the more active interplay of household, occupation, and civic areas for both sexes. There are no historical precedents for this, so the resocialization has to take place without adequate role models.

After examining the historical experience, we will look at the reconstruction of social roles that is currently going on—the massive re-education that society is generating for itself in the intersecting arenas of household, workplace, and civic life. Finally, we will look at what more might be done to assist this dynamic but painful process.

What is the community of women? It is the mutual aid community across households and ages traditionally bonded in the care of the human species. It tends to birthing, marrying, and dying, and the preparation of communal feasts. In societies where gender segregation is strongly institutionalized by purdah or other customs, the community of women may be all-encompassing for women in that all childrearing, domestic maintenance, and economic production tasks are undertaken, and all celebrations are held, within women's quarters. Another special form of women's community that reappears across the centuries is the lesbian community, which today proudly bears its name in memory of the poetess Sappho and the school/community she founded on the Isle of Lesbos. Lesbian communities are historically unique in providing an extremely limited social role, if any, for men in the microsociety. Socioemotional, sexual, and economic needs are all met within the community of women.[3]

Such extreme gender segregation is uncommon. In no society, however, is an identifiable community of women entirely absent. It is most clearly defined in such institutions as convents, girls' schools, and women's clubs. Sometimes praised, sometimes deplored, the community of women is a social fact of every culture.

The community of men with men is the mutual aid community across households and ages traditionally bonded in the blood of the battlefield and in men's willingness to defend by force their common polity. It controls decision making and resource allocation within and between households and trains male children to carry on that work. The community of men maintains institutions to enhance the physical fitness of their kind, including athletic games and war. It utilizes community surpluses for the training of artists, philosophers, and scientists for the cultural order, and trains a priesthood to maintain the moral and religious order. In societies where gender segregation is strongly institutionalized, all male economic activity is carried out in male work groups, and public celebrations are for men only. In certain historical periods, all-male subcultures have provided for the deepest emotional and sexual needs of men, within their own community; if they mated with women it was for reproductive purposes only. Homosexual or gay communities may or may not include a dependence on women to maintain their life-style.

While extreme segregation is uncommon, in no society is an identifiable community of men completely absent. It is most clearly defined in such institutions as monasteries, boys' schools, men's clubs, including sports and huntsmen organizations, armies, and gay bars. Sometimes praised, sometimes deplored, the community of men is a social fact of every culture.

The community of women and men is that mutual aid group most frequently, but not exclusively, found in households. There women and men united by bonds of kin, contract, and varying degrees of affection, collaborate in carrying out some basic maintenance functions of life: physical (and perhaps emotional) nurturance and sheltering, and the reproduction and rearing of children. The household in its modal form, husband-wife/wives-children, has become the order-creating template for society after society, in numerous local variations, arising again and again out of the vicissitudes of social interaction in the human search for survival and reproduction. The household has been the site of the most violent clashes between women and men, and the site of their most dedicated and sensitive cooperation. It has been subject to far more stress than the community of women with women, or men with men, because it has involved a daily propinquity and interdependence not found in the other communities. It has often been described as a prison by both sexes. In spite of its bad press, the household has been the primary organizational format in which women and men have interacted in any society.

Men-men, women-women, and women-men communities contribute jointly to the social definition of gender roles in the societies of which they are a part. Male and female sexual characteristics, however irrelevant to gender-assigned tasks, form the basis for social role assignments in a macrohistorical process of sex stereotyping which is matched in absurdity only by the variety of pseudocharacteristics ascribed now to the male, now to the female. Sometimes heavy load lifting is assigned to the female, as the less sentient of the species. Sometimes the handling of money and bargaining tasks are assigned to females, on a similar premise. More often, the reverse role assignments prevail: women are supposed to be too weak to lift heavy loads, and too sensitive to handle money. Whatever the culturally defined attributes are, women's groups, men's groups, and the mixed familial group for the most part cooperate to reinforce socially approved gender behaviors and to discourage disapproved gender behaviors.

The importance of the collaborative process among the three communities cannot be overestimated, because culturally defined gender roles set the limits within which socialization takes place in each society. By setting minimum gender performance standards which must be met, and setting definitive ceilings (or floors) on individual aspirations for each sex, they also establish the boundaries within which societal development takes place. While the pattern varies from culture to culture, there has been a gender-based division of labor in every known society, and this division of labor has been anchored in familial groupings organized by households. Today Plato's old question about that division of labor is being raised again. In Book VIII of *The Republic*, Plato proposed the abolition of private property and the family and the development of a high civic culture with a guardian class of men and women who would share the same education and the same responsibilities. He reversed himself in *The Laws*, prescribing a "second-best but attainable" society in which women would carry out familial duties in the traditional manner of his time.

As Susan Okin has so well conveyed, the functionalist view of women as a part of the natural order, as over against the view of men as a part of the civic order, the *polis*, repeatedly overrides the recurring perception that physiological sex differences are not related to differences in intellectual and civic capabilities.[4] This functionalist view appears to stem from an intuitive conviction on the part of an array of male philosophers and thinkers down through the centuries that society could not function without keeping women in a primary maintenance-service role for the community of men, who need to be freed for civic decision making and social invention. The human rights legislation of the twentieth century has not erased the juridical articulation of this concept from twentieth-century lawbooks. We will explore how this particular form of gender-based division of labor became so pervasive, how it has affected the social development of men and women, and what kinds of societal learning are taking place to prepare for the future.

The Household: Historical Anchor for
Gender Role Concepts

History, archaeology, and anthropology all bear witness to the universality of the household unit. The Perigordians and the Aurignacians lived in familistic groupings in the cave apartments of the valleys of Europe in 35,000 B.C. Nomadic peoples had moveable campfires but identifiably familistic food and shelter patterns.

As urban life developed in the Fertile Crescent and on other continents, houses and walled courtyards became familiar features along with palaces and temples in royal cities. Familistic groupings became more literally households. In medieval Europe, laboring and serving classes maintained "households" in the corners of their masters' quarters or in tiny houses or apartments just big enough to sleep in,[5] sending infants to rural baby farms for survival.

Every variety of household type that has ever existed still exists today. In the industrial west we may find familial households consisting of husband/wife/children, or single parent/children, lesbian or gay couples with/without children, small groups of unrelated people living in communes, group houses or group marriages, or the mobile one-person household. In the traditional sectors of the less industrialized world, the household may consist of a husband with several wives each farming her own bit of land and handling her own finances, or frerêche-style town housing for well-to-do, upper-middle-class, entrepreneurial, extended families.

The civic and decision-making assemblies of most societies have consisted of male heads of households.[6] The exceptions are often located so far back in antiquity that it is difficult to separate history from myth. This fact gives us a clue both to the historical utility of the household as the basis for sociopolitical organization, and to the utility for men of maintaining power over the resources within each household.

THE HOUSEHOLD AS A UNIT OF SOCIAL ORGANIZATION
AND A UNIT OF REPRODUCTION

Familial household units are so omnipresent a feature of human society because they provide the maximum in human services with the minimum of regulatory mechanisms. As Litwak pointed out in his classic essay,[7] the family (read extended family, familial grouping, household) in complex societies forms a partnership with bureaucratic organizations to individualize the latter's services in all arenas—

manufacturing, protection, medical care, education of children, and old-age security—making those services fit the needs of individual family members. Bureaucracies could not work without that family intervention process, because their services could never be made to fit idiosyncratic human needs. Even more important, intrahousehold and extended family interhousehold services provide far more resources, and more efficiently, than any public regulatory system. In the United States, James Morgan estimates that intrafamilial grants-in-aid add up to 30 percent of the total GNP, as compared with a modest 10 percent of the GNP in public sector aid to households and a meager 2 percent contributed by private sector aid (including churches and foundations) to households.[8] Data on interhousehold family aid are sparse, but two studies suggest substantial aid-in-kind as well as financial transfers: Hill's study of intergenerational decision making and aid[9] and Fischer's study of extended kin networks in California.[10] The historical value of households to every society does, however, rest on one all-important social fact: households perform as effectively as they do primarily because of interhousehold women's networks which help cushion families against both major and minor stresses and crises.

THE HOUSEHOLD AS A CIVIC UNIT

The political and legal context of family mutual aid has been a social order based on the concept of included interest. The interests of women, children, and slaves and servants, if any, are included in the interest of the male head of household. While the concept in that form was first described by James Mill in 1924, its origins lie in the distant past of tribal councils, when every male head of household was also a potential warrior who represented the interests of his household's women-tended sacred hearth at councils of war and peace. Going back even further, as I have argued elsewhere, this representational role of the male as head of household has its roots in the hunting and gathering stage of human existence. Men's greater mobility in the hunt, unfettered by childbearing and nursing, gave them knowledge of more extended geographical and social terrains. It brought them into more frequent contact with distant villages, and gave them by default a set of trading, negotiating, and resource-allocation roles based on that wider knowledge. The development of the male political community, the council of elders, capable of mobilizing the resources of each represented household in times of famine and war, was a logical next step. Once the council of elders was in place the knowledge gap between women and men widened. The included-interest concept left women as hidden collaborators in the household economy, their personal well-being dependent on prevailing norms of respect and affection as these were observed by the household head.

As societies became wealthier the economic value of the household came to be a primary consideration along with the need to protect the sacred hearth. Male children took on increasing importance as developers and extenders of household wealth, and women came to be seen as bearers of males who could continue household lineages. Political and economic developments reinforced one another to enhance the authority of male heads of households. The system was further reinforced by the obvious advantages in public decision making of only having to listen to one voice in each household. Ancient empires depended heavily on this system, and its shadow remains today in the male head-of-household concept.

THE IMAGE AND THE REALITY

Household-based social orders created a sharp division between public space, occupied by male household heads in their politico-economic roles of decision makers and traders, and private space, occupied by the women of each man's household who functioned as hidden partners in household enterprises. While some cultures have been more equalitarian than others, civic councils remain predominantly or entirely male. The occasional powerful female landowner or entrepreneur or reigning queen are the exceptions that prove the rule.

The hidden partners in the household economic enterprises were not "housewives" doing "housework" in the modern sense. Women have always worked in market-bound economic production activities in house or field or craft shop or factory, often with hours to walk between home and workplace. Home maintenance has always been a small part of the work that women have done.

It is startling that the legal fiction of the male representing his household, which juridically places every woman under the authority of a male head of household, whether father, brother, husband, or son, has continued over the centuries in the face of the social reality that at any one time or place in history, including the present, roughly one-third of adult women are unpartnered; of these, a substantial number function independently of a juridical "protector." These women may be never-married, widowed, divorced, or separated. United Nations figures on the marital status of women[11] confirm the strong impression gained from a reading of historical materials in many different societies, that substantial numbers of women live and have always lived in de facto women-headed households. They have been without civic rights, but they have reared children, worked as laborers, managed enterprises, or developed their abilities as artists, scientists, teachers, and doctors in convents.

Historically, women have always had to be prepared to act autonomously on behalf of their children and themselves even while having no separate civic existence, and supposedly being without knowledge of the larger world. This has been particularly true in wartime, when women have had to ensure family survival in the absence of men, often having to face enemy males unprotected. It is also true in any time of rapid social change. The skills of the community of women in building mutual aid networks for survival under crisis conditions are what make possible the survival of that other community, the community of men and women in households.

The Breakdown of Household-Anchored Gender Roles

It is hard to pinpoint a historical moment when the household shell that symbolically hid women from society began crumbling. It is hard because, Plato's recantation notwithstanding, there has been an unbroken chain of male and female voices through time proclaiming the absurdity of women's civic hiddenness. Two separate developments unfolded slowly on the European scene out of the intellectual ferment of the Renaissance and came to a head in the nineteenth century, laying the groundwork for a basic redefinition of the relationships of women and men to one another, and to the household which had so long held them together. One was an enriched understanding of the meaning of humanism and an extension of those meanings to women. The other was the series of scientific and technological revolutions lumped together under the label "industrial revolution," which produced industrial society and changed working conditions for women as well as for men.

By the mid-1800s, middle-class women began protesting their legal status and turning their rapidly growing international mutual aid networks to the task of gaining civic rights for themselves and their sisters. The human rights covenants of the United Nations now ensure that women have some de jure rights as civic beings in every member state, although de facto rights still lag behind badly.[12] The traditional all-male tribal councils have disappeared in theory, but not in fact.

The parallel phenomenon that gave substance to women's demands for civic rights was the claim laid by the new industrial work force on the household. Women could no longer be the hidden partners in family enterprises. Now their long walk to the family workshop was replaced by a long walk to factories or stores owned by strangers, and the fruits of their labors came in money wages. Hours were longer, working conditions not "child-friendly" as in the preindustrial society. Women's traditional triple role as "breeder-feeder-producer" became much harder for the industrial poor. At the same time a new "nonworking" group of women emerged from the middle classes, leaving family workshops to engage in civic labor in the bleak public spaces of industrial society.

The gap between the de jure and de facto status of women as civic beings and as workers is enormous, and the injustices to women in both statuses severe. The tragedy is that everyone looks to the household to help regain the social equilibrium lost by rapid social changes in the economic and civic spheres, and then cries doom to society because the household is not functioning as it used to. Once women became civic beings with their own legal identity the doctrine of included interest was gone forever, and with it the role of the male head of household as primary decision maker. Now households consist of adult males and females whose voices count separately. These adults are constrained in decision making regarding household matters, including children's welfare, by each other's civic rights and by the emerging civic rights of their children. (The latter still figure as an "included interest" but with some caveats and legal resources available to them.) Having an independent voice can be frightening, and not all women want it. Others want it so badly that they can not wait for the slow interpersonal negotiations at the household level, and simply move out of the family. The consequence is much social confusion among women (and men) about their new identities. The larger community of women, itself divided and confused, has nevertheless in some of its parts been preparing for this situation for a long time. There are role models and support networks to be found for those women who know where to look.

There is much compassion for the displaced homemaker, the woman who was not ready for the new role but had it thrust upon her by widowhood, or by a husband who was impatient for change.[13] There is relatively little compassion for the displaced male household head. The tribal warrior may not have lost his place in the council of elders, but many have lost their female support systems. The community of men has been slow in responding to the new situation. They were caught unprepared, with few role models and little wisdom available. Now, slowly, painfully, belatedly, men's support groups are forming so the community of men can take up this new mutual aid task. While political and economic structures are still overwhelmingly male, that basic organizational unit on which all other structures are based, the household, is not the same. Instead of one voice, the head-of-household voice, there are now many voices. Old patterns of policy consensus are breaking down in the tribal council as well as in the household.

Most difficult of all, gender has broken down as a de jure basis for social role allocation. Its continuance as a de facto practice cannot long survive the creative new inputs to economic and political life and to science and the arts coming from women whose capabilities have for the first time been allowed public exercise. The process of occupational stereotyping, on which traditional household organization was based, has been upset by the human rights concept that work opportunities should be determined by ability and not by gender, age, religion, or ethnicity.

Not only has gender broken down as a basis for occupational role allocation, it has also broken down as a basis for marital roles. Gays and lesbians have the human right to partner and live in connubial bliss. Churches and secular organizations provide spiritual and emotional, as well as legal, support for these couples. Adoption agencies may no longer deny homosexuals the right to adopt children simply on the basis of their sexual preference.

With such rapid changes taking place in supposedly familiar social institutions, everyone, male and female, becomes to some degree a socially displaced person. This produces much social pain, but also much social creativity. The three gender communities—the community of women with women, of men with men, and of men with women—are all creating new ways of dealing with old tasks, not least in the household itself. The same terrain that has become a battleground for women and men is also the soil in which seeds of new relationships are being planted.

The Reconstruction of Social Roles for Women and Men

The breakdown of the old head-of-household mode of social organization has changed the nature of the public-private interface in society, for both women and men. Formerly, women were privatized and it was only men who moved back and forth between the public and the private spheres of life. Now, both men and women move back and forth, and only the household itself remains private, offering spiritual and emotional sustenance to its members in hidden spaces that are entered voluntarily, and left voluntarily. We will examine the demographics of the present transition era and some of the new responses to the transition upheaval.

THE DEMOGRAPHICS OF TRANSITION

While the drama of gender role change has in the past been played out primarily in urban areas, the decade of the 1970s produced a reversal of a centuries-long rural-urban migration. In the United States, the open country and small towns distant from metropolitan areas, which were still losing population in the 1960s, had by the 1970s gained roughly 15 percent of new population. Demographers are predicting changes in overall settlement patterns in all parts of the United States away from metropolitan areas, and an increasing preference for rural life-styles.[14] With the divorce rate leveling off, the remarriage rate high (.49 for black women, .73 for white women, within five years of divorce) and *expectations* of marrying showing no decline over the past two decades,[15] gender relations in the new households being formed between now and the end of the century may work themselves out in less stressful settings than high-pressure cities.

At the same time, a comparison of attitudes toward marriage in the 1960s and the 1980s, based on data from several different longitudinal studies,[16] also indicates an increasing acceptance of singleness as a way of life, and a more relaxed attitude toward the marriage choice. The new view, reported in western Europe as well, is that one does not *have* to be married to be happy. The rapid increase in the number of single-person households in the United States since the 1950s and the decline in five-, six-, and seven-person households from the beginning of the century, suggest that the future is for singles and small families. (The phenomenon of group houses, to be discussed later, is a third household alternative.) The population is aging. The median age today is 30.3. By 2050 it will be 41.6. The population booms of the twentieth century are gradually drawing to a close.

Paralleling the more relaxed attitude toward marriage is a rising expectation on the part of women (and to a lesser degree men) that women will continue in the paid labor force through their adult life, married or single, childed or childless. As of 1981, 60 percent of all women work, and 43 percent of the work force is female. Two-thirds of that female work force *must* work because they are either single, widowed, divorced, or separated (45 percent) or their husbands do not earn a subsistence wage (21 percent). The number of working mothers has increased more than tenfold since 1940: 59 percent of all mothers with children under eighteen are in the work force, and 50 percent of all women with preschoolers. Women head 16 percent of all households and from 50-70 percent of poverty households, so outside economic activity is a *choice* for relatively few women. Nevertheless, their earnings continue at 59 percent of the earnings of men and have shown no signs of improvement over several decades of efforts to achieve equal pay.[17] This situation is worldwide and is to a substantial degree due to the failure to end occupational gender stereotyping of women as mandated by human rights legislation nationally and internationally. Contrary, however, to a worldwide trend to increase public child care facilities for working women, the United States has steadily decreased its child care facilities since World War II, greatly adding to the economic and social stress of working mothers.[18]

Prolonged unemployment and increasing poverty, a continuing arms race, increasing rates of drug and alcohol abuse, and violence, intrafamilial and on the streets, provide the broader context for the somewhat conflicting trends in familial and occupational demographics. We may eventually be heading for a period of greater stability, but prospects for the next decade look grim. The struggle for social survival is intense, whether for individuals, families, or nations. There is little surplus energy for working at new gender definitions to replace the old stereotyped ones. Yet new gender perceptions may hold the key to solving many of our other social problems. How are the communities of women and men dealing with this problem?

New Occupational Roles

The workplace has been the primary focus of action by the women's community in its effort to implement the new freedom of action for women established by law. There are several reasons for this. One is the factor of visibility of workplace activities as contrasted with the invisibility of the home. It is easier to focus a critical mass of public attention on the workplace. Another is that the majority of women have to be in the workplace anyway, as primary breadwinners or as essential secondary breadwinners, and they are angry at the dullness and lack of advancement in the job sectors to which they have been historically confined. Studies of women's work attitudes show that they generally enjoy working, feel committed to their jobs, have lifetime work aspirations which increase with their years in the work force, and are increasingly aware of dead-end job traps.[19] A comparison of women of the World War I cohort of the teens and 1920s, of the World War II cohort of the 1930s and 1940s, and of the baby boom generation of the 1950s and 1960s, shows intensity of work commitments increasing with each generation as well as with age and years spent in the work force. We can anticipate that young women entering the work force in the 1980s and 1990s will insist on a greater variety of job opportunities than their mothers and grandmothers pushed for.[20]

The change-resistant character of workplace role structures for women is in part due to the cultural lag in men's understandings of women's roles in the contemporary economy. The hearth-tender image is still in men's minds, and the workplace commitment of women frequently is not perceived as anything more than "helping out." Service roles and low-skill roles are often seen by men as being sufficient for women. The women's community has launched a major drive to open up new job opportunities for women, in response both to rising aspiration levels and to urgent need for higher incomes for women heads of households. In the blue-collar world, this has meant a slow but steady increase in women holding the skilled jobs that have hitherto been a male prerogative, and earning the higher salaries that go with them.

These slow gains must often be achieved in the face of refusals to allow women into the apprenticeship programs that would qualify them for skilled trades. Women also endure on-the-job hassling by men. The ones who hang in eventually earn respect through sheer grit and competence. Nowhere is the exclusionary effect of male bonding on women more evident than at the workplace. Male workers in heavy manual labor become close mutual aid teams. Since the work is often dangerous and injuries occur, each worker must know the others' weak points—a weak back, a tricky shoulder—and compensate for that. Men who have weak hearts can be carried for years on a construction team by co-workers who will see to it that their mate never does heavy lifting at all.[21] Not only will men not extend this kind of help to new women workers on their teams, they sometimes deliberately leave women to lift unaided equipment and materials men would normally not try to lift alone. If a woman does not complain and handles herself well, she may eventually be treated as part of the team.

In every traditionally men's occupation the story of resistance and harassment is the same. Community education, political pressure, and legal action are required to open up job opportunities. Without the help of the women's community in finding training for new kinds of work, and in providing support groups to turn to in the face of harassment and sexual abuse, women would not enter these new sectors in any numbers and traditional segregation practices would remain intact. Obstacles and the need for support are present everywhere. Two examples are women entering the ministry[22] and women in the sciences.[23] The Association of Women in Science (AWIS), which publishes a quarterly newsletter, provides a helping network for women in all the sciences. Each discipline in the natural and social sciences also has its own helping network for women (in sociology, for example, it is Sociologists for Women in Society [SWS]). Women scientists in universities face a double hazard: negative attitudes of male colleagues in the laboratory and negative attitudes of academe toward tenure for women.[24] Women in the arts have similar networks to help women find studios in which to work and market outlets. Women in the military have created their own support networks inside the armed forces with courage and humor.[25]

Women in the professions have gone from being lone doctors and lawyers to forming highly articulate mutual aid networks. The American Women's Medical Association has both medical students and doctors in membership, and the American Medical Students Association has a special section for women in medicine. There are many new women lawyers' groups in addition to the prestigious older National Women Lawyers Association. They have worked with the Judicial Selection project of the National Women's Political Caucus to get a 200 to 300 percent increase in women on the bench over a seven-year period. They organize "shadow bar associations" and utilize an informal national network to assist women lawyers in getting important public assignments and in finding promising job openings. Business women's associations are rapidly proliferating locally, regionally, and nationally. One magazine for executive women, *Savvy*, lists women's business groups by region each month in a special networking section. The National Association for Female Executives publishes its own bimonthly magazine, *Executive Female*, and offers a nationwide network of women business contacts to its members.

The positive side of this activity by the women's community is that women are actually breaking out of the traditional job molds, albeit slowly. In twenty years the number of women engineers has risen from 1 percent to 4 percent, women physicians from 6 percent to 14 percent, women in natural sciences from 9 percent to 22 percent. Women are now nearly half of all bus drivers and 40 percent of postal clerks and accountants. Women have been a significant new factor in the world of team sports, going well beyond the traditional women's sports—swimming and tennis. They have revitalized earlier women's sports associations and formed new ones for help in the struggle for recognition. In mining, women have gone from 0 percent to 2 percent to 3 percent. Half of all divinity students are now women, as are nearly half of all students in schools of agriculture. Women of the next generation will work in many settings where their mothers could not go.

The dark side of this picture is the negative response from the male work force. While there are supportive men, and the number of men willing to accept women as colleagues is increasing, women are more aware of the hindrances than the help. On the one hand, there is the deliberate noncooperation and harassment in the blue-collar world, and the subtle failure of white-collar men to pass on to women colleagues information necessary for good job performance.[26] On the other hand, there is the systematic erection of barriers to women's achievement. As Blumrosen notes in her careful study of wage discrimination and job segregation, job evaluation procedures are systematically used to underrate the work women actually do, often in very blatant and easily identified ways.[27] There may be differential job descriptions for the same job according to whether it is done by a man or a woman, or, more commonly, by simple job segregation, and by placing women in dead-end positions that are not on the organization's career ladder. In field or factory or laboratory or university or corporation, women are clustered in the lower-paid jobs, with a few token women in top positions. This in spite of the fact that nationally the average woman worker has the same level of education as the average male worker—12.7 years of schooling, and generally the same or lower absentee rates. The Women's Bureau reports that women with four or more years of college education earn the same income as men with one to three years of high school education.

Because many women accept men's lower evaluation of them, the problem is triply rooted: in men's psyches, in women's psyches, and in the structures of the social order itself. With all the efforts of the special women's networks, and of multipurpose action organizations like NOW (National Organization of Women) and Women's Equity Action League, little dent has been made on the misuses of women's capabilities in the paid labor force.

The tragedy is that the solid wall of the fleshy faces of the community of men that many women perceive everywhere they turn makes for bitterness and rage against man's kind. In the public sphere, the lunacy of the arms race and the lunacy of an ever more shrunken welfare policy are seen as *male* lunacies, enunciated on television, radio, and in newspapers by those same continually recurring fleshy faces. The fact that women know they have been assigned the care and feeding of those lunatics, and that they in fact *comply* with the assignment, makes the rage all the deeper. There is of course an answering rage from men at women who will not stay where "in the nature of things" they belong.

The problem is deep and difficult, because men and women do not have any models for relating to each other in the public sphere of work and politics. They only have the private, domestic models of an earlier age available. These models are not only inadequate to workplace relations; they are harmful in that they violate both work norms and norms of human respect for colleagues. It is hard for both men and women to develop a new gender identity which includes having "opposite-sex" workmates as colleagues, when the new culture which can support this collegiality has not yet been developed.

VALUE CLASHES IN THE WORLD OF WORK:
THE OLD VERSUS THE NEW

The deeper struggle going on here is not only between women and men, but between old and new values for women, and old and new values for men. Many indications at present suggest that resolution of those clashes may in the long run bring a convergence in the valuing of lifeways between women and men. Here we will discuss value clashes only in terms of work roles, but later we will see that the same conflicts lie at the heart of perceptions of the family and the polity.

Women are torn three ways in how to handle their work roles. The traditional good-wife-and-mother mandate calls for zero work force commitment and a willingness to work outside the home only under financial pressure. This implies a docile work role. Yet the women with newly released high aspirations and newly discovered self-confidence may find satisfaction in beating highly competitive men at their own game. Other women with high aspirations, remembering the ugliness of machismo, may want to humanize the world of work and use a more nurturant, interactive style with their colleagues, putting more emphasis on good communication flows than on hierarchical authority for getting work done. Women have made important contributions to changing work styles. Rosabeth Moss Kanter has not only impressively described these new work styles, but has developed a new type of business consulting to enable firms to make work-style changes.[28] Colwill describes new reciprocities in male-female work relationships.[29] Harder than changing work styles, however, is the change in self-concepts needed for women to integrate long-term career aspirations with their sense of inner personhood and growth. Hennig and Jardim point out with great compassion how hard it is for career women to feel whole, as compared with men who have known they would be "career men" ever since they were little.[30] Little girls dream of being mommies, not breadwinners. Freer childhood dreaming may well hold the key to a new wholeness for both men and women. Lack of wholeness may lead successful women to the "topping out" phenomenon—abandoning the rat race—just at the social moment when the rat race formula is being rejected by men as well.[31] The most recent signals on this topping out phenomenon are that some executive women are leaving the corporate world to start their own enterprises in a setting where they can develop their own preferred models of economic enterprise. It is too early to evaluate this as a "trend," but it may have long-run significance if the current merger mania wreaks economic havoc in the corporate world. Women's experiments with small-scale enterprises and different managerial styles may provide answers for future economic crises.

Men's struggles are different. They have always known they would work all their lives, but a surprising number of men do not enjoy competition. They experience a forced socialization into an aggressive style of male dominance through athletics during childhood and youth.[32] Yet as adults they may prefer a quiet niche in the workplace where not more is asked than they feel they can handle. Even for men bursting with energy and self-confidence, the race to the top is not necessarily fun. Once, these achievers wrote poetry and dreamed dreams. A part of them is atrophying, shriveling up, and many would like to break away from the insistent high-pressure demands of work. They may get little pleasure out of their men's club activities, traditionally the prized secret center of the male world, and they resent their dependence on the women in their lives, who have their own secret world.[33] They *must* work or they will have no identity. The only thing they were ever expected to be was breadwinner. If a man becomes unemployed, he is literally nothing.

If anything, men's work-role situation is more complicated than women's in this transition era. A man is in the situation of competing at work—his only source of identity—with women while at the same time he feels emotionally dependent on women in his private life. He can not turn for nurturance and support to other men as women can to each other, because male talk is not "personal" talk. He hurts and he can not cry.

He can be inventive, however, and he is. One of the first efforts to humanize the modern workplace started well before the contemporary women's movement, with the conceptualization of group dynamics by Kurt Lewin and his associates, first at the Massachusetts Institute of Technology and then at the University of Michigan. Group dynamics gave rise to the National Training Laboratories in Bethel, Maine, where small groups of businessmen in the early 1940s learned to listen, to empathize, and to care. Group dynamics reached out into many parts of the white-collar world of work, and into the trade union movement as well. A more recent development along similar lines is the rapid expansion of mediation and conflict resolution training programs that produce individuals prepared to operate with sensitivities and skills not normally valued in the community of men. The human potential movement in psychology first developed with male leadership. These developments have paved the way for the entry of men into highly nurturant occupations such as preschool and elementary school teaching, nursing, and social work. The movement of men into what are for them nontraditional, or women's occupations, is slower than the movement of women into traditionally male jobs, but it is happening.[34] The fact that the movement is two-way is important. The fact that men tend to earn more than women at women's jobs is part of the cultural/structural lag that continues to make a mockery of equal opportunity for most women workers.

In spite of the maddeningly persistent inequities in job status and wages, the new developments in the men's work world, as well as in the women's work world, open up large areas where men and women can and do work together in mutually enhancing ways. Just as women are learning to modify their own working styles to fit new occupational sectors, so men are learning to modify their working styles in their traditional occupational sectors to fit new understandings of human capacity and human productivity in the broader social sense. It is in face-to-face collaboration in the workplace under gradually rewritten rules that the rage of women and the rage of men may gradually dissolve into a more realistic acceptance of common human values. The alternative is a continuing power struggle between the sexes.

New Family Roles

What does a man really want? As already indicated, men have been taught to want to be breadwinners, with emphasis on "winner," from nursery days. From the life-span perspective, increasingly used by sociologists to analyze social roles, the breadwinner aspiration is a thin one. And so men apparently find it, as we see in studies like Levinson's *Seasons of a Man's Life*.[35] The career goal works for a few years. The young man leaps from school to job and begins plowing away on his career line with just enough time out to start the family that belongs to his life-style. He wears the labels "husband" and "father" proudly, but invests little time in family activities. Somewhere around the age of forty a midlife crisis occurs: Am I in the right career? Am I ready for the top, and to be a mentor for others? Who am I, anyway? I think I'm stagnating. Is this all there is to life?

If a man is lucky, he finds good answers to these questions and either changes his career or hangs in. But then he has to go through it all over again at around age sixty-five. Not only does he have to step down from his job, but from his other "authority roles" as well. He has to find another answer to "Who am I?" He gets more interested in his family, his grandchildren. But if he hangs around the house too much his wife may tell him that she "married him for better or worse, but not for lunch." If a man is lucky, he now taps hitherto hidden sources of creativity and has a delightful couple of decades as an active retiree, ready for the view from the bridge when he reaches the more severe limitations of the really elderly at eighty-five or ninety. Many men are not lucky, and have a miserable life after retirement.

What does a woman really want? A job, a family probably (but not just yet), and life-in-relationships most of all, says the young girl graduate. As Carol Gilligan has so eloquently put it, her wants are "in a different voice."[36] While her partner is climbing his career ladder, she is moving in and out of the labor force, bearing children, making a home, exploring the community, building a network of relationships, trying out life, juggling the inevitable double roles that modern women expect. Partly because she takes time off for childbearing, and to meet family crises, her career does not advance much in those prime years between twenty and forty (this is not to discount the above-noted effects of male prejudice against women in the workplace). They are busy years, exhausting, but many have fun in them too. While her husband is having his midlife crisis, she is just reaching a happy stage of newfound freedom. Not needed by young children, still with her youthful energies flowing, she can now (with retraining) throw herself into the work she may have been dreaming of. The years between forty and sixty-five simply fly by, and the menopause is not such a big deal—only one more freedom gained. She is still carrying that double load, but it is much lighter than when the children were home, and the job has more rewards than frustrations. Nevertheless, energies diminish in the sixties, and the long years of the double load have taken their toll. She begins to dream of freedom from that double load, freedom to explore new aspects of life she has not yet had time for, and finds herself joyfully anticipating stepping down from her job. She enters retirement with the same anticipation that she entered her work-force career. New horizons beckon, but the pace can be more leisurely now, and each moment tasted.

A life cycle phenomenon that promises a more pleasurable companionship between women and men in their older years is what is sometimes called the androgyny of aging.[37] Men become gentler, more person and family-oriented, and women become more assertive, more ready to test out what they know about how the world works. With each shifting towards the other's style of interaction, men and women can in fact become more interesting to each other in their later years as they present each other with changing personalities. If the two spouses can find complementary rhythms, these can indeed be golden years, and both will be ready for the view from the bridge. I have of course described ideal types, not real human beings, and yet the patterns are familiar.

TRANSITION STRATEGIES

How in fact are men and women in heterosexual households handling these transition years and role changes? With difficulty. Some of the saddest casualties of the transition are the displaced homemakers, traditional women who have been "fired" from marriage by their liberated husbands and have no skills for even managing a home alone, let alone entering the work force. André estimates that there are at least three million displaced homemakers in America today—including the suddenly widowed as well.[38] We hear more about the displaced husbands—men whose wives have become liberated and simply left home, with or without the children. The third category of transition casualties—those divorced by mutual consent—are the most numerous, but they are also the men and women best equipped to restructure their lives. Separation and divorce are one important way to deal with role conflict, although the battle is uneven and women lose far more than men in divorce. Another way is through joint struggle, slow changes in values and attitudes, and more emphasis on the writing of special-purpose contracts between men and women that spell out new rights and preferences.[39] The whole area of family law has radically changed in the past fifteen years. New legal precedents are being established out of battles between men and women over property and joint custody, and an entirely new set of family law textbooks is now being written.[40]

Change is hard. Women do not want men to be so helplessly dependent on them at home, yet keep men out of "their" kitchen, guard the mysteries of the domestic arts, and do not teach their husbands household skills. Men do not want to be trapped in the breadwinner role, yet resent sharing with wives the wider freedom of movement the job world entails—and being offered aprons in exchange. Ambivalence is high on both sides. Because women are socialized to be compliant, they will continue roles they resent and keep the anger inside until too late for constructive conflict resolution.

In terms of surface attitudes, men seem to be more ready for change than women. Joseph Pleck reports that more husbands than wives say that they feel husbands should do more housework than they now do. In families where both spouses work, only 65 percent of wives, but 79 percent of husbands, say husbands should do *some* housework.[41] However, reports of attitudinal changes can be misleading; reports focusing on actual behaviors do not show men rushing to take over housework. André reports Detroit Area Study findings comparing hours spent in housework by wives and husbands in 1965 and 1975. In 1965, women employed outside the home were doing 28.1 hours a week of housework and men 11.3 hours. By 1975, men had increased their work around the house by an average of six minutes a day and were doing primarily nonroutine home chores (yardwork, repairs, and so forth).[42]

Men's involvement in the full range of home-related work will change slowly, but it is changing. A special issue of the *Family Coordinator*, devoted to changing men's roles in the family, included a two-generation study showing that sons reported fathers should be more actively nurturant and less active as provider than their fathers reported. The differences are not large, but there is a trend.[43] Studies of fathering behavior show fathers responding as nurturantly as mothers to newborns.[44] The turn toward involving husbands not only in birth preparation classes but in birth itself has in fact produced a new generation of fathers who delight in intimate contact with their children from infancy onwards. Fathers carrying infants in snugglies (infant carrying packs) is not a frequent sight, but is becoming less rare. One study projected an increase in lone-father families from 10 percent of all single-parent families in 1960 to 30 percent in 1985.[45] There is no doubt that fathering is becoming more popular. Writing on the subject by men suggests a real feeling of being "liberated" into fatherhood.[46] The Rapoports, themselves a husband and wife research team, have studied what they call coordinate marriages in which career responsibility and parenting and homemaking responsibilities are equally shared between men and women. Studies in Britain, Norway, and the United States all document high marital satisfaction in such marriages.[47]

While we may have more home-based production in the future than we now have, it is extremely unlikely that this will become a major form of economic activity in the foreseeable future. What is important is a new note of flexibility in considering possible lifeways. If there are work-sharing rural and small-town families, there are also increasingly work-sharing urban families. An examination of popular women's magazines shows a new relaxed acceptance of a lifeway that involves children and work sharing in the marketplace and at home. McCall's new magazine, *Working Mothers*, has none of the frantic self-questioning that characterized earlier women's periodicals on the issue of women's working. Informational and feature articles are all geared to helping women manage more complex life-styles with grace and enjoyment. *Essence*, a magazine for black women, has exactly these same qualities. If there is still frantic self-questioning, it is more apt to be found in magazines like *Savvy*, where professional women's woes are still fresh enough and new enough to warrant breastbeating.

There are other household life-styles open to women and men. Communes and group marriages are still part of the social scene, though less frequent than in the 1960s and early 1970s.[48] A more popular option today is the group house, a household composed of unrelated people living together for primarily economic and life-style reasons. One quarter of all United States households are "nonfamily households," and some substantial percentage of these are group houses containing from three to ten or more people. The homes in which they live were built for the larger families of yesteryear.[49] Some are all men's houses, some all women, but the majority are mixed. This provides yet another example of the more relaxed attitude toward marriage and family. Singles may live in a group house anywhere from one to ten years, and after marriage either set up a separate household or continue in group living. Group housing is a welcome haven for the recently divorced as well as the newly married who can not afford separate housing. Resource sharing, friendship, and nurturance all take place, but within well-defined limits. This makes of group housing a low-key support network for men and women who want something less involving than a commune or a separate marital household.

There remain, however, substantial numbers of men and women who are struggling through to new roles in traditional familial households. They are not managing unaided. Wives are more likely to have women's support groups to turn to than husbands are to have men's support groups available. This is because the tradition of women supporting women is a more highly evolved interpersonal phenomenon, geared to a greater variety of crises, than is to be found in traditional men's groups in our society. Male bonding relies heavily on sparring and rough physical pounding to show affection and support. Alternatively there is humor, as in the long list of self-satirizing clubs men form: the Baldheaded Men, the Procrastinators, the Dull Men's Club. When men really need help and emotional support from other men, it is often given in masked form, not named as help or nurturance. In spite of, or rather because of, this difficulty for men in naming the hidden nurturer in themselves, an important part of the gender role changes in these decades has been the development of men's support groups.

MEN SUPPORTING MEN

The men's movement is complex, multifaceted, and still emergent. If the publication of Betty Friedan's *The Feminine Mystique* in 1963 marked the beginning of the contemporary women's movement, then the publication in 1974 of Marc Fasteau's *The Male Machine*, Warren Farrell's *Beyond Masculinity*, and Pleck and Sawyer's *Men and Masculinity* marks the beginning of the contemporary men's movement. (A more recent publication in this genre is James Doyle's *The Male Experience* [1983]). Also, in 1974 the National Conference on Men and Masculinity was founded and has met annually ever since.

Helped in its birthing by the women's movement, it has consistently supported equal rights for women. In the intervening years, however, it has developed divergent orientations.

One set of groups using the acronym MAN (Men's Awareness Networks), takes a strong profeminist stance typified by the journal *M.—Gentle Men for Gentle Justice. M.* "is dedicated to discussing issues important to changing men; affirming a healthy life-loving nonoppressive masculinity; and supporting the network of women struggling to end sexism" (from *M.'s* editorial guidelines). The *M.*-associated groups focus on the problems of male violence against women and children, and have developed a nationwide network of supporting groups for abusive men. Their goal is to help abusers control their own behavior. RAVEN (Rape and Violence End Now) in St. Louis, EMERGE in Boston, and AMEND (Abusive Men Exploring New Directions) in Denver are three of the best known of these groups, which are organized on an all-volunteer basis. The volunteers in these self-help projects for men show a skill, sensitivity, and dedication that is awe-inspiring. They also support childcare and women's shelter projects. *Network News*, obtainable through RAVEN in St. Louis, gives national coverage of their activities. *Learning to Live Without Violence: A Handbook for Men Who Batter* by Sonkin and Durphy is an outgrowth of the RAVEN project.[50]

In addition to this crisis-oriented work, *M.* helps a broader network of men's consciousness-raising groups stay in touch with one another. As Pleck and Sawyer summarize its goals, men's liberation involves: (a) closer friendships with men; (b) a freer showing of emotions; (c) recovery of psychic energy; (d) fuller relations with spouse; (e) fuller relations with children; (f) more social skill and trust, less violence and competition; and (g) a change in values, with less need for dominance.[51] While the women's movement helped the men's movement get started, many women are not aware of the great supportive efforts on behalf of women carried on by MAN and similar local groups across the country.

A different branch of the men's movement, while continuing to support the ERA, has gone more in the direction of men's rights—in divorce, in child custody, in paternity. These groups are sometimes called Free Men, and the *American Man* is their journal. If the gentler gender groups define their tasks largely in relation to feminism, the Free Men lean toward a reformist version of the traditional male bond. Both groups are struggling to define what the men's community should mean for men. There is poignancy in the realization that women-helping-women, and men-helping-men, constitute a kind of precondition for women and men to be emotionally free to help each other without getting tangled in pathological dependency relations. This is the basic message of the gay and lesbian liberation movement.[52] Women-identified women and men-identified men can more easily achieve love with autonomy, work-sharing with dignity, nurturance without infantile dependency, because they are less caught up in gender-defined, dominance-submission relationships.[53] At their best they represent, in their one-gender households, the ideal of what man-woman relationships could be. Nor should we be surprised if they often fail to achieve this ideal in their own households, since they have been as exposed as the rest of us to the poison of sex-role dominance.

THE DARK THREAD OF VIOLENCE

The dark thread which runs through the social tapestry of the community of women and men in households is the threat of violence of the male against the female.[54] Such violence erupts in more than 50 percent of all marriages in the United States, and in one of four marriages physical abuse is chronic—monthly or more often.[55] Once started it usually escalates, and one-eighth of all homicides are committed by spouses killing spouses. What men's support groups are helping abusive men to understand is that their violence is a learned behavior and it can be unlearned. Most men who batter their wives love them and are devastated when their partners leave for a women's shelter. It is their desire to reconstruct the broken relationship that makes them willing to participate in men's groups like RAVEN and EMERGE. The resocialization process is long and painful but it can be done. Men who really thought they had no control over their own behavior are learning that they can control themselves. By the same token, women and men who are child abusers, yet love their children, also learn self-control in such support groups.

An analysis of the rage and lack of self-control in people who also feel love for their partners would be too complex to attempt here. But the analysis would include attention to the divisions in male-female parenting relations of the traditional family unit. The differential roles and power relations between mother and father serve to reproduce gender-related expectations and characters that are inimical to a more humane society.

Our society owes an enormous intellectual and spiritual debt to Dorothy Dinnerstein, who had the wisdom and courage to point to mother-rearing, the very foundation of the household pattern of social reproduction, as a major source of human maldevelopment in society as we know it.[56] If her analysis is correct, a sharing of parenting responsibilities, from participation in birthing onward, may be a significant contribution to a more humane socialization of young people.

Would men and women become more alike? No, more different, because with shared parenting a fuller individuation of each personality would be possible. Whatever biological potentialities are present in individuals will have freer play with the fuller maturity that comes from sharing nurturance and service roles between men and women. The link between gender and occupationally defined social roles will have been broken. Nor would the three communities I have been speaking of disappear. What we have learned from the study of communities of women-identified women and men-identified men is that same-sex relationships have special qualities that can unleash creativity and joy. Women do not have to be lesbian or engage in sexual relations with their kind to enjoy women, any more than men have to be gay and engage in sexual relations with their kind to enjoy men. The greater freedom to move back and forth between male bonding, female bonding, and male-female bonding will further enhance individuation. With greater individuation, gender identity will evolve in dimensions now hidden under the facade of occupational stereotyping.

New Civic Roles

If the spheres of work and family are profoundly touched by changing values about what men and women should do, the civic sphere is equally affected. The civic sphere, like the work sphere, suffers from a lack of role models of public civic partnership between women and men. The maintenance of the public social order has traditionally been men's work, but women have always had certain niches in which to work, providing for the health, education, and welfare of the local poor and disadvantaged. Women have often been the actual deliverers of services, while men make the administrative decisions.

It is hard to compare men's and women's participation in social and economic activity because so much that women do is through informal networks and does not show up as formal civic activity. Smith and Macauley's massive study of social and political participation in the United States measures only formally defined participation.[57] They do not find any difference in the overall rates of participation for women and men, only in the character of the participation in terms of status, resources commanded, and so forth. What they do find is a consistent upper limit on the percentage of the population working as volunteers in organizations with altruistic purposes—16 percent. The same figure holds for women as for men. The authors also find special characteristics in people who work in voluntary organizations, notably above-average education, self-esteem, and capacity for social empathy.

Most of these findings relate to the more traditional participation of women and not to newer movement activities. Since women have traditionally had few opportunities to gain self-confidence in the public sphere, that women should show participation rates equal to mens', however different the status roles, is very interesting. I suggest that their relatively strong showing in formal organizational structures, and the self-confidence this reflects, has to do with the fact that the activities all require local knowledge, and that women are par excellence the experts on neighborhood affairs. They know who has what, who needs what, and have excellent mental maps of local resources of every kind. Men who become house-husbands and stay home to care for children usually find themselves very helpless in the first weeks of their new role because they do not have this kind of mental map and do not know how to access resources for themselves or other family members.

The changes brought about by the movements within the women's communities and the men's communities have partly been changes in mental maps, and partly changes in the skills of translation from the small to the large scale. The women's networks have helped women become familiar with new social terrains, and to gain the courage to translate what they know of small-scale interactions, with appropriate adjustments, to large-scale interactions. The result is that the neighborhood and the world are now firmly linked in the minds of growing numbers of women, and they are able to think in the policy terms once considered men's preserve. At the same time, more men are discovering the relevance of the local to the global, and realizing how little they know about the most basic processes of social production and reproduction.

For women, the new knowledge has led to an explosion of political activity, as they discover the full extent of the absurdity of existing social and economic policies in terms of local human need.

While women have always consistently showed a preference in opinion polls for less military expenditures and more expenditures for social welfare and environmental conservation, this enduring preference has only recently begun to show up in voting patterns. Political alignments have never been simply pro or con human welfare, but women are now finding ways to translate welfare interests into political interests. The 1982 elections in the United States brought into public awareness a "gender gap" in voting. The gender gap is felt the most strongly in local and state elections. Presumably it will not stop there, particularly since women are now themselves aware that they are playing a leadership role in the formation of public opinion on economic and quality of life issues.

A very important feature of this new development is the growing alliance between the activist women's community and the activist "new men's" community. Obviously neither sex alone is going to change political life or the social order. The old alliance between women and men in the radical activist movement of the 1960s came to a disastrous end as women became aware that they were being exploited by their male colleagues. It was in fact the intensity of that revolt of women during the civil rights and peace movements of the 1960s against male dominance that helped energize both radical feminism and political lesbianism in the 1970s. By the same token, the pain of men over that loss helped energize the Men's Awareness Network. The coming together out of pain separately faced has brought a new and deeper meaning to the buzz word, "equality." The same phenomenon is taking place in Europe, in some countries predating the American movement, in others contemporaneous. In France, Germany, the Netherlands, England, and Scandinavia in particular, there is a linkage of ecology and militarism issues in the women's movement, and a new visibility of women, sharing leadership roles with men, in the dissenting wings of old political parties and at center stage in the new political parties.

National leadership at the parliamentary level is slower in coming for women. If state and local trends continue, however, what Jessie Bernard calls the tipping point will eventually be reached,[58] and a new balance of male-female participation in national politics will be achieved. Some of the trends that will contribute to reaching that tipping point are the rapidly increasing national networks of local problem-focused organizations of the women's community. The National Congress of Neighborhood Women (NCNW), which has expanded from New York City to cover the country in ten years, is a stirring example of local vigor gone national. Women are teaching each other how to reconstruct decayed neighborhoods, sweep corruption out of public housing, provide better schooling for children and neighborhood community colleges for adults, and form business enterprises which are economically viable and meet the needs of local communities. The NCNW is now moving into international networks as well, as they see the linkage between the quality of life in local neighborhoods and world peace. The NCNW is one of a great many special networks generated by the women's community to deal with the public interests of women.

In short, the women's community is beginning to develop civic bonding comparable to the civic bonding that has always existed for the men's community. The third type of civic bonding, the bonding of women and men in joint civic work, remains weak because of the history of men giving housekeeping roles to women in organizations open to both. That bond will become stronger only as men demonstrate that they can work with women as colleagues, and as women learn to trust that colleagueship. Where the civic bond is presently strongest is perhaps in the churches, where traditional service roles for women are so clearly indispensable to the day-to-day survival of a parish or congregation that some degree of public recognition has always had to be accorded to this fact. For women to move from service to ministry roles, however, is a big step in any local church, and one that denominations are taking only very slowly and hesitantly.

Human bonding in a congregation, in a political caucus, or in a family, is a strong blend of love-and-duty. All bonding involved in civic service is a blend of love-and-duty. The more love there is, the less the discipline of duty is needed to ensure that humans will serve one another. The teaching of the Catholic church about "duties of state," meaning responsibilities one must take on because of one's specific life situation, takes a straightforward position toward the love-duty problem: it is simply up to the individual how much love can be mustered in the carrying out of the duties. The miracle is that the capacity of men and women to do things for one another for love has not been destroyed by centuries of male head-of-household dominance. If the power asymmetries can be removed, men and women will be the richer for the experience of collaboration in the civic and workplace spheres, as in the household. Collaboration in one cannot substitute for collaboration in the other two. Human and social development require all three.

The struggle that men and women have been going through has left its traces on both. The 1982 annual survey of entering college freshmen notes a sliding downward of scores on altruism in response to questions on social objectives, in comparison with the 1960s. But,

the decline in "altruism and humanism" is not as great as the rise in the desire for money and power. The reason? The survey shows that women in recent years have "adopted a lot of stereotypic attitudes" associated with men. Women were formerly less concerned with money and influence. The gap has narrowed so that greed and power quotient is up.[59]

Developing the new balance will not be easy, and the difficulties must not be underestimated. In Sweden, the country that has gone farthest in legislating equality in workplace and home for women and men, with shared maternity/paternity leave now a settled policy, a sympathetic male observer sees serious problems. Men are nervous and disoriented. "The factors that are responsible for restraining women from being able to cover the last gap are so intricate and webbed with tension that setbacks multiply. And so the clarity of the vision recedes."[60] In spite of a national policy of shared birthing leave, the work of fathering and help with routine household chores in Sweden remains at the level of tokenism, and the resulting conflicts place the marriage choice itself in doubt for many young Swedes. Far-reaching changes will be required in architecture and town planning, not only in economic structures and school curricula, says Chhabra.[61] No one is ready for changes of that order of magnitude. In short, nothing like the revolutionary changes in gender roles called for by Dinnerstein have taken place in Sweden. A few fathers participating in the birthing of their children is not enough.

Unlike orderly, plan-conscious Sweden, the United States is a topsy-turvy society swept by conflicting currents. The enormous expenditures of social energy needed to reconstruct male-female relationships cannot be summoned by any one of the many competing interest groups on the American scene. This is all the more true because there is an important subgroup within the community of women which resists the changes described here and fights vigorously to retain traditional ways. Phyllis Schlafly, founder of the Eagles, is an articulate spokeswoman for this group. Yet many changes in gender-role attitudes and behaviors *are* taking place in the midst of all the apparent social flux. The changes are of small dimensions yet consistent with one another, and they may be read as signals of larger changes to come, not in the lifetime of anyone now living, but perhaps in the fifth or the tenth generation down the line. It would be a mistake to think of present trends as fads that will disappear. The social clock of evolving human relationships ticks on, and cannot be turned back.

This is all the more important to realize because surface trends in the mid-1980s are now apparently reversing in the United States. Affirmative action and equal opportunity directives are being overturned, and civil rights legislation is being challenged. This is a sign of the unevenness in the rates of social change in different sectors of society, and of differences in exposure to new social learnings. With the public's attention riveted on status struggles carried on by a dedicated minority of women, the mass media and the school systems have gone on reproducing old stereotypes for the general population. The longer-run agendas that can provide a context for learning new gender roles have scarcely begun to be addressed. For example, with an aging population, there will be a war of the young against the old unless firm alliances develop between them now while there is still time. The alliance between younger and older women will be particularly important in meeting the new social stresses created by the new tasks of providing care for a growing group of dependent elderly.

What will speed up rates of societal learning and increase the capacity for creative responses to the new forms of gender and age struggle that lie ahead? The answer lies in part in more attention to the situation of women and men at different stages in the life cycle, more awareness of the special needs of each age from preschoolers to the old-old. Social effort tends to be carried on at the midpoint of the age spectrum, ignoring the two ends. Intensive attention to the learning and developmental needs of very young and growing children, which have taken a back seat to the agenda of women's liberation, is crucial for building a resilient, autonomous citizenry able to make real choices and not be mesmerized by media hype. New creative forms of collaboration between women and men mean nothing if they are not prepared and carried out in all stages of the life cycle.

Ultimately society is neighborhood, and it is in neighborhood that men and women have to discover their new humanness. A strong focus on the quality of human services, the quality of voluntarism, the quality of lifelong learning experiences available at the neighborhood level for each human being living there will give substance to the new partnership between women and men. We know that we live in an interdependent world, but we are apt to forget that we live in interdependent neighborhoods too. The neighborhood focus puts the spotlight on the neighborhood elementary school, almost the last remaining viable neighborhood institution widely used by local residents. This is the one part of the school system most amenable to change, since specialization is at a minimum, and the pattern of using parent volunteers is well established in many elementary schools. Here is one place to begin involving men and women in practicing new roles which can serve as models for children. It is not just textbook reform that will bring about a change in gender roles; it is face-to-face behavior modeling.

What will bring men and women to elementary schools? Putting more neighborhood services in the elementary school—clinics and classes and family counseling and aids of all kinds—will help men be more adequate in their fathering and home maintenance duties because they will know where to go for help, and will also give children a chance to see men and women doing a greater variety of things than the media stereotypes suggest. (Fathers who are scientists are invited to do demonstrations in science classes; mothers who are scientists are invited to bring cookies.)

Society is at once our creation, our instrument, and our teacher. It also stands over against us, challenging our skill in crafting better lifeways, better human beings. The key to meeting society's challenge does not lie only in devising better human support structures from daycare to job retraining, or devising better strategies for luring men to fathering and women to public decision making. The key lies in tapping the secret stirrings in each person, in remembering that those secret stirrings are there from birth to death in every girl and boy, every man and woman. They are society's seeds in us. Whether we are educators, parents, scientists, or policymakers, there are ways for each of us to nurture those stirrings in others in the course of our daily work, so that every human being has the opportunity to become a microcosm of the better society we seek.

FOOTNOTES

1. Lionel Tiger, *Men in Groups* (New York: Random House, 1969).

2. Jessie Bernard, *The Female World* (New York: Macmillan, 1981).

3. Charlotte Perkins Gilman's *Herland* (New York: Pantheon, 1979) gives a fictional account of such a community which is valuable for the plausibility it gives to lesbian personhood. It is also a fine novel.

4. Susan Okin, *Women in Western Political Thought* (Princeton, N.J.: Princeton University Press, 1979).

5. Lewis Mumford, *The City in History* (New York: Harcourt Brace Jovanovich, 1961).

6. It is interesting to note that the earliest historical records of the great civilizations of the East contain references to an earlier time when women sat in councils of elders. This is true of China, India, Sumeria, Crete, and Egypt. In North America, the famed women's councils of the Iroquois served as senior consultants to the men's councils, especially in matters of war and peace, but they did not sit with the men's councils.

7. Eugene Litwak, "The Use of Extended Family Groups in the Achievement of Social Goals: Some Policy Implications," *Social Problems* 7 (Winter 1959-60): 177-87.

8. James Morgan, "Intrafamily Transfers Revisited," in *Five Thousand American Families: Patterns of Economic Progress*, vol. 6, ed. Greg L. Duncan and James Morgan (Ann Arbor, Mich.: Institute for Social Research, University of Michigan, 1978).

9. Reuben Hill, "Decision Making and the Family Life Cycle," in *Social Structure and the Family: Generational Relations*, ed. Ethel Shanas and Gordon F. Streib (Englewood Cliffs, N.J.: Prentice-Hall, 1965).

10. Claude Fischer, "The Dispersion of Kinship Ties in Modern Society: Contemporary Data and Historical Speculation," *Journal of Family History* 74 (Winter 1982): 353-75.

11. Elise Boulding, Shirley A. Nuss, Michael A. Greenstein, and Dorothy Lee Carson, *Handbook of International Data on Women* (New York: Halsted Press, 1976).

12. Even the de jure rights are slow in coming. In January, 1983, Greece adopted legislation giving married women an equal voice with their husbands in family matters and abolishing the legal concept of the male as head of household with final say on all matters. Marvine Howe, *New York Times*, 30 January 1983.

13. Rae André, *Homemakers: The Forgotten Workers* (Chicago: University of Chicago Press, 1981).

14. Larry Long and Diana DeAre, "Repopulating the Countryside: A 1980 Census Trend," *Science* 217 (September 17, 1982): 1111-1117.

15. Arland Thornton and Deborah Freedman, "Changing Attitudes toward Marriage and Single Life," *Family Planning Perspectives* 14 (November/December 1982): 297-303.

16. Ibid.

17. See *Employment in Perspective: Working Women*, Report No. 665 (Washington, D.C.: Bureau of Labor Statistics, U.S. Department of Labor, 1982); "Workforce," *Women Today*, 2 December 1982; and Ruth G. Blumrosen, "Wage Discrimination, Job Segregation, and Title VII of the Civil Rights Act of 1964," *University of Michigan Journal of Law Reform* 12 (Spring 1979): 395-502.

18. For reports from other countries on policy issues relating to women's work, see Jean Lipman-Blumen and Jessie Bernard, eds., *Sex Roles and Social Policy* (Beverly Hills, Calif.: Sage Publications, 1979) and Naomi Black and Ann Baker Cottrell, eds., *Women and World Change: Equity Issues in Development* (Beverly Hills, Calif.: Sage Publications, 1981). The child care situation in the United States would be even more desperate than it is if it were not for churches taking on the provision of child care for working mothers. Of the 18,000 licensed day-care centers identified from a 1977 study done for the U.S. Department of Health and Human Services, the vast majority were run by churches. See *New York Times*, 15 January 1983.

19. Judith Agassi, *Women on the Job: The Attitudes of Women to Their Work* (Lexington, Mass.: D. C. Heath, 1979).

20. George Masnick and Mary Jo Bane, *The Nation's Families: 1960-1990* (Boston: Auburn House, 1980).

21. This phenomenon was commented on by both men and women workers in the boomtown areas where the Growth Impact group of the Institute of Behavioral Science (University of Colorado) worked. I personally heard such stories from men workers. See Elizabeth E. Moen, Elise Boulding, Jane Lillydahl, and Risa Palm, *Women and the Social Costs of Economic Development: Two Colorado Case Studies* (Boulder, Colo.: Westview Press, 1981).

22. Jackson W. Carroll, Barbara J. Hargrove, and A. Loomis, *Women of the Cloth* (New York: Harper and Row, 1983).

23. Margaret W. Rossiter, *Women Scientists in America: Struggles and Strategies to 1940* (Baltimore: Johns Hopkins University Press, 1982).

24. Jennie Farley, *Academic Women and Employment Discrimination: A Critical Annotated Bibliography* (Ithaca, N.Y.: New York State School of Industrial and Labor Relations, 1982).

25. Jeanne Holm, *Women in the Military: An Unfinished Revolution* (Novato, Calif.: Presidio Press, 1982); Judith Stiehm, *Bring Me Men and Women: Mandated Change at the U.S. Air Force Academy* (Berkeley, Calif.: University of California Press, 1980).

26. It sometimes appears to women that men do all their communicating and decision making in the men's toilet and in "men only" city clubs, and none at all in the office where the women are.

27. Blumrosen, "Wage Discrimination, Job Segregation, and Title VII of the Civil Rights Act of 1964."

28. Rosabeth M. Kanter, *Women and Men of the Corporation* (New York: Basic Books, 1977.

29. Nina L. Colwill, *The New Partnership: Women and Men in Organizations* (Palo Alto, Calif.: Mayfield Publishing Co., 1982).

30. Margaret Hennig and Anne Jardim, *The Managerial Woman* (New York: Doubleday, 1976).

31. Trudy Heller, *Women and Men as Leaders* (New York: Praeger, 1982).

32. See the thought-provoking volume by Donald F. Sabo and Ross Runfola, *Jock: Sports and Male Identity* (Englewood Cliffs, N.J.: Prentice-Hall, 1980).

33. Joseph H. Pleck, "The Male Sex Role: Definitions, Problems and Sources of Change," *Journal of Social Issues* 32, no. 3 (1976): 155-64; Joseph H. Pleck and Jack Sawyer, *Men and Masculinity* (Englewood Cliffs, N.J.: Prentice-Hall, 1974).

34. See the delightful volume by Mark Wandro and Joani Blank, *My Daddy Is a Nurse* (New York: Addison-Wesley, 1981), for a glimpse of nontraditional work roles for men.

35. Daniel J. Levinson, *The Seasons of a Man's Life* (New York: Ballantine Books, 1978).

36. Carol Gilligan, *In a Different Voice* (Cambridge, Mass.: Harvard University Press, 1982).

37. Elise Boulding, *Childrens' Rights and the Wheel of Life* (New Brunswick, N.J.: Transaction Press, 1979), pp. 105-6.

38. André, *Homemakers.*

39. Lenore J. Weitzman, *The Marriage Contract: Spouses, Lovers, and the Law* (New York: Free Press, 1981).

40. The legal ferment these changed behaviors are generating is reflected in Doris J. Freed and Henry H. Foster, "Family Law in the Fifty States," *Family Law Quarterly* 16 (Winter 1983): 289-383.

41. Joseph H. Pleck, "Men's New Roles in the Family: Housework and Child Care" (Paper prepared for the Ford Foundation/Merrill Palmer Institute, Detroit 1975, cited in André, *Homemakers*, p. 26).

42. André, *Homemakers*, pp. 25-26.

43. Deanna Eversoll, "A Two Generational View of Fathering," *Family Coordinator* 28, no. 4 (1979): 503-7.

44. Douglas B. Sawin and Ross D. Parke, "Fathers' Affectionate Stimulation and Caregiving Behaviors with Newborn Infants," *Family Coordinator* 28, no. 4 (1979): 509-513.

45. Arnold J. Katz, "Lone Fathers: Perspectives and Implications for Family Policy," *Family Coordinator* 28, no. 4 (1979): 521-28.

46. Warren Farrell, *The Liberated Man: Beyond Masculinity* (New York: Random House, 1974).

47. Lotte Bailyn, "Career and Family Orientations of Husbands and Wives in Relation to Marital Happiness," *Human Relations* 23 (April 1970): 97-113; Erik Grönseth, "Work-Sharing Families: Adaptations of Pioneering Families with Husband and Wife in Part-time Employment," (Paper prepared for the third annual ISSBD conference, 1975; cited in *Fathers, Mothers, and Society: Towards New Alliances*, ed. Rhona Rapoport and Robert Rapoport (New York: Basic Books, 1977); Laura Lein, Maureen Durham, Michael Pratt, Michael Schudson, Ronald Thomas, and Heather Weiss, *Work and Family Life*, Final Report, National Institute of Education, Project No. 3-3094 (Cambridge, Mass.: Center for the Study of Public Policy, 1974), cited in *Fathers, Mothers, and Society*, ed. Rapoport and Rapoport.

48. Rosabeth Kanter, *Communes: Creating and Managing the Collective Life* (New York: Harper and Row, 1973); Larry Constantine and Joan M. Constantine, *Group Marriage: A Study of Contemporary Multilateral Marriage* (New York: Macmillan, 1973).

49. Nancy Brandwein, Jill MacNeice, and Peter Spiers, *The Group House Handbook* (Washington, D.C.: Acropolis Books, 1982).

50. Daniel J. Sonkin and Michael Durphy, *Learning to Live Without Violence: A Handbook for Men* (San Francisco: Volcano Press, 1982).

51. Pleck and Sawyer, *Men and Masculinity*.

52. B. D. Adams, *Lesbian/Gay Challenges to Social Theory* (New York: Irvington Publishers, 1983); E. M. Ettore, *Lesbians, Women, and Society* (London: Routledge and Kegan Paul, 1980); Martin P. Levine, *Gay Men* (New York: Harper and Row, 1979); Nancy Myron and Charlotte Bunch, eds., *Lesbianism and the Women's Movement* (Baltimore: Diana Press, 1975).

53. I base this statement on the reading of a number of student papers by gays in recent years describing the fluidity of the household division of labor as they have personally experienced it in their couple relationships.

54. Some husband-wife violence is female initiated, but by far the largest part is male initiated. See Murray A. Straus, Richard J. Gelles, and Suzanne K. Steinmetz, *Behind Closed Doors: Violence in the American Family* (Garden City, N.Y.: Anchor Press, Doubleday, 1980).

55. RAVEN, *Men, Women, and Violence* (St. Louis, Mo.: Rape and Violence End Now, 1982).

56. Dorothy Dinnerstein, *The Mermaid and the Minotaur* (New York: Harper and Row, 1977).

57. David H. Smith and Jacqueline Macaulay, *Participation in Social and Political Activities* (San Francisco: Jossey-Bass, 1980).

58. Jessie Bernard, *Women, Wives, Mothers* (Chicago: Aldine Press, 1975).

59. John Walsh, "Survey Shows Freshmen Shift on Careers, Values," *Science* 219 (February 18, 1983): 822.

60. Rami Chhabra, "Some Are (Still) More Equal Than Others," *M.*, No. 9 (Summer-Fall, 1982): 27.

61. Ibid.

CHAPTER VI

Social Heterogeneity, Democracy, and Democratic Pluralism

RICHARD PRATTE

Introduction

The relatively modest aim of this chapter is to examine the status and place of social heterogeneity in the United States and especially to establish the relationship of today's social heterogeneity to American democracy. Specifically, I wish to ascertain the relative salience of social heterogeneity when Americans reflectively debate among themselves about what it means to live, work, and play in a democratic United States of America.

Social heterogeneity is a personal as well as a professional concern to me. It has been a part of my personal life since birth, and I have written about it for over three decades. Since childhood I have looked across three generations, from my own to that of immigrant grandparents. The social heterogeneity or cultural diversity of America has been a first-hand experience for me, since I was born and raised in a northeastern city, in southeastern Connecticut, with a mixed population of ethnics—Poles, Italians, Russians, Irish, French-Canadians, and Portugese. Although French-Canadian, I went to an Irish-run Roman Catholic elementary school, and generally tended to revel in the cultural fabric of Roman Catholicism stretched and tested by such diverse groups. Sometimes exasperated and perplexed by the process of assimilation, my Americanization was completed by the time I finished elementary school: I was a capitalist, a fledgling businessman—a paper carrier—and could not speak French, but my mother and older sister could. I was called "Dick," rather than "Rishard," and I was proud of the fact that I spoke English without a French accent. Today, much older and a little bit wiser, I strongly regret not having a French-Canadian cultural identity.

148

Social Heterogeneity

The phrase "social heterogeneity" has become indispensable in the discussion of American problems and issues. However, the relationship between social heterogeneity and democracy is complex and elusive at best. The problem is compounded because the terms we use to define social heterogeneity and democracy are themselves inescapably multivalent and can be employed in many different senses. For this reason alone, it is desirable to be as explicit as possible about the terms "social heterogeneity" and "democracy" at the outset.

Social heterogeneity will be employed here interchangeably with cultural diversity. While it is true that cultural diversity is itself a loose term and questions may be raised about its lack of precision, it can be plausibly argued that the imprecision accurately reflects the indeterminacy of the phenomena to which both social heterogeneity and cultural diversity refer. Moreover, in common usage these terms are more or less synonymous. Both express, in a very loose sense, the taken for granted fact of everyday life that American society is an evolutionary mixture of many associational collectivities reflecting in all cases a diffuse enduring diversity. Socially and culturally, there are of course strains, but the diversity acts as an antidote to everything that is bland and homogenized.

Among the most important associational collectivities are ethnic groups. Ethnic groups are self-conscious collectivities of people who, on the basis of selected differences such as a common origin or a separate subculture, maintain over generations a distinction between themselves and others. Thus an ethnic group may be cultural or racial, as long as the above criteria are met.

Although there has been disagreement in the social sciences over the usage of the term ethnic, the notion of a self-conscious collectivity of people who, on the basis of selected differences, maintain over generations a distinction between themselves and others is basic to most definitions.[1] The maintenance of separateness may be manifested in the circumscribed social participation of the group's members with others, in a restricted geographic territory, in a distinct pattern of thought, values, or ideology, or simply in a consciousness of a historical past.

The inclusion of racial groups as ethnics is herein maintained. In everyday usage the word race is most often employed to mean people of different skin colors; thus racial groups are considered the nation's nonwhite groups, indigenous and immigrant alike, while the term ethnic is reserved for whites. This distinction between racial groups and ethnic groups implies that ethnic groups are only whites and racial groups are not also ethnic groups, both points that are obviously false. Thus all groups in the United States, regardless of race, are defined as ethnic groups, if they meet the above criteria.

With these caveats in mind, I shall comment briefly on religious differences in contemporary American life, in order to consider and make clear how social heterogeneity, as a condition of social life, can exercise considerable influence in our daily affairs.

RELIGIOUS DIFFERENCES

First, it is a well documented fact that institutional religion and religious values have played and continue to play a vital role in shaping the American social experience. For instance, there has been an unusually close relationship between religion and civic life in the United States, so much so that civic republican themes have often been carried out by religionists employing religious purposes, language, and practice. This is clearly seen in the social program called the "common school" movement of the first half of the nineteenth century. Protestant clergymen led the way in establishing free, public schooling for the masses, and it is no coincidence that the curriculum of these schools was dominated by Protestant religious values.[2] Other examples can be given, but perhaps this point can be made in terms of the civil rights movement in the latter half of the twentieth century. Black southern clergymen, most notably Martin Luther King, Jr., gave leadership to this fight, again casting the themes of resistance and struggle in the accents, verbs, and metaphors of religious experience.

To grasp this relationship between a religious and a civic conscience is to sharpen significantly our understanding of social heterogeneity. The religious toleration that colonists sought in America was protected by royal decree even before the American Revolution. Different Protestant sects, and even the Catholic church, coexisted in the agrarian countryside and in such urban centers as New York and Philadelphia. From colonial times until the close of the nineteenth century, these various denominations contributed both to the individuals' sense of personal virtue, which resided in piety and hard work, and to the mores of the civic culture. While conceptions of piety might differ with different religious commitments, the divisive potential of those differences was balanced by the recognition that a social conscience must be founded on civic, rather than religious, virtues. The laws of the civic culture, then, were grounded in and buttressed by civic *principia media*, social values held in common across religions.

The twentieth century, however, brought a new conception of personal conscience to American life, one that was more civic and secular in nature. Due in part to the intellectual impact of a Darwinian view of reality that posited an evolving, organic world in which truths were not absolute (as religious truths had been) but were functions of scientific method, and due in part to the turmoil of cities bursting with unprecedented immigration, poverty, and explosive labor problems, the concept of personal conscience rapidly became grounded in what was good for temporal society's demands rather than in what was good for one's eternal salvation. The leaders of moral society were not clergymen but civic officials and private citizens. Personal conscience became more synonymous with civic virtue as the dictates of faith grew less powerful than the conclusions of empirical data. The good (pious) person emerged as less important to society than the good citizen.

The surprising thing about religion and civic life today is not that religious conscience is no longer strongly held by most Americans; it surely is. Rather, what surprises is how religious zealots (moral absolutists) are reacting to this changed situation, namely, the ongoing secularization of civic life in which a civic conscience is marked by a more open society, a broadening or widening of alternative life-styles, a questioning of mores, a relativistic social ethic. The point is simple, but the problem is not.

Traditionally, the religionists' conscience—a framework of strongly held moral values—mirrored the civic culture and seemed to reflect, as it were, an ethic of justice and rights, a clearly enunciated conception of a public that comprised the entire religious community. The consensus encompassed elements of three large religious groups in the United States—Catholic, Jew, and Protestant—as well as many other religious sects. But the mood of America has changed. Religious conscience has been called into question by some and it has to deal with formidable competitors: relativism, science, and technology.

The secularization of American society is not opposed by all religionists, indeed not even by most. However, it is strongly rejected by religious zealots who judge secularization as a violation of religious conscience and, of course, their religious privilege. One result has been to remedy the defects of a secular society, at least in the public sphere. A fusillade of books, articles, media presentations, lobbying efforts, and popular movements aim at a vigorous, searching, and fundamental attack on secular humanism, situation ethics, utilitarian values, and so on. Citizens are asked to consider education, from kindergarten through university, as suffering from misplaced emphases ranging from the taking over of domestic functions that properly belonged to parents to the exclusion of religion, without which, it is argued, education could have no ultimate purpose.

Consider this situation carefully. The religious zealots constitute a dedicated and active body of believers with a tightly formulated set of dogmas and doctrines, who believe they are duty-bound, by religious conscience, to perpetuate the faith by seeing to it, through diverse methods and righteous indignation, that public policy, including educational policy, be changed by a return to religious principles embodied in religious conscience. Also, they attract support from a growing number of citizens who do not generally favor the same lines of action taken by educational policymakers of recent years.

It is apparent in this case that the religious zealots have a conscience more suited for the conduct of private life than for the conduct of public life. At present, conservative biblical or fundamentalist religious views are essentially bodies of thought about moral life that are calculated to inform the lives of individuals for the private and intimate spheres of life, not for a civic coexistence in terms of membership in a public, interdependent, civic community.

A religious conscience, in other words, seems to offer one route in life, guidance of deeper truths, fundamental laws, one's relationship with God, and so on, and this seems deeply meaningful because a religious conscience takes us more significantly beyond our limits, and is the reason for connecting with possibilities that go beyond living in the day-to-day world.

To have a religious conscience is not merely to have a conscience, but to be restricted to taking account of the range of factors handled by religion. Religion cannot and should not be linked to anything and everything. Perhaps this, not professional chauvinism, explains why philosophers often have considered philosophical thought (not religious thought) and contemplation the highest activity. The problem of religious conscience and civic conscience is created by limits. That is, to be one thing and not another is to have limits. It seems, then, that religious conscience can apply only in a limited sense. A religious conscience is distinct from a civic conscience in that it is thought to specify an answer to the question of the meaning of my life, not our life.

Perhaps the point can be made clear in this way. Religious conscience and civic conscience are not necessarily connected. First of all, civic conscience engages us in the problem of "building a better society." Among other things, such a task requires us to ask certain questions about doing now what is undesirable or even unjust in order later to do what is beneficial and just. In developing a civic conscience, judgments are needed within the context of some public membership. Thus civic competence is not only involved with the individual but with the member of society, not only with individual morality but with the member's morality. In other words, civic competence more often than not entails a civic conscience that sacrifices one's own self-interest for the interest of others, sometimes at a cost of moral principle (as in the making of civic promises, keeping of contracts and conventions, and being obliged to exercise one's civic duties, such as jury duty), while being tolerant of others' views quite incompatible with one's own, and acting honorably.

This last point is highly illustrative of the basic difference between religious and civic conscience. The honorable citizen acts according to molded social character, and this virtue has always been a moral push of civic life. Yet to be honorable is to hold one's actions to civic standards—a social code of law and custom which sets norms for civic conduct—in response to a shared civic predicament, sometimes for civic survival itself. The virtue of honor offers citizens a shield against informal, private criticism, and can obscure judgments of a personal, even religious sort.

Religious conscience, on the other hand, has to do with questions of what is good for me to do in my understanding and covenant with God, but not with what is good for us, as members of a civic community, to do. No just society would, if it had the choice, allocate decisions about what is good for the community so unevenly. This is not to say that a religious conscience is basically unjust, but rather that large-scale collective matters are, by definition, indisputably in the public, not the private, sphere. A religious conscience is intimate, private, and limited to what individuals choose to share with one another about themselves—in families, for example, or with friends and colleagues.

Still another factor is involved, adding to the dangers of commingling civic and religious conscience in the public sphere. A religious conscience principally concerned with moral principles or moral character alone has often led to fanaticism, to a retreat into irrationality (do what is right though the heavens may fall), and to elevating personal, religious conscience to the status of moral principle. Similarly, a civic conscience primarily concerned with honor and civic character alone has too readily championed chauvinism. But in the design of democracy, in the operation of the public sphere, although precise division is not always possible, the two consciences must be separated. This requires continued attention, rebuilding and repair of the informal values and formal laws of society, but eternal vigilance is the price of maintaining a vital democracy.

This last remark suggests that one way to elucidate the complex relationship between religious conscience on the one hand and civic conscience on the other is to consider what would be involved in a democracy in achieving a common project, to bring about some good recognized as a shared good by all those engaged in the project. A modern example of such a project would be the founding and carrying forward of a school. Those who participated in such a project with a dominant religious conscience would need to value the qualities of mind and character which would contribute to the realization of their religious common good. That is, they would need to organize and set the school's curriculum in such a way as to render the doing or achieving of a religious purpose or purposes. Although the school would teach its students what kinds of actions (good works) would gain them grace and perhaps salvation, ultimately the relation between the individual and God is a private affair. There is no communal provision for entering into or achieving a state of grace.

Those who participated in the project of founding and maintaining a secular school would also need to identify certain types of action (good works)—those democratic practices that would promote individual self-development and thus strengthen the bonds of community, identity, and privacy. Moreover, the table of civic virtues promulgated in such a school would teach its citizens what kinds of action would gain them merit and honor; and the table of legal offenses would teach them what kinds of actions would be regarded not simply as bad, but as illegal. The commission of such offenses could result in a citizen being excluded from the community, if the community is not to fail.

The point is that the monopoly of grace by religions is not harmful so long as it does not extend to political power, the government, and the state. Religious disagreements and dissent set limits on the reach of religious conscience in a civic culture, limits that eventually take the form of a separation we have come to know and appreciate: the wall between church and state. To extend the reach of religious conscience beyond its proper limits to the public sphere is to impose and/or coerce private values, and this is properly called tyrannical.

Of course, all the evidence is that the converse is true. We must recognize that the standards of the community may encroach upon the private affairs of citizens in the guise of a guardian of public matters. Thus the question of the relationship between public and private, being a good citizen and being a good person, becomes central, and knowledge of the variety of possible human relations, religious and secular, provides the background to the asking of that question.

What is at stake are the values of human dignity, mutual respect, concern, caring, and tolerance. The good state has no right to attack gratuitously the fundamental religious convictions of its citizens, and this finds its basic expression in freedom of religion. To attack someone's convictions is an act of violence against that person, and it is a denial of human dignity, mutual respect, concern, caring, and above all, tolerance. Citizens may have to be reminded periodically that in addition to having rights, including freedom of religion, other citizens have value. The fact that a majority of people controls the public decision, one way or another, while others can only object to it, cannot be a sound basis for communal living. If citizens are to defend their decisions against complaints, they need to be able to give principled reasons for them, particularly when those decisions offend religious or secular convictions.

Finally, religious conscience does exist and thrives in the United States today. Its ready application in the public sphere complicates policymaking and enforcement perhaps more than any other cultural factor, excepting race. Religiously tinged issues such as abortion, prayer in public schools, and public support for schools of religious denominations are debates over the public interest and are not likely to disappear in the near future. The battle lines are drawn, but we must not be blind to the invasion of the public sphere by religious conscience in pursuit of goals regarded as overriding moral concerns. Public sphere activity should not be a matter of religious conscience but of civic competence, a function of the office of citizen, any more than religious activity should be a matter of civic conscience.

The above remarks clearly point to a fundamental issue: the fundamentalist sects are attempting to impose religious values upon civic life. Yet we note that they are not appealing to religious values that are civic *principia media* across a variety of religious sects, but to religious values that are narrow, even absolutist. In short, we confront the basic issue of tolerance in a democratic society. Perhaps the example of Martin Luther King, Jr. is instructive here. He was certainly zealous, but he was not so absolutist as to claim his opponents were the agents of Satan, as some fundamentalists claim about their opponents. Moreover, King applied religious values to civic issues. The difference between what King advocated and what the fundamentalist sects advocate is that King appealed to religious values that crossed denominational lines. Jews, Catholics, and all kinds of Protestants found religious support for the civic conscience King enunciated in religious language. Today's fundamentalists are guilty of trying to impose their religious values upon civic issues on which other, perhaps most, religious groups hold contrasting views. They fail, in other words, to recognize that a civic conscience in a heterogeneous religious society stems from common civic values, not from the unique values of a single religious perspective. In short, the fundamentalists' rigidity about their own values and their lack of tolerance of the values of others is not just a problem for coexistence of religions in a heterogeneous society, but a problem for different cultures as well.

ETHNICITY AND ASSIMILATION

The story of America's social heterogeneity cannot be told apart from a consideration of ethnicity and assimilation. According to ordinary usage, *assimilation* is the process by which diverse ethnic groups come to share a common culture and have access to the opportunity structure of society. Assimilation, then, is a process whereby groups with diverse ways of thinking, feeling, valuing, and behaving become *fused together in a social unity with a common culture.*

Obviously, assimilation has been more than an ideal in the United States. It was and is a hoped for result for many Americans. Much has been said about the role of the school in the social order in terms of promoting the "fusing together in a social unity" of diverse groups, what we commonly call *integration*, that is nonsegregation with respect to social participation and residence, and equal access to education, jobs, and other societal opportunities. However, equally important has been the school's effort to bring about the second component of assimilation, *acculturation*, that is, helping diverse ethnic groups assimilate by becoming similar in their thinking, feeling, valuing, and behavior.[3]

The achieving of intimacy between members of different ethnic groups has always been considered by assimilationists to be the main link between ethnicity and assimilation. Intergroup intimacy posits that people from culturally diverse backgrounds, if given the chance to know one another in meaningful ways, would become cordial neighbors, members of the same business associations and social clubs, perhaps even close friends, and their children would eventually intermarry. This contact hypothesis, however, is predicated on the value that the assimilative process is a good, and that a common culture is something to strive for purposely. Assimilationists reject the view that social heterogeneity might be a value worth maintaining, and that ethnicity has valuable social, economic, political, and psychological functions in modern society.

Put differently, an assimilationist American society can be likened to a melting pot, a single, unitary melting pot. However, assimilationists have also not focused upon the degree to which assimilation as an ideal may ignore relations of domination and subordination, that is, where one group may impose its values and attitudes either overtly or covertly on others in the name of assimilation and, of course, in the name of unity.

Pluralists, on the other hand, reject the assimilationists' metaphor and suggest instead the idea of a tossed salad to depict social heterogeneity in America more exactly. Rather than fusing into one mass society, ethnic groups are encouraged to display their differences proudly, each distinct from the other, but making a lovely, appetizing salad. Thus rather than disappearing or becoming invisible, ethnicity evolves into new cultural forms and expressions enriching an evolving society.[4]

Pluralists have made of social heterogeneity a badge of honor. Thus ethnicity today has come out of the closet and can be voluntarily displayed in the presentation of self (recall my personal note at the beginning of this chapter) and is used in both personal and group strategies to achieve certain objectives in American society, such as gaining a greater share of society's goods and services. This is a major reason for today's revitalized, accepted, proudly displayed ethnicity.

A second and enduring reason why social heterogeneity persists in the United States is a continuing stream of immigration. Sometimes it was their own national disasters that sent immigrants flocking to America, sometimes it was wars or revolutions, and sometimes it was simply the lure of the New World. Whatever the reasons, the influx, which was first recorded in 1820, roughly follows the ups and downs of the United States economy. Overwhelmingly northern and western Europeans dominated at the beginning of the nineteenth century, but today the ethnic mix has become steadily more varied, a trend that is accelerating each day.

We are, indeed, a nation of immigrants. Pluralists see an accommodation among ethnic groups as basic to society's well-being since a premise of pluralism is that a multitude of ethnic groups can cooperate in a single society, at least to the extent necessary for their continued existence.[5] The issues of prejudice, discrimination, and bigotry are thus a central concern of pluralists, for if unchecked, hostility might divide and weaken a pluralist society beyond repair.

It is this point that makes tolerance of others so basic to the pluralist view. They claim that America has nurtured and been nurtured by its ethnic groups, and does not require, either by law or decree, that ethnic groups meld into a single entity—a homogeneous American. Rather, the history of America is that everyone is asked to subscribe to a certain cultural and political ideal: a democratic pluralism. The implication is that somehow everyone is allowed, even encouraged, to maintain and nurture one's ethnic identity, if that is his or her desire. But, as Americans, we are asked to believe in the civic culture. One may have an identity as a hyphenated American, but the hyphen is regarded as connecting rather than separating. From this perspective, then, America is strengthened and not weakened by the fostering of social heterogeneity.

Democracy

The term "democracy" has many meanings, but the most common and most accepted meaning is caught in the notion that citizens must govern themselves. As Abraham Lincoln said, democracy is government of, by, and for the people. A number of astute observers, many from foreign lands, have long understood the durability, strength, and significance of Lincoln's words. To most, they suggest a nation of free individuals, people with freedom of conscience, with the right of open inquiry without fear of the consequences of that inquiry, and a government to which they accede voluntarily, and which they manage and control. There is one further inference here. Good citizenship and good government go hand in hand. Citizens must be prepared to devote some time to the political process, if it is to work. This means inducting children into the norms of civic virtue which can be defined as the willingness to subordinate private self-interest to the public interest and general welfare. Thus the concept of a civic culture "wraps up" or includes the notion of civic virtue or citizen participation and is central if participatory democracy is to work and prevail.[6]

The defining feature of participatory democracy is not the formal sovereignty of the people whose will must somehow be obeyed. Nor, certainly, does it lie in a simple choice by citizens between representative members of various elites who will make decisions or take action for them. On the contrary, the point of participatory democracy is that those involved, those who will be most affected by the decision to be made or the action to be taken, actually take part in the discussion and take the decision, and the responsibility for the decision, themselves. Of course, the notion of democracy as direct participation and discussion by those involved in decisions to be taken is precisely what Lincoln's words meant: government of, by, and for the people.

It is not my purpose to trace the origin and development of our idealized political democracy (the American Creed) as well as our basic democratic norms as embodied in the great documents: the Declaration of Independence, the Bill of Rights, the Gettysburg Address, our legal codes, and significant Supreme Court decisions. Suffice it to say that democratic norms do exist and these serve both in a legal and moral nonneutral way to help secure a public sphere in which citizens exercise their abilities, values, and capacities as their conceptions of civic virtue allow.

Put differently, the civic culture defines what it means to be an American by establishing an American adherence to values and institutions, stressing freedom, equality, rights and duties, tolerance, participation, and above all, a *political* union. America is, lest we forget, first and foremost a political union, not primarily a cultural, linguistic, religious, or racial union.

E pluribus unum suggests the above. The *unum* demands that each citizen wants to become a citizen, is willing to perform as a good citizen, and believes in the political ideals of the republic. Yet, at the same time, the *pluribus* requires that people be allowed, even encouraged, to preserve their cultural, linguistic, and religious collectivities. Hence, the civic culture is the glue, the basic foundation for balancing social heterogeneity and individual political rights. For instance, an American may be as ethnic as he or she wishes in private actions, but in public actions, the informal and formal rules of the civic culture are binding. In fact, the consensus over the civic culture has been so pervasive that it can easily go unrecognized. That is, we Americans *are* a highly ideological people. That one does not ordinarily notice this fact is remarkable, made possible, to a large extent, because practically all have accepted the same ideology!

What, then, is American democracy? As suggested above, it is defined by adherence to a civic culture. One becomes an American not by rushing headlong into the American mainstream, seeking to adopt indiscriminately new manners, clothes, technology, and sometimes names, but by manifesting an attachment to the values of the civic culture and, relatedly, to the nationalism of the United States.

In his *Politics*, Aristotle argued that justice in a democracy requires that citizens rule and be ruled in turn.[7] Citizens, in other words, must take turns governing one another. In American society today, as opposed to the small Greek city-state, this principle of democracy is inapplicable since citizens are too many; they cannot be guaranteed a turn. Moreover, we are well aware that, as a simple matter of fact, some citizens wield more power than others and, consequently, they receive an unequal benefit of society's good and services. Clearly, then, inequalities of rule abound.

But in his *Politics* Aristotle also argued that the proper end of the state was the attainment of the very highest good, and the state should use its power to enhance the moral development of the citizen. Those who care about participatory democracy subscribe to the belief that ruler and ruled alike are bound to the laws of the land, and although the system at times fails, a commitment to the civic culture, the democratic process, is rewarded in the long run.

The two points proposed by Aristotle are seen at work today in the public sphere, the arena where political decisions are carried out. A dominant force at work is the ready acceptance of the legitimacy and value of social heterogeneity. Currently, ethnic groups are seeking redress of grievances and the satisfaction of their demands through intervention by federal, state, and local government. For example, because of poverty and prejudice, many Mexican-Americans in the Southwest were, in effect, denied an education. One result is that many now in their fifties and sixties do not speak and read English. Still, they are citizens, with the right to vote, but how are they to exercise their right except with a ballot printed in a language they can understand?

In the 1970s, this issue came before the courts, and several decisions held that if voters otherwise eligible could not understand English, they must have voting materials prepared in a more accessible language. In 1975, the Voting Rights Act amendments said that there must be bilingual ballots if more than 5 percent of the voters in a district were members of a "language minority group." The only such groups eligible under this ruling were American Indians, Alaskan natives, Asian-Americans (most significantly, Chinese and Filipinos), and Spanish-speakers.

Today, as never before, ethnic groups are undertaking collective and corrective action for improving their position within the larger system of participatory democracy. The public sphere, which now mediates ethnic demands for making real the promise of civil participation for all, has become a field teeming with competing groups. In this struggle for societal resources, the shift away from assimilation is clear and enduring.

This last point is illustrative of a fundamental problem. If we take seriously the democratic ideal—that a democracy is government of, by, and for the people—then the officeholders we elect to head our federal, state, and local affairs are not the government; they are only the executors of the people's government. If we take seriously the ideal that a democratic polity, at least in theory, is coextensive with self-government, then equality before the law is essential. Every citizen has the same guaranteed legal and political rights, and must be allowed to exercise these; everyone's vote is to be counted in the same way, and my word in a court of law has the same weight as yours. In other words, equality before the law is a necessary condition for fostering and guaranteeing the rights of citizens.

So it is that ballots in parts of the country are printed in Spanish, or Chinese, or Tagalog, along with English. (This is true even though anyone applying for naturalization must still pass an English-proficiency test. From this perspective, the apparent inconsistency reflects the linguistic reality that many native-born citizens have not learned English.) This fact is akin to giving concrete meaning to the principle of democratic rights and obligations and the prideful activity they can engender for all citizens. The glory of participatory democracy is that it is always and necessarily a moral order, requiring equal rights or civic equality, not equal power, not equal office holding, and not the equality of turns. Minimally, civic equality involves guaranteed opportunities to exercise power in the form of voting rights, the rights of assembly, association, petition, office holding, and speech. These rights are the infrastructure of the political union and must be permanent guarantees because this is what we mean by democracy. It is not that we all rule, but the opportunities and occasions for the exercise of power in the form of rights are civic equality, the glory of a democracy, and this must be guaranteed to all.

What public arrangements should we seek? To what extent, why, how and by what means should we again move toward assimilation of ethnic groups or toward fostering a pluralistic society? Although it is useful to isolate and examine the myriad voices competing for attention on this issue, the debate is much less clear in reality.

For instance, the formulation of a debate over a national policy on language would compel citizens, the ruled, and their officers, the rulers, to articulate and examine in detail language and language-related issues. Moreover, a national debate on whether to make English the official language of the United States for government affairs would resolve the often conflicting language policies that the United States has randomly and almost unconsciously followed to date. The National Defense Education Act (NDEA) of 1957 and the Title VII of the Bilingual Education Act of 1968 epitomize this conflict. The former affirmed the significance of foreign languages as integral components of national security; the bilingual education legislation, by contrast, was designed to foster the rich linguistic experiences of the immigrant and indigenous minority communities in the United States.

To establish a debate over a national policy on language requires the recognition that the integrating mechanism of any society is language. Again, we note that the *unum* in *e pluribus unum* demands only certain things of the *pluribus*, but one of them is that, as a practical reality, English be recognized as the language of commerce, government, and mobility. But the *pluribus* suggests that, in principle, it should not be this way. Hence, we have the volatile issue of a national policy on language. This is a fundamental issue of social heterogeneity and of a democracy. A democracy ought to be able to debate this issue as a political matter, since culturally different groups will respond to proposed public policy and public policy will respond to culturally different groups.

The American Experience: An Evolving Nation

Just how rich and varied is American social heterogeneity? How rich and diverse are the social and cultural dimensions of our society? Since 1820 the story of social heterogeneity has been told from the records of immigration. It may be that one may truly paraphrase the historian Herodotus's remark that "Egypt is the gift of the Nile" by saying "The United States is, in large part, a gift of immigrants."

A qualifier "in large part," is included because we must not neglect by an error of omission the fact that significant intergroup contact occurred on the frontier of America between the immigrant settlers and America's indigenous people, native Americans, as well as between the immigrant settlers and Hispanics in the Southwest. In both cases there was conflict over land and its use.

The Old World culture helped shape the New World experience as well as contributing to the phenomenon of social heterogeneity. Early in the nineteenth century came the great flood of Irish, over 2 million between 1815 and 1860, and 1.5 million Germans, some driven westward by political persecution, but more by hunger and hardship. In response, "nativists" in Philadelphia attacked Irish-Catholic churches and burned Irish homes.

The next wave was more than twice as large—10 million from 1860 to 1890—but these were still mostly Northern Europeans: English, Dutch, Swedes, and Norwegians. The third wave was even bigger: 16 million from 1890 to 1914, including a still unmatched record of 1.3 million in 1907, when the United States population was only 87 million. To the dismay of the newly established Irish and Germans, more than 80 percent of the newcomers were Southern and Eastern Europeans: Italians, Bulgarians, Poles, Greeks, Slavs, and Jews. This was the period in which Emma Lazarus wrote the Statue of Liberty's welcome to the huddled masses yearning to be free. Table 1 shows the volume of immigration from 1820 to 1930, its peak period. Table 2 shows European immigration by decade and the percentage coming from either Northern and Western Europe or Southern and Eastern Europe.

TABLE 1

IMMIGRATION TO THE UNITED STATES, 1820-1930, BY DECADES

1820-1830	151,824
1831-1840	599,125
1841-1850	1,713,251
1851-1860	2,598,214
1861-1870	2,314,824
1871-1880	2,812,191
1881-1890	5,246,613
1891-1900	3,687,564
1901-1910	8,795,386
1911-1920	5,735,811
1921-1930	4,107,209

Source: U.S. Immigration and Naturalization Service, Annual Report (1946).

TABLE 2

EUROPEAN SOURCES OF IMMIGRATION TO THE UNITED STATES
DISTRIBUTION BY PERCENTAGES AND DECADES, 1820-1920

DECADE	TOTAL EUROPEAN IMMIGRATION	NORTHERN AND WESTERN EUROPEAN (PERCENT)*	SOUTHERN AND EASTERN EUROPEAN (PERCENT)
1821-1830	98,817	68	2
1831-1840	495,688	82	1
1841-1850	1,597,501	93	.3
1851-1860	2,452,660	94	.8
1861-1870	2,065,270	88	2
1871-1880	2,272,262	74	7
1881-1890	4,737,046	72	18
1891-1900	3,558,978	45	52
1901-1910	8,136,016	22	71
1911-1920	4,376,564	17	59

*Percentages may not total to 100 because of rounding and European immigration from other countries.

Source: Based on data in Marian T. Bennett, *American Immigration Policies* (Washington, D.C.: Public Affairs Press, 1963).

Initially, from 1820 to 1880, the United States had no systematic immigration policy. This was, in effect, a free period of immigration, although some states did have immigration restrictions. Immigration policy changed, however, between 1870 and 1924. From the very start there was a strong element of racism involved, but restrictions did not proceed solely on this basis. Following the passage of two bills suspending all Chinese immigration, the first Chinese Exclusion Act was passed in 1882. The Immigration Act of 1891 was concerned with other classes of aliens—"undesirables" such as the insane, the diseased, criminals, and paupers—and the Immigration Acts of 1903 and 1904 excluded aliens such as anarchists and children unaccompanied by their parents.[8]

The immigration restrictions based on racial grounds, inspired to exclude Chinese, were extended to the Japanese in 1907-08. In that year the United States and Japan negotiated a "gentleman's agreement" which limited immigration from Japan to former resident aliens or relatives of resident aliens. The aim of the agreement was to stop further Japanese immigration. In 1924, Japan was given no quota in the quota act of that year, and immigration from Japan amounted to a mere 3,503 from 1931 to 1950.[9]

During the early 1900s, the immigration policies of the United

States grew like topsy. Piece after piece of legislation was added, but with no systematic or overall policy. Such a process began in 1907, with the appointment of the Immigration Commission, chaired by Senator William Dillingham, of Vermont, and continued through the late 1920s as successive national origins acts were passed.

The Dillingham Commission produced a study comprised of forty-two volumes that laid the ground work for the immigration laws of the 1920s, that is, an overall policy of "national origins": America's new citizens should resemble its old ones. Hence, under the national origins system introduced in 1921, quotas for European immigration preserved the "racial preponderance" within the American population. Ireland, for example, could send each year 3 percent as many immigrants as there were foreign-born Irish-Americans counted in the U.S. Census of 1910. Moreover, in 1924 the quotas were the most restrictive of all immigration legislation, which were essentially in force until 1965. They were reduced from 3 to 2 percent of the ethnic representation among Americans, foreign-born, and native-born, shown not in the 1910 Census but in the 1890 Census. In effect, the national origins system was designed as a shield against the new immigration of Poles, Italians, Slavs, and Eastern European Jews.

With the passage of the national origins law of 1924, the ethnic balance of the American population was supposed to be preserved. But with the coming of the Great Depression, immigration ceased to be an issue at all. During the 1930s, more people left the United States than entered. For more than forty years, the United States had a breathing space. The cycles of assimilation were able to run undisturbed for more than a generation, slowly bringing the masses of new immigrants into the wider market place and civic culture.

The second revision of immigration policy issues from one of the many acts of the Great Society: the Immigration and Nationality Act amendments of 1965. For the first time in America's history, it put limits on the numbers that could enter from Mexico, the Caribbean, and elsewhere in the Western Hemisphere, but the laws did revolutionize the nature of the immigrant population: national quotas were replaced by international ones. The United States announced that it would look impartially on the world. The Turk, Ethiopian, or resident of Calcutta would now compete on equal footing with the German or Englishman. The United States would open itself to the racial and ethnic balance of the wide world. Thus the flow of immigrants changed drastically. From 1930 to 1960 about 80 percent of America's immigrants came from European countries or Canada. From 1977 to 1979, 16 percent came from those sources, while Asia and Latin America accounted for about 40 percent each. In 1979, the nine leading "source" countries for legal immigration were Mexico, the Philippines, Korea, China and Taiwan, Vietnam, India, Jamaica, the Dominican Republic, and Cuba. In tenth place, with 3 percent of the total, was the United Kingdom.[10]

Equally important, under the post-1965 immigration code, places in the immigration queue are assigned with great indifference to ethnic origin but with careful attention to family ties. The immediate relatives of American citizens—parents, minor children, and spouses—are admitted without limit. The law's premium on family connections means that each new arrival eventually makes many others in those countries eligible for admission.

Additionally, the law provides for 270,000 immigrants each year (no more than 20,000 from any one country) in the "numerically limited" categories, which heavily favor less immediate relatives. Eighty percent of the 270,000 places are allotted to the adult children or the brothers and sisters of United States citizens, plus the immediate relatives of noncitizens who are here as permanent resident aliens. The remaining places go to those with skills considered valuable to the American economy, or to those who would simply like to come.

Furthermore, under the McCarran-Walter Immigration and Naturalization Act of 1952, skilled workers had an advantage in qualifying for admission. Since 1965, first come the immediate relatives of United States citizens, defined as spouses, children under twenty-one, or parents of citizens over twenty-one, who were admitted without limit.[11]

This short history of immigration and its restrictions is only part of a larger history of an evolving nation. That evolution has brought both the inclusion and exclusion of racial and ethnic groups, as documented by immigration and immigration restriction. Both sets of factors, inclusion and exclusion, bear mightily today on the American experience.

The Changing Face of America

Without too much exaggeration it could be said that the fact of social heterogeneity is the single most important element of change in the United States today. In only one state, Hawaii, are whites a minority, making up one-third of Hawaii's population; Asians and Pacific Islanders are the majority there. At the other extreme, only one state, Vermont, is more than 99 percent white, but New Hampshire is a close second at 98.9 percent.[12]

Making up the largest minority group are the 28.6 million blacks, up about 6 percent since 1980. The growth rate among blacks, however, has been declining for more than three decades.[13]

The 16.8 million Hispanics make up the next largest minority group. This ethnic group has increased 14 percent in four years (1980-84). The increase from Mexico alone (legal immigration) from 1970 to 1980 is 35 percent. Three states now have more than 1 million Hispanics (California, Texas, and New York) and nearly two-thirds of the nation's Hispanics live in those states.[14] (Puerto Ricans do not count as immigrants, since their island is part of the United States and they are citizens at birth.)

The smallest racial or ethnic part of the United States population that can be accurately estimated is "other races." The latest estimate shows that 6.7 million members of "other races" include about 4.8 million Asians and about 1.3 million Native Americans.[15]

High relative growth among Hispanics and Asians and their concentration in only a few states mean they will influence taste, fashion, and politics beyond their numbers. For instance, Asians will likely account for one out of every twenty-five Americans by the turn of the century, with the country's fastest growing minority heading for the 10 million mark, a mere fifteen years ahead. Thus by the year 2000, Asian-Americans will comprise almost 4 percent of the United States population.[16]

As the immigrants continue to arrive, American society is an ever-changing mixture of many ethnic groups, and this is viewed with mixed feelings. From liberals and conservatives alike, the alarm bells have begun to ring. There are warnings about the implications. Carl Rowan, a black Democrat, coined the phrase an "immigration nightmare." Richard Lamm, the controversial white Democratic governor of Colorado, said that our immigration policy is making us poorer, not richer. It is dividing our wealth and resources. Clare Booth Luce, a highly respected Republican, has claimed that the "new" immigrants will be more difficult to absorb because they are not white. Labor leaders have issued statements saying that immigrant workers are stealing Americans' jobs. Immigrants, they say, more narrowly divide the economic pie.[17]

On the other hand, a very different approach suggests the value of immigrants, not only because they provide labor—new workers in the labor force as well as extra purchasers in the national market—but because they represent additional people as people. From this perspective, the ingenuity, perseverance, and hopefulness that immigrants possess can and do make the economy richer, because immigrants will adapt and innovate and sacrifice in ways that nonimmigrants are too comfortable to try. In essence, immigrants make the pie larger for everyone to share.

It is clear that the best-known "facts" about today's changing America and its consequences are, in most cases, hotly disputed. Still there is little dispute that an "immigrant personality" exists, and that its elements are the same ones that, in retrospect, were apparent in the nation's previous immigrants. That is, immigrants tend to be more resourceful and determined. At best, they arrive with specific talents ranging from Australian Rupert Murdoch to Soviet artists Alexander Solzhenitsyn and Mikhail Baryshnikov, but most immigrants are still the tired, the poor, the huddled masses whom the Statue of Liberty traditionally welcomed to New York Harbor. Most arrive as uprooted foreigners, ignorant of the language and the mores that comprise their new culture. They have come from the lower, but not the bottom, ranks of their native societies. They are people without advantages of birth who are nonetheless on the way up with a high willingness to adapt.

Consequently, the most important questions about the new makeup of American society are these: What is happening? What are the immigrants doing to us? Will they adapt by accepting our language? Will they be so numerous and powerful that they will alter social and political relations? Will they learn to respect the civic culture, the formal and informal rules, that allow this nation to cohere?

These questions are not really asking whether the new Americans can be integrated—they must be—but rather how the United States will be changed by that process. What will be their individual or particular and cumulative impact on our society?

Economic Impact

For many of the recently arrived, the pivot on their visions for the future is work. Finding a niche in the market place is a different experience for each newcomer, but often a pattern emerges that was set by earlier immigrants. Newcomers, in a place where everything is new, often flock to certain fields for a variety of reasons, cling to a thread of familiarity by clustering in certain trades, and thus dominate their chosen field by long and hard work. They gravitate to a field because their countrymen are already there. For example, Albanians do not show up in great numbers in the Census, but their presence is felt in classic immigrant fashion because they cluster in Brooklyn, in a part of New York City, in a particular occupation, managing apartments. But not every immigrant can find something familiar. More often, the newcomers move into jobs that other groups are leaving. Additionally, they tend to live frugally, becoming prodigious savers.

Cab driving is probably the occupation that most clearly reflects the impact and prospects of immigrants. It provides flexible time for other occupational training as well as to study English and numerous opportunities to practice speaking English. It is raw, unskilled labor that requires little training and cabbies can work eighteen to twenty hours a day, if they wish.

The Urban Institute, which conducted a study of the California economy in the 1970s, reported that Southern California, "[received] more immigration than any other [state], and its per capita income increased by 25 percent, also higher than the norm."[18] It is also true that immigration was not the only factor in these increases. The study notes this point, but the findings suggest that "at least at the aggregate level, the large-scale immigration did not depress, and perhaps increased, per capita income in the state."[19] Put differently, the newcomers did not divide the pie into smaller pieces for all. Overall, the study said, the immigrants contributed economic benefits in the form of new human energy, entrepreneurship, adaptability, and these outweighed the deficits and the costs that primarily came from their use of public services, such as schools and hospitals.

Immigration is a divisive issue along the Texas coast, in Miami, Philadelphia, and in numerous pockets elsewhere. In Texas, fighting broke out between Vietnamese shrimpers, who began arriving in the late 1970s, and the American fishermen who were already there. The Vietnamese, through their industry, frugality, and clansmanship, have prospered where others have not been able to. Tensions have mounted and led to violence, leading to at least one death in Corpus Christi. Several Vietnamese boats have been destroyed by fire, and Ku Klux Klansmen have burned crosses to intimidate the Vietnamese. However, these conflicts have not stopped them. A decade after their arrival, they are becoming solid members of the Texas middle class.

A similar sense of disaffection prevails in Miami. Immigration is a divisive issue there, although no one disputes the economic bonus the Cuban community now represents. Cubans have achieved the most within the Hispanic fold. The first to flee Castro were mainly professionals and businessmen, who soon repeated their success there. The second and third waves were less select, more like America's typical immigrants; still they were absorbed into Little Havana, where they opened shops and restaurants and thrived. In Dade County, which encompasses Miami, Cuban family incomes average $25,000. Miami's Cuban population has helped make it the entrepot for Latin American trade.

The sense of dissatisfaction in Miami stems from the fact that the sheer number of Cubans enables them to colonize big chunks of the city and live in insularity. To many Americans, putting it bluntly, this is un-American, and this feeling is fed by a blatant racism. The barrios are viewed as "foreign," drug-ridden, and controlled by street gangs of unruly youth. Miami's garment district, once run chiefly by Italians and East European Jews, is another field dominated by Cubans. In Miami, more than 400 Cuban-born executives hold the rank of vice president or higher in Miami's banks.

Another example is the Hmong hill tribe of Laos, many of whom were recruited by the CIA to fight communist forces, who migrated to Powelton Village in West Philadelphia in 1981. They were an agrarian people with an animist faith and a language that had no written form until thirty years ago. They came with little knowledge of American life, and were overwhelmed by their new circumstances. Some 2,000 were placed in inner-city neighborhoods, but distrust and ignorance of one another led blacks and Hmong in West Philadelphia to hate one another. The mutual resentment bred violence in the streets. Less schooled in urban violence and survival than the blacks, all but 400 have scattered to other locations after falling frequent victim to street crime.[20]

According to Barry Chiswick, of the University of Illinois, the offspring of immigrants earn 5 to 10 percent more than others of the same age and educational level whose parents are native-born.[21] Although the immigrants themselves, compared with native-born, start out at a big earnings disadvantage, in a matter of years the first generation catches up with and then passes the native-born. This "earnings crossover" occurs after fifteen years for Mexican immigrants and after eleven for black immigrants.

Underlying the tension and hostility shown by both whites and blacks toward the newcomers is a good deal of resentment based on a recognition that the determined immigrants are achieving a measure of economic success that surpasses native-born whites and blacks. Whites and blacks are watching the new immigrants from Asia, Latin America, and the Pacific Islands flourish where they have not. For example, the median household income of Koreans, Vietnamese, Haitians, Cubans, and Mexicans has climbed past that of blacks.[22] The 1980 census showed that median household income for Asians as a whole was $22,000, exceeding not only that of American families in general ($19,900) but also the level reported by whites ($20,800).[23]

Poor whites and blacks tend to regard the immigrants as frustrating their efforts to gain part of the nation's wealth and services. The most fundamental objection is that immigrants take jobs away from native Americans. That is, they are displacing Americans, directly or indirectly.

Donald Huddle, of Rice University, contends that citizens do want the jobs immigrants now hold. He says that it is misleading to talk about "immigrant work" because even illegal immigrant work ranges from $4 to $9.50 an hour.[24] Clearly the victims of immigration are the marginal workers with low education, who tend to be the market for unskilled jobs and low-skilled entrepreneurial opportunities.

It is instructive here to return to the situation of the Vietnamese on the Gulf Coast. In Kemah, Texas, the commercial fishermen who had long worked the Gulf Coast found new competition with the Vietnamese. The working-class whites of the region had tolerated the newcomers when they took low-income jobs cleaning fish or working in restaurant kitchens, but when they became fishermen and competitors, the attitudes and tolerance quickly changed. Overall, the Vietnamese have won; their extended family structure cheapens labor costs and they work harder and longer and under more difficult conditions than do the white fishermen.

But perhaps the most burning economic issue regarding immigrants is the illegal alien. Some advance the claim that illegal aliens are flooding into the occupations of this country, performing jobs that Americans will not do. The jobs are so onerous, so poorly paid, that if illegal aliens did not exist to take them, the jobs would not exist. Therefore, the story goes, the aliens are filling jobs no one really wants to do and thus have not really displaced anyone else. They do the dirty work of society. Employers like it, because they will work harder, complain less, and they are available.

A contrasting view of illegal immigration holds that the aliens are displacing working Americans, directly or indirectly. It is contended that it is misleading to talk about "immigrant, dirty work." The argument goes like this: if there were no illegals, the jobs would change, they would be different. The current jobs are dirty and low paid precisely because there is such an abundance of cheap labor.

The consensus concerning the element of illegal immigrants suggests that both views are partly right and partly wrong. Immigrants can and do make the economy more efficient, but they can hurt one element of the working class, the lower class. We gain an efficiency from immigration and the cost is what we lose in upward mobility from the lower class. This latter category includes farm workers, dishwashers, laborers, garbage collectors, building cleaners, restaurant employees, gardeners, maintenance workers, to name a few occupations performing useful, often indispensable work, but the remuneration is poor, the training needed is gained on the job in a matter of days, and there is a large pool of persons available for these jobs.

Thomas Muller, an immigration expert at the Urban Institute, a Washington-based think tank, argues that the large numbers of illegal aliens in the United States are less a problem than a manifestation of American economic dynamism. The central argument of immigration reformers and restrictionists, the possibility of a backlash against newcomers, is not easily dismissed. Historically, we know that early immigration policy was written with the aim of barring Chinese and other Asians. Muller, however, believes there is now more tolerance and less racial animosity than at any other time in United States history.[25]

Just as immigrants redefine cities, they have transformed the working world. There is good evidence that their grit and courage impart productive energy to the society they join, although work means back breaking and demeaning work for many newcomers. Immigrants built the United States with muscle and brains. We, of all people, should realize they are an asset.

Social and Cultural Impact

Even if we assumed that immigration, including illegal aliens, made our economy work more efficiently, does that tell us all we need to know in order to understand the impact of immigrants on society? Of course not, for society and culture, the foundation of a national ethos, are affected by the arrival of newcomers. Strains and conflicts occur, values are tested, a civic culture is stretched, and language, dress, taste, morals, and habits of life are altered. In the past, the United States has prided itself on building a society and culture, a nation, out of diverse parts. The question today is this: Can democratic pluralism still prevail?

This question arises and is real because many of today's immigrants share one trait: their native language is Spanish. Is this a threat? If not a threat, it is certainly an inflammatory issue in American education.

The conventional wisdom about American society, with its varied languages, is that the national culture is held together by official rules and a formal language. In the old days, it is said, immigrants were eager and willing to assimilate as quickly as possible, especially as regards their children. These were placed in English-language classrooms, and they were expected to learn English, and helped their parents to learn English. Perhaps the English language was America's most powerful assimilative force, at least "in the old days," and for most immigrants, success was possible only after the enigma of culture and language was solved.

But now the situation is quite different. Hispanics (people who have Spanish as the native language) do not all wish to follow the pattern of forced assimilation of the old days. Many are insisting on bilingual education and ballots. This shift in the pattern began in the 1960s when the policy of the United States government moved away from the forced assimilation approach after surveys in New York and Texas showed Puerto Rican and Mexican-American youths dropping out of school early. There was the recognition that equal educational opportunity was a myth for large numbers of students not able to learn in English.

The turning point in the pattern came with *Lau v. Nichols*, a case initiated in 1971 involving Chinese-speaking students in San Francisco.[26] They sued for "equal protection," on the grounds that their unfamiliarity with English denied them an adequate education. In 1974, the U.S. Supreme Court ruled in their favor. The ruling did not say that school systems had to start bilingual education programs, but the federal regulations and state statutes that implemented the decision obliged many districts to set up a system of "transitional" bilingual education that has since become the focus of controversy.

Although the rules vary from state to state, they generally require a school district to set up a bilingual program whenever a certain number of students (usually twenty) at one grade level belong to one language group and do not speak English well—that is they are limited English language proficient (LEP). In principle, bilingual programs are expected to assist students in keeping up with the content of, say, history and mathematics courses, while preparing them to enter the English-language classroom. In other words, the principle aimed to generate optional instruction that would help non-English speaking students learn English quickly. Meanwhile, the students were to move ahead in their school work by using their native language as much as necessary.

Today, more than 1.3 million students whose primary language is not English are enrolled in federal, state, or local study programs that provide instruction in their native tongues. These programs are conducted in at least eighty languages, ranging from Spanish to Lithuanian to Micronesian Yapese. The current annual cost is well over $350 million.

Bilingual education is highly controversial and has become a debated public policy issue. It is inflammatory in large part because of what it symbolizes to different groups. Backers of bilingual education include those who applaud the easing of the transition to English in a nonhostile environment so that students learn the English language well as well as those who hail it as promoting one's ethnic heritage. The backers view bilingual education as a sane way of learning English and as a symbol of cultural pride in that one's culture is not being denigrated, intentionally or unintentionally.

On the other hand, detractors view bilingual education as a threat to America's national culture either from the position that today's ethnic groups are asking for special consideration; they are changing the operating rules that have bound the society together for so long, or it is said, mastery of English is not emphasized, and such mastery is the key to economic mobility. We may be perpetuating a large group of unemployed citizens.

This debate, however real and inflammatory, seems to be a battle over three disputed issues: (a) the use of public funds for special educational programs for students with limited proficiency in English, (b) the extent to which language, and not other socioeconomic and cultural factors, is responsible for academic fortune, and (c) the function of language as a bonding or polarizing force in society. There is no gainsaying that forced assimilation, the sink or swim classes in

English, has ignored sensitivities that lie behind the sentiments of immigrants and non-English-speaking students. A denigrated or confused ethnicity is a heavy burden for the individual and society to bear since it wastes resources and damages individual lives.

The goal for an integrated bilingual education for Hispanics appears to be a significant step toward minimizing the differential minority status to which they have been socialized for generations. But to view this question only as a battle between a national culture and ethnic pride is mistaken. It also is a question for factual resolution, at least in part. The choice between bilingual education and intensive instruction in English is a choice between methods and between values, but it should not be a battle between ideologies. It is hoped that better designed and more thoughtful research will study a new cohort of Hispanic students who are followed throughout their schooling experiences in integrated settings to determine the dimensions of student ethnic integration as well as student achievement. The results, of course, of such research will not be sufficient to decide the issue, for values must be considered. But, significantly, no one has proved beyond a doubt that students with limited English proficiency learn faster or better by bilingual instruction than by any other methods, including the old-fashioned "sink or swim" or "submersion" approach in a classroom where only English is spoken. To date, the evidence suggests that sometimes bilingualism works and sometimes it does not, and most of the time, it makes no difference at all.

But, in another crucial sense, it does make a difference. To Hispanic activists, it is a symbol that they are at least taking their place in the sun; to many other Americans, it sounds like a threat not to assimilate. And this is the ideological issue; it is not an educational issue. The choice seems to be between ideologies.

Should linguistic minority groups have the right to participate fully in American life without being completely in the mainstream culture? The issue is far from being resolved. Clearly it is deeply embedded in such matters as economic and cultural attitudes toward immigrants and indigenous minorities. Moreover, it is hard to examine the pedagogical value of bilingual instruction without becoming entangled in such sensitive political issues as the right and status of alien workers.

The importance of going beyond ideology is crucial here. The school should nurture the rich linguistic resources that ethnic minorities provide by affirming children's rights to maintain their home language when it is other than English. And importantly, we need to foster the acquisition of second language among English-speaking students. The urgent need is for critical research that would support programs to implement what *Lau* was intended to achieve: equal educational opportunity for America's linguistic minorities.

Race and Racism

Although it has been argued that the concept of race should be collapsed into the broader category of ethnicity, there is a very good reason for separating out race and racism at this point. The fact of race itself is not of special interest in a discussion of social heterogeneity but the brute circumstance of racism is. The historical essence of black racism in the United States reflects what results from a "caste" group status. Historically, blacks in the United States have suffered a unique history, begun in the institution of slavery and sustained over generations by racist justifications, prejudice, and discrimination. The current status of blacks must be understood within a context of a postslavery caste status and policy of continued immigration.

Thus no discussion of social heterogeneity in the United States would be complete without a consideration of race and racism. The wonder of American society is its civic culture and its role in fostering ethnic identity. But the shame of the society is its concern about racial makeup: racial distinctions that separate groups from one another allegedly as a result of some notion of superiority and inferiority.

It will be recalled that the turn-of-the-century immigration restrictionists agreed that there were different races and some were superior to others. What we are left with today, then, is the nasty question of how much residue of their belief still exists with regard to the children of the old immigrants and the new immigrants themselves? How much resistance to social heterogeneity and to the virtue of tolerance arises merely from color prejudice? Clearly some of it does; it is part of American history, but it is ignoble and ugly, and it deserves to be stamped out.

Historically, there is no more obvious strand in our social past than concern about social change. Members of successive ethnic groups have continually changed the so-called "American" character. The original British and Dutch Protestants were joined by Catholics and Jews, Central and later Eastern Europeans, and, most slowly and arduously of all, people of color.

What is crucial to grasp is that the concept of race is far from a useful scientific concept, especially in terms of a classification to divide the human species. No fixed racial classification system is without its detractors. Why, then, use the concept? If it is granted that race, for instance, is a legitimate concept, it is not clear what the scientific implications are of the existence of races. Why typologies of race and for what purpose? Since it serves no legitimate scientific purpose, then what purpose does it serve? The most likely candidates are racism, prejudice, and discrimination.[27] This is not to say that there are not innumerable differences between human populations, but it is no longer accepted that there are certain *ineradicable traits*. Today we know that ethnic groups are different from one another. They have different religious preferences, different eating and drinking habits, different patterns of marriage, and different criteria of economic success.

The theme of racism is tied to the ineradicability of ethnic traits.[28] Racism assumes it is meaningful to allege racial differences between human populations based upon connections between biology and human conduct. Like antisemitism, racism is a form of prejudice and/ or discrimination, taking specific forms involving different groups and situations. Most commonly, people use the term "racism" today to refer to antiblack prejudice as well as beliefs and actions by whites toward Hispanics, Asians, Pacific Islanders, and American Indians. Ethnocentrism is also seen at work here. It refers to the tendency of groups to consider themselves, their own physical appearance and way of life, as superior and most honorable, while their respect for the physical appearance and way of life of others is a function of how much these characteristics approximate their own.

Ever since the first slave ships unloaded their human cargo over 350 years ago, black Americans have witnessed a succession of determined immigrants weather discrimination to achieve a measure of acceptance and economic success that has far surpassed their own. In America's large cities, the earlier settlers have moved out to the suburbs leaving the inner cities to blacks. Today, in most cities, Cambodians, Albanians, Filipinos, Cubans, Vietnamese, Central Americans, and so forth are moving into areas that for at least a generation have been home to American blacks. Predominantly black areas of Long Beach, for example, are becoming centers for Cambodian and Vietnamese merchants, doctors, and dentists. In Miami, native blacks are beginning to feel like spurned foreigners as ambitious Cubans give the city a Latin rhythm and take over what were once bastions of black business.

To many American blacks, it seems obvious that the new immigrants have been more warmly welcomed than the blacks, who have been here all along. With a mixture of animosity and admiration, blacks are watching the new immigrants achieve what others did before them. They see that jobs they previously held—porters, maids, parking lot attendants, hotel workers—are now being filled by immigrants. And, adding to the bitterness, is the perception held by many blacks that a "racist" system benefits the new immigrants. Too many of the gains made by the immigrants, it is believed, come at the expense of blacks. Marvin Dunn, a black psychologist at Florida International University in Miami, says,

When the first wave of Cubans moved in, there was a deep resentment at all the financial assistance and resettlement aid the government was giving them, at the expense of social programs for people who had been living here. Now there is resentment at a system that would prefer to hire Haitians because they work more cheaply and complain less.[29]

For example, in 1960 blacks owned 25 percent of the gas stations in Dade county; by 1979 they had only 9 percent, while the percentage of Hispanic-owned stations grew from 12 percent to 48 percent. Moreover, the average income of a Hispanic business in Dade county is now $84,000, almost twice that of a black business.[30]

Some black officials express fear that immigration is harming the black lower class. The new immigrants are successfully competing with blacks for entry-level jobs and jobs at depressed wage rates. But what is most important is that willing foreign workers give employers less incentive to find a place for black teenagers. Here is the gut issue. Many black youths who have grown up in single-parent families, especially boys without fathers, are on the verge of a hopeless future. Some will not work rather than hire themselves out for what they consider insultingly low pay. A high volume of children are growing up outside a family network, a trend that could create a violent black underclass. This is the group that could threaten the rest of America, black and white. And regardless of such a threat, the well-being of that black underclass is a sensitive moral and social issue.

The problem addressed here is a sensitive question: Why have blacks failed to repeat the classic immigrant experience? Clearly some have. Millions of black Americans have climbed up the ladder to create a stable and growing black middle class. There may be two black Americas. One is doing very well, better than ever, by taking advantage of the system and moving up. The other, getting larger as a group, is stuck at the very bottom of society.

America must come to grips with the fact that blacks, due to their unique history as slaves in American history, have faced generations of racism, not just a decade or even a few generations of prejudice and discrimination. Strictly speaking, the black lower-class or underclass problem is not directly connected with immigration; it merely exacerbates the situation. The issue is what makes a society cohere, hang together, and give people the faith and trust necessary to continue to maintain the society? We know that there must be confidence in the system. The black underclass is, alarmingly, from fragmented families and households, who appear to live for the now, who have little ambition, no hope of a better future, and appear less capable of economic survival than the tenacious new immigrants. The fact seems to be that the culture of the black underclass leaves its members worse equipped for economic advancement than immigrants who start out with less.

Perhaps we should be cheered by the realization that school desegregation based on race is now illegal, but the hard questions raised by desegregation—such as how much attention should we pay to magnet schools, to maintaining housing integration in mixed neighborhoods, to inequities in busing, to elimination of discriminatory suspension in desegregated schools—require value judgments that must be addressed if we wish to nurture and support our black youth.

If we have one major social challenge it is this: It is not only the issue of integrating the Cubans or the Vietnamese, no matter how far down the road that may be, but coming to terms with the culture of the black underclass, that part of American society most estranged from the rest, by giving its members a reason to feel that they ought to—and in fact can—join their fellow Americans, a reason to feel that they belong. This means encouraging a cohesive black cultural identity, an orientation for success, and institutional structures that make such success more likely.

Articulating a Democratic Pluralism

Perhaps the most awesome thing to learn about the United States is about the people themselves. There is a dizzying variety of groups that proliferate in a sort of ethnic shopping mall. They came from everywhere, for all kinds of reasons. Immigration has permanently changed the face of America, and continues to do so by altering its landscapes and cityscapes, its taste in food, clothes and music, and its perception of itself and its way of life. Thus one of the conditions of being an American is having to—and being privileged to—come to grips with a great many people around you who are different, different in their origins, their religions, their values, and their life-styles.

Our present situation, with its massive potential for change and conflict, is not too far removed from the social conditions of the nineteenth century and early twentieth century which harnessed and nurtured a public life, however imperfectly, within economic and social conditions that did not seem completely antagonistic to the hopes of the stream of immigrants. Americans consciously sought, and found, political traditions that could buttress and reinforce the cultural bases of a highly diverse democratic society.

Traditionally, it has been widely held that uniformity is the best guarantee of the sturdy virtues of citizenship that would then lead to civic cooperation in the local community, particularly when nurtured by the political ideals of the American Creed. Thus the guiding purpose of American society, particularly its schools, has been to create citizens who will cooperate to produce a democratic culture under the conditions of a weakening social heterogeneity.

Disputes about American democracy today issue, at the deepest levels, from the above guiding purpose and the continuing fact of social heterogeneity. There are no instant recipes for this situation, no patent medicines, no easy fixes. It is enough to realize that a vital citizenship must build upon our still living and renewed traditions of democratic pluralism and tolerance wherever they may be found, but it cannot take the older forms and resources of society for granted. For some, the struggle and conflict caused by social heterogeneity is a threat, for others it may not be worth the effort, but for an increasing number of Americans, with a hopeful view of the nation's future, a culturally diverse America that rests not on assimilation but on democratic pluralism promoting a culture of justice, tolerance, dignity, and fellowship is a wondrous possibility.

But even with the best of intentions on all sides, the question of how to fit all the varieties of ethnic groups into a relatively coherent democratic pluralism, socially and culturally, remains difficult at best. The present ambiguous situation of American society has been generated far less by rampant social heterogeneity than by the residue of racism that accompanies the erection of forced assimilative processes. To counter this, democratic pluralism is the absolutely necessary condition for the enhancement of the dignity of the individual or groups, for the destructive aspect of forced assimilation is that it undermines the sustaining web of civic democracy. It must be recognized that neither cultural assimilation nor social heterogeneity is necessarily democratic-pluralistic in nature.

Again, however, the culprit is not social heterogeneity. On the contrary, American society has suffered from the lack of a continuously developed and coherent public philosophy adequate for celebrating social heterogeneity as well as cherishing fundamental democratic values. The real culprit is a lack of commitment to the democratic values of human dignity, mutual respect, an ethic of tolerance. If ethnic membership systematically denies these in the public sphere, then ethnicity may be taken as the villain of the piece, but this is merely an illusion. The central tension is not between democracy and social heterogeneity but between selfish private interests or group interests and moral collective responsibility embodied in the idea of nation-community.

Democratic pluralism is a possibility in the United States if we are able to instill in citizens the need to go beyond ethnic group identification to the forming of publics or communities of interest through which citizens can express a multiplicity of different, even incompatible values, but embodying in their deliberations the value of mutual respect and an ethic of tolerance in building a democratic society. The publics, the new political constituencies, would be created to bridge the gap between the need for *unum*, national unity, while all the while protecting the *pluribus*, social heterogeneity, within a democratic culture. We can label this state of affairs "democratic pluralism."

The strengths of this position have the combined result of suggesting that the initial and indispensable first effort at promoting democratic pluralism is to have recourse to a political agenda bolstered by the moral values of mutual respect and an ethic of tolerance. This effort demands opportunity for the many different ethnic groups or factions to come together for discussion as well as a free circulation of ideas, evidence, and the like in political debate. Recent developments such as movements for police review boards, consumer protection, Mothers Against Drunk Driving, Students Against Drunk Driving, along with an increasing desire on the part of citizens to support the imperative to live according to collective moral principles, a common good, suggests the living out of a renewed civic practice as well as a public philosophy.

The working approach to a rapprochement between democracy and pluralism is not an unrealizable ideal. If we take seriously communities of interest, we can revitalize our civic culture. In this view, it is both necessary and good that the public interest not be ignored or relegated to second status. Moreover, a sharing of a moral compact based on human dignity, mutual respect, and an ethic of tolerance holds hope for a renewed struggle toward a "great community," a nation-community worthy of respect and trust by all.

The theme of a reinvigorated democratic pluralism must be based on, and show a deep concern for, the moral compact or moral infrastructure of democracy. To do so is to recognize the interdependence of the entire nation-community as well as to embrace a moral of mutual responsibility for each other. Just as self-interested political motives are a deficient element of democracy, so too is a group-interested political motivation lacking in terms of a viable moral civic culture.

What must bind Americans together, regardless of the fact of social heterogeneity, is a civic culture consisting of active associations and political organizations and forums in which the meaning of good citizenship could be developed on a moral basis. These structures must provide regular opportunities for opinion and judgment to be intelligently and publicly shaped as well as for learning and passing on the subtle habits of public inquiry, responsibility, and initiative. This kind of general civic competence is fundamental to the proposition that democratic pluralism is only possible through a life that values freedom of association and, concomitantly, helps citizens to identify themselves in terms of the broader social interdependence, the common good, in which they live.

A democratic pluralism has its justification in the right of all to equal influence and consideration in matters that affect us collectively, and correspondingly more say in those that affect us more closely. This view would seem to be best realized in a society in which as many opportunities as possible exist for democratic participation at all levels including those that affect the individual most closely in his or her daily life. Democratic pluralism, then, is a genuinely associational activity since it involves sharing responsibility for acts that create a quality of life different from the mere sum of individual satisfactions.

Pluralism and participatory democracy are thus bound together because citizens must be taught the value and skills of discussion and willing cooperation. They need to try to understand and attempt to accommodate others' points of view, to be respectful of the values of others, and to see reasons as genuine reasons and not merely as obstacles to one's own will or to what one sees from one's own point of view as the common good.

Citizens should learn that humans are by nature social beings, living together requires a shared life, and a shared life is possible only when the members of a community trust and respect one another. Thus children of different ethnic groups must come together in a common schooling that shows them that, despite differences that exist between them, there are many bases for a shared life. To achieve this, students need to learn how to get along with people whose values, tastes, attitudes, and understandings differ from theirs. Moreover, there are some academic things all citizens need to know, such as having some understanding of citizen duties and responsibilities if democratic pluralism is to function properly.

There is another point, closely connected to the foregoing. Given that social heterogeneity is a good, we also need to be clear that a democratic solution to the problem of competing ethnic group interests is not one that overrules the other's position by means of a majority vote, or a mere compromise that results in no one's getting more than half of what is wanted. Rather, it is one that promotes both (or all) interests, and such a solution is most likely to be found when each one involved in the discussion understands more of what the other wants than the other has yet put into words.

Clearly education must play a vital role in the above in that its products are to learn that democratic pluralism demands that we choose ends and means not only for ourselves but also for others. The beauty of America is not in its buildings, not in its artifacts or its arts. Its greatest beauty is found in its democracy. Freedom is the ultimate value, whether aesthetic or political. It would, of course, be dishonest and unfair to ignore the dreadful ethnic scars and blemishes of the United States, both past and present, but they are themselves the result of our failure to find an accommodation between social heterogeneity and democracy. Without a doubt social heterogeneity can be dangerous—competing ethnic groups help create great ruptures and divisions within the society. Yet social heterogeneity also holds out the value of diversity and hope, and a democracy must allow, even encourage, people to be different, to hold contradictory views, and, certainly, to tolerate one another.

These are indeed noble sentiments. But are they more than lofty, abstract hopes and aspirations? I believe so. Democratic pluralism has its justification in the development and maintenance of a widely shared sense of moral values, including mutual respect, the human dignity of the individual, and an ethic of tolerance, all of which place constraints on self-interested striving and influence matters that affect citizens collectively. A restructured civic culture, then, would seem to be realized in a society where many opportunities exist for participatory democracy at all levels, including those that affect citizens most closely in their daily life. `

In conclusion, to address the problem of the relation between democracy and cultural pluralism is to arrive at the central tension in the American moral order. In democratic pluralism men and women either subscribe to the moral compact which is the foundation of the civic culture or they do not. Democratic citizens, obviously, have a choice: if they want to invest their sense of self-development only in ethnic group membership then they must be prepared to abandon the view that the members of society are equal, and that mutual respect and tolerance are basic to the civic culture. If they want to perpetuate these values, then they must find ways within existing ethnic groupings to become committed to broad political membership. And these are the only choices. But this choice itself is significant because it derives from the existence of a democratic community of citizens, a civic culture, which values choice, and is thus not compatible with the destruction of the community of citizens or its transformation into an enclave of warring ethnic factions.

FOOTNOTES

1. Cynthia H. Enloe, *Ethnic Conflict and Political Development* (Boston: Little, Brown, and Co., 1973), especially chap. 2, "Varieties of Ethnicity"; Joseph Hraba, *American Ethnicity* (Itasca, Ill.: F. E. Peacock, 1979); Andrew M. Greeley, *Ethnicity in the United States: A Preliminary Reconnaissance* (New York: John Wiley and Sons, 1974); *Race and Ethnicity in Modern America*, ed. Richard J. Meister (Lexington, Mass.: D. C. Heath, 1974); Nathan Glazer and Daniel P. Moynihan, *Beyond the Melting Pot* (Cambridge, Mass.: M.I.T. Press, 2d ed., 1970); William Petersen, Michael Novak, and Philip Gleason, *Concepts of Ethnicity* (Cambridge, Mass.: Belknap Press of Harvard University Press, 1982); Peter Schrag, *The Decline of the Wasp* (New York: Simon and Schuster, 1970); Howard F. Stein and Robert F. Hill, *The Ethnic Imperative* (University Park, Penn.: Pennsylvania State University Press, 1877).

2. David Tyack, "The Kingdom of God and the Common School: Protestant Ministers and the Educational Awakening in the West," *Harvard Educational Review* 36 (Fall 1966): 447-69. See also, David Tyack, "Onward Christian Soldiers: Religion in the American Common School," in *History and Education: The Educational Uses of the Past*, ed. Paul Nash (New York: Random House, 1970), pp. 212-55.

3. Milton Gordon, *Assimilation in American Life* (New York: Oxford University Press, 1964), especially chap. 3.

4. Michael Novak, *The Rise of the Unmeltable Ethnics* (New York: Macmillan, 1973).

5. Thomas F. Green, *Education and Pluralism: Ideal and Reality* (Syracuse, N.Y.: School of Education, Syracuse University, 1966), pp. 14-15.

6. Richard Pratte, "Civism and Its Problems" (Normal, Ill.: Philosophy of Education Society, 1985).

7. Aristotle, *The Politics*, 1283, trans. Ernest Barker (Oxford, Eng.: Oxford University Press, 1946), p. 157.

8. Marian T. Bennett, *American Immigration Policies* (Washington, D.C.: Public Affairs Press, 1963), pp. 21-22.

9. Ibid., p. 23.

10. "Immigrants: The Changing Face of America," *Time*, 8 July 1985.

11. Hraba, *American Ethnicity*, p. 21.

12. U.S. Census Bureau, July 1984 Estimates, American Demographics, cited in *Columbus Dispatch*, 18 September 1985, p. 16.

13. Ibid.

14. Ibid.

15. James Fallows, "Immigration: How It's Affecting Us," *Atlantic* 252 (November 1983): 48.

16. U.S. Department of Commerce, Census Bureau, *1980 Census*, Vol. 1, Part 1, Chapter C (Washington, D.C.: U.S. Department of Commerce, 1983), p. 163.

17. U.S. Census Bureau, July 1984 Estimates, cited in *Columbus Dispatch*, 18 September 1985.

18. Fallows, "Immigration," p. 55.

19. Ibid.

20. "Immigrants: The Changing Face of America."

21. Fallows, "Immigration," p. 55.

22. "Immigrants: The Changing Face of America."

23. Ibid.

24. Fallows, "Immigration," pp. 60-61.

25. "Immigrants: The Changing Face of America."

26. *Lau v. Nichols*, 414 U.S. 563 (1974).

27. The case for deleting race from the language is argued at length in Ashley Montagu, *Man's Most Dangerous Myth: The Fallacy of Race* (New York: Oxford University Press, 1974). See also John Higham's classic *Strangers in the Land* (New Brunswick, N.J.: Rutgers University Press, 1955) for an understanding of Anglo-Saxon racism.

28. Petersen, Novak, and Gleason, *Concepts of Ethnicity*, pp. 5-6.

29. Fallows, "Immigration," p. 94.

30. "Immigrants: The Changing Face of America."

CHAPTER VII

Elite Power and Democratic Ideals

STEVEN TOZER

Social Forces Influencing American Education, the most recent
yearbook of the National Society for the Study of Education to deal
explicitly with the complex relationships between school and society,
was published in 1961. In that same year, two events revealed
contrasting assessments of power in the United States: the publication
of Robert Dahl's *Who Governs?* and President Dwight Eisenhower's
farewell address to the nation.[1] Dahl's book was a major contribution
to the pluralist school that dominated political science in this country
during the 1950s—and which, not surprisingly, Havighurst embraced
in the 1961 NSSE Yearbook.[2] Pluralists argued that, despite being
governed by a very small group of decision makers, modern societies
are consistent with democratic ideals so long as the governing groups
represent competing political interests and are accountable by election
to the general population. That this normative account of democracy
described political conditions in the United States was virtually an
article of faith in the pluralist camp, and *Who Governs?* was intended to
provide empirical data to bolster that faith. It came as some surprise,
then, that President Eisenhower would warn the nation in 1961 of
"the potential for the disastrous rise of misplaced power" of a
"military-industrial complex" under which "public policy itself could
become the captive of a scientific technological elite."[3] While Dahl's
work strengthened the pluralist position as the received view in
American political science, Eisenhower's speech echoed the leftist
critique of power that C. Wright Mills had advanced five years earlier
in *The Power Elite*.[4] In Mills's analysis, which the pluralists took pains
to reject, the important power in the United States was concentrated
in the hands of a powerful elite made up of those in leadership
positions in government, in the military, and in the corporate
establishment. For Mills, this elite was neither open to competition
from other interests nor significantly accountable to the citizenry.

Paul Violas suggested the basic framework of this paper as a way to focus the
unwieldy subject of power in contemporary society. Frank Margonis and Lawrence
Parker made substantial contributions and criticisms.

Eisenhower was warning the nation, in effect, that Mills was closer to the truth than the pluralists cared to admit.

In 1973, when Theodore Lowi wrote of "the old and stalemated battle between the elites and the pluralists,"[5] it was not clear what "old" meant. One finds variations of this conflict between the democrats and aristocrats of classical Athens and between the Federalists and Antifederalists in early United States history. It is likely, however, that Lowi meant to recall only the social science dispute following World War II over whether the political order in the United States is organized consistently with democratic ideals. The pluralists, beginning with Schumpeter in 1943 and extending most prominently through Riesman, Dahl, and Kornhauser in the 1950s and 1960s, argued that the political system has remained consistent with democratic ideals, while those who argued from the "power elite" position took the opposite view.[6] Whether this debate is stalemated due to the inconclusiveness of the arguments or due to the stubbornness of ideology is an important question. Certainly, each side has continued to develop its own spokesmen in the quarter century since the 1961 NSSE Yearbook. The purpose of this chapter is not to settle the debate between the pluralists and the elite theorists, but to see what recent contributions to the dispute reveal about power and democratic ideals in the United States today. Further, it will be argued that the conditions of power in contemporary society both rely upon and contribute to the miseducation of citizens.

A Working Conception of Power

This chapter is not a philosophical treatment of the concept of power. Rather, I will treat the concept of social power itself as relatively unproblematic, recent philosophical treatments notwithstanding.[7] A useful working conception of social power can roughly equate power with influence. This is not new in political science usage, of course, and it seems to have the virtue of commonsense understanding. People or organizations are said to have power if they influence others or influence conditions that in turn influence others. It must be noted that this conception says nothing about *intent*. One can unintentionally have influence over others, and this may also be an important kind of power.

So conceived, power may be used to liberate, or to enslave. Like energy in physics, which influences bodies at rest or in motion, power in social relations denotes influence upon others, or upon the conditions that influence others. Bertrand Russell expressed this idea as follows:

The fundamental concept in social science is Power in the sense in which Energy is the fundamental concept in physics. Like energy, power has many forms, such as wealth, armaments, influence on opinion. No one of these can be regarded as subordinate to any other, and there is no form from which the others are derivable.[8]

It is thus possible that a child has power in a relationship with a parent, although it will be of a different kind and degree than the parent's power over the child. Similarly, it can be argued that the working class has power in its relations with the ownership class, if it has any influence at all, but it is of a different kind and degree than the power of the owners over the workers.

Power-as-influence is thus seen as distinct from such power-related notions as prestige or authority, for example. Prestige can enhance one's power or influence, as advertising agencies demonstrate in hiring celebrities to sell their products. A position of authority can similarly enhance one's power; it is doubtful that Ronald Reagan could have had as much influence upon social policy if he had remained an actor.

For the purposes of this paper, a further virtue in this working conception of power is that it favors neither the elite theory nor the pluralist perspective. Pluralists have been using a power-as-influence conception at least since Dahl's treatment in 1957 and continuing through Verba and Orren's work in 1985. Elite theorists, too, use conceptions of power compatible with the notion of power as influence, although they use different terms. Mills implies influence in defining power in terms of who exercises it: "By the powerful we mean, of course, those who are able to realize their own will, even if others resist it."[9] Domhoff invokes Russell's definition, and Dye focuses on those who are in a position to "affect the conduct of others."[10]

Pluralists and elite theorists agree that some people or organizations have disproportionate influence; thus they have disproportionate power. This raises the normative question of most concern here: Is the constitution and distribution of power in contemporary society consistent with democratic ideals? It is here that pluralists and elite theorists disagree most fundamentally.

Pluralist and Elite Theory Accounts of Society

In the first chapter of this volume, Kenneth Benne refers to the tradition in democratic thought, rooted in Mill, Rousseau, Dewey, and in such modern theorists as Pateman, that locates much of the significance of democracy in its educative effects on citizens. Bachrach refers to this as the "self-developmental" tradition in democratic theory: democracy is good because participation in the decisions that affect one's life contributes to personal and intellectual growth.[11] The pluralist tradition in democracy, which Pateman calls "contemporary democratic theory," argues that such participatory decision making is no longer possible in modern, mass society, and that most important political decisions must be made by relatively small groups of people.[12]

While there are differences among those who are commonly referred to as "pluralist" political scientists, their various treatments share several fundamental, distinctive components. These are perhaps nowhere summarized better than by Bachrach:

Owing to the dramatic growth of elite power, most leading theorists regard the self-developmental approach to democracy as an anachronism. To continue to advocate such a theory in today's world, it is argued, is bound to foster cynicism toward democracy as it becomes evident that the gap between the reality and the ideal cannot be closed. Thus it is said that there is no alternative but to recast democracy, emphasizing the stable, constitutional, and liberal nature of the system of elite pluralism; the competitiveness of political elites, their accountability to the electorate at periodic elections; and the open, multiple points of access to elite power for those who bother to organize to voice their grievances and demands.[13]

The three features of the pluralist position considered in this chapter are the alleged competitiveness among elite groups, their accountability to the people, and the openness of the elite system. Both pluralists and elite theorists agree that United States society is "stable, constitutional, and liberal." Any disagreement regarding those terms tends to raise questions not of descriptive accuracy, but of their democratic significance. Jefferson, for example, argued that stability is not a good in itself, for it can well serve tyranny. Similarly, it has been argued that the Constitution itself was written by elitists who provided that only half of one of the three main branches of the federal government would be elected by the people. And such analysts as Karier and Kolko have shown that "liberal" social policy is not necessarily good if it serves the interests of the powerful rather than the majority of people.[14] While pluralists and elite theorists may agree that contemporary society is stable, constitutional, and liberal, the elite theorists would not find these qualities necessarily consistent with democratic ideals.

With regard to the degree to which political elites in the United States are competitive, accountable, and open, however, there is disagreement of a different kind. As Pateman has pointed out, there is some unclarity among pluralists about whether such criteria as these are offered only as normative components of a "contemporary democratic theory," or whether they are also intended to describe the contemporary political order. It can fairly be said of the pluralist account that it serves both purposes. Dahl's study of New Haven city politics is one example of an effort to illustrate explicitly that the social order is pluralist in nature. As Verba and Orren comment in their recent pluralist treatment: "Usually at issue is the question of who actually governs rather than who ought to govern."[15] Pluralists argue not only that the system ought to be competitive, accountable, and open, but that in general it is. As Verba and Orren state:

Those who take a fairly benign view of the pluralist struggle see the system as somewhat biased and yet relatively open: groups differ in the amount of political resources they control, but all groups control some, and the disparity between sectors of the society is not severe. More important, they view the system as open to new groups challenging the established order. Entry into the political market is regarded as relatively easy, though successful competition in that market is somewhat more difficult.[16]

The pluralist account of the criteria for modern democracy thus serves both to establish norms and to show that political organization in the United States is consistent with these norms. As Dye remarks, "Pluralism . . . is an integrated body of theory that seeks to reaffirm the fundamental democratic character of American society."[17]

The strength of the pluralist argument need not be determined by the validity of the criteria—openness, competitiveness, and accountability—themselves. As already argued, the pluralist criteria are not consistent with the self-developmental, participatory view of democracy that Pateman and Bachrach support. Even if one grants the pluralists their criteria, however, empirical questions remain. How open, both to new individuals and to new groups, is the power structure in the United States today? How much competition exists among the groups that share significant power? How accountable is the leadership of these groups to the public? Each of these questions is more answerable today than it was twenty-five years ago. Each of the last three decades has witnessed a considerable amount of research, much of it by elite theorists, that helps clarify the constitution and distribution of power.

The elite theory positions argued by such contemporary political scientists as Bachrach or Melman in the 1960s, Prewitt and Stone in the 1970s, or Dye and Domhoff in the 1970s and 1980s all are rooted more or less explicitly in the analysis put forward by Mills in *The Power Elite*. Here Mills gave first clear expression to the concentration of power after World War II that was echoed in Eisenhower's "military-industrial establishment."

At the top of the economy, among the corporate rich, there are the chief executives; at the top of the political order, the members of the political directorate; at the top of the military establishment, the elite of soldier statesmen clustered in and around the Joint Chiefs of Staff and the upper echelon. As each of these domains has coincided with the others, as decisions tend to become total in their consequence, the leading men in each of the three domains of power—the warlords, the corporation chieftains, the political directorate—tend to come together, to form the power elite of America.[18]

Characteristic of Mills's position—and of all elite theorists after him—is the emphasis on power as constituted in institutions and institutional leadership. Mills again:

No one, accordingly, can be truly powerful unless he has access to the command of major institutions, for it is over these institutional means of power that the truly powerful are, in the first instance, powerful. Higher politicians and key officials of government command such institutional power; so do admirals and generals, and so do the major owners and executives of the larger corporations. Not all power, it is true, is anchored in and exercised by means of such institutions, but only within and through them can power be more or less continuous and important.[19]

Neither Mills nor any other elite theorist argues that institutions are all-powerful, nor that institutional leaders may enact their will unencumbered by resistance from others. How *much* power the elite exercise, and how it is exercised, are precisely what elite theorists seek to determine. As Prewitt and Stone write, "The amount of power in the hands of the elite is a matter for analysis, not definition."[20]

Are Elites Open, Competing, and Accountable?

To what degree is the exercise of power in contemporary society "open"? In *Who's Running America?*, first published in 1976 and then revised during the Carter and Reagan Administrations, Thomas Dye agrees with Mills that power resides not primarily in individuals, but in institutions.[21] Dye's approach is helpful for getting a concrete look at what positions exercise major influence throughout the society of the United States. Dye identifies three major sectors of society: the corporate, the public interest, and the governmental. By identifying, for example, the most powerful positions in each of the top one hundred industrial corporations, the top fifty utilities, communications, and transportation companies, the top fifty banks, the top fifty insurance companies, and the top fifteen investment firms, Dye finds that 4,325 positions carry extraordinary influence in the corporate sector. In the public interest sector, he identifies 2,705 positions in the mass media, in education, in philanthropic foundations, in the most prestigious law firms, and in civic and cultural organizations. In the governmental sector, Dye identifies the most influential committee positions in Congress, the most powerful positions in the legislative and executive branches, and the key positions in the military for a total of 284 governmental positions. The total from these three sectors is 7,314 positions that, according to Dye, wield the major decision-making power in the most powerful institutions in political and economic life.

The influence of these institutions, and those who run them, is remarkable, in Dye's account. The positions in Dye's list control, for example, over half the nation's industrial assets, over half the utilities, banking, and transportations assets, over two-thirds of the nation's insurance assets, over half the endowed assets in the nation's private colleges and universities, and over 90 percent of broadcast news. In addition, these positions control one-third of the nation's daily newspaper circulation; they dominate the legal field and investments and securities, all of the major standing committees in the House and Senate, the Supreme Court, and the four branches of the military. These are the positions occupied by those whom Mills called "the power elite," and whom Prewitt and Stone have more recently called "the ruling elite."

OPEN ACCESS TO ELITE POWER STRUCTURE

Dye's enumeration of the corporate, governmental, and public interest elite allows some initial observations about the alleged "openness" of the contemporary power structure. There are two senses of "open" that should be considered. One is the degree to which elite positions are available for occupation by the mass of citizens, which Prewitt and Stone, for example, treat as the "recruitment" of elites. The other is the degree to which elite positions and institutions are available for occupation by new interest groups, a process Prewitt and Stone refer to as the "circulation" of elites.

Classical Athens had a model of institutional leadership intended to be structurally open in the first sense, that of "recruitment." Citizens became members of the main legislative body, the assembly, not by competition for votes, but by lot. Every citizen who wished to serve had an equal chance to do so, because it was chance that determined the membership of the assembly. Because the assembly numbered 500 and the Athenian citizenry only several thousand, and because legislative tenure was strictly limited to one or at the most two years, citizens had reasonable expectations of "ruling and being ruled in turn," as Aristotle said. In contrast, the very numbers cited in Dye's analysis show the difficulty of entering into institutional leadership positions today. If there are only roughly seven thousand such positions, then the average citizen in a society of 230 million people has about three-thousandths of a percent (.003 percent) chance of gaining any one of those positions. This assumes, of course, that everyone starts with an equal statistical opportunity, which is not the case. Of the "top seven thousand" institutional elite positions Dye identified, only 4.3 percent were filled by women, and they were found primarily in philanthropic foundations, education, and civic organizations rather than in corporate or government leadership. Only 0.3 percent of the "top seven thousand" institutional positions were filled by blacks. In 1700 corporate leadership positions, only three were filled by blacks. Those blacks and women who do make it to the top tend to be ideologically "safe," such as the conservative black Nixon appointee Samuel K. Pierce or conservative Reagan appointees Sandra Day O'Connor and Jeane Kirkpatrick.

Even among white males from privileged backgrounds, the chances of entering the ruling elite are very slim, as Prewitt and Stone point out. They calculate that even for a Harvard Law School graduate whose father is a corporate lawyer, the chances are 100 to 1 against rising to a ruling elite position, while for the average white male, Prewitt and Stone's prediction is slightly more optimistic than,

but similar to, that based on Dye's figures: the chances are 100,000 to
1.[22] For the sake of comparison, the chances of being murdered in the
United States are a thousand times greater for males: 1 in 100,
according to recent FBI figures.[23]

The question of socioeconomic origins raises another limitation on
recruitment of elites. Dye's research confirms Prewitt and Stone's
finding that 90 percent of all those in elite positions come from the
upper 20 percent of the socioeconomic strata. The remaining 80
percent of the public contribute only 10 percent of the membership of
the ruling elite.

The mechanisms and processes that so effectively screen women,
blacks, and low- and middle-income citizens from eligibility for elite
positions are complex and varied, and they need not be detailed here.
Elite recruitment is but one of many manifestations of deeply rooted
sexism, racism, and class bias, and it is important to recognize that
these inequalities make a mockery of the claim of "openness" in the
elite power structure, if by openness we mean that elite positions are
even roughly equally open to all.

A pluralist response to this line of argument could emphasize that
leadership positions in a democratic society need not be open to all
citizens, but open to those with sufficient talent and preparation to
lead well. This is the "meritocratic" argument incorporated into the
functionalist theory of stratification first articulated by Davis and
Moore in the mid-1940s. On this view, recruitment to elite positions
is open to those who merit such positions on account of their
distinctive talents and training. The democratic character of such an
arrangement is said to reside in the opportunity of talented people
from any walk of life to enter the institutional elite. Unfortunately, the
meritocracy myth does not explain why the elite consists almost
entirely (with some well-publicized exceptions) of relatively wealthy
white males. It is not plausible that these persons, representing a small
minority of the public, are born with much more talent than the
majority population of females, minority group members, and
members of the lower and middle classes. It is plausible, however, that
they have access to educational institutions and social contacts that are
direct routes to power. Domhoff and Dye are among many who
document the importance, for example, of attending expensive eastern
prep schools, graduation from which opens doors to Ivy League
institutions and beyond. The significance of attending such a prestige
prep school is detailed by Persell and Cookson.[24] Those who attend

such schools are not particularly distinctive for their talent but rather for the social-class backgrounds that allow them to attend high schools in which tuition and fees average $10,000 yearly.

The meritocracy myth has been exposed repeatedly in recent years by economists, sociologists, and educational theorists who have shown that social rewards are not distributed on the basis of talent but rather on the basis of systemic processes favoring some ethnic and economic groups over others. As Prewitt and Stone point out, talent and achievement are not enough in themselves; one must demonstrate them in the arenas valued by the elite who control the recruitment process.

The used car salesman may be as skilled, as personable, and as hard-working as the president of General Motors, but he was born into the working class, not the upper classes; he attended a local junior college, not Harvard Business School; his friends also sell used cars, rather than direct corporations that manufacture them; he votes from time to time, but does not contribute thousands of dollars to political candidates. When the list is compiled of possible appointees to the Cabinet or possible candidates for the ambassadorship, it seems never to include the skilled, personable, hard-working used car salesman, but almost always includes the head of the company whose cars he sells.[25]

The significance of the place of "meritocracy" in the ideology of the ruling elite who themselves hold the pluralist view will be examined shortly.

Pluralists also argue that institutional leadership is open because it is available to new groups, a situation to which Prewitt and Stone (following Gaetano Mosca and Vilfredo Pareto) refer as the "circulation" of elites. This does not refer to simple turnover of personnel in elite positions, for such turnover exists in many elite systems. Nor does it refer, in the sense intended here, to the rise of selected individuals from lower economic classes to elite positions, an event which also takes place in some few instances. Rather, what is at issue here is whether significantly different "types" of social groups attain elite power status. The rise to power of corporate industrial capitalists at the end of the nineteenth century, for example, represented the rise of a new group to the status of power elite. It has been argued by some that a managerial revolution in the mid-twentieth century has brought yet another group, the middle-class managerial stratum, into power. But in response to these examples, one must ask what distinguishes these groups as different "types" from the wealthy aristocracy who constituted the first elite of the nation. In neither case was the new group brought to power by an electorate demanding that new interests be represented. Rather, changes in the means and organization of production created new opportunities for wealth and power—opportunities often defended by force against laboring classes. Whereas two hundred years ago, wealth and power resided in landholdings and a growing merchant class, and nearly a hundred years ago in the hands of corporate industrialists, today a corporate executive officer is likely to exercise considerable power and amass considerable wealth. This is evidence not of a circulation of groups representing fundamentally different interests, but evidence of different historical developments in the production of wealth and the power that accompanies it.

While significant elite circulation has not been documented, there is upward social mobility in the United States, particularly for white males. However, the attainments of particular individuals do not constitute the circulation of elites. In 1986, twenty blacks serve in the House of Representatives, and eventually, one or more of them may obtain a key committee chairmanship or some other "ruling elite" position of influence. Yet, such isolated cases of individual accomplishment cannot represent a circulation of elites, for there has been no turnover in the interests served by those in ruling positions.

This is not to claim, say elite theorists, that other groups, such as labor, farmers, and feminists, do not have measurable influence. They do. But, in Mills's terms, the same power elite continues to exercise "continuous and important" power. In Domhoff's view, this power elite "sets the terms of the interaction" with all other social groups in society.[26] Domhoff's analysis denies that groups with significantly different interests have access to elite circulation; it focuses instead on whether the power elite as currently constituted includes groups with competing interests. This introduces the second major claim made by pluralists: that the modern political-economic system in the United States is democratic because the competition for power among elite groups serves as a check-and-balance system to keep any group from amassing disproportionate power.

COMPETITION AMONG ELITES

Elite theorists argue that both shared class interests and shared ideology limit the competitiveness among elite groups. Domhoff's conception of the power elite focuses on the relations between social class and elite power. He writes in *The Powers That Be* that his is a "class-hegemony paradigm."[27] For Domhoff, one could be a member of the institutional elite without being a member of the "social upper class," a class notable for its wealth and privilege. For Domhoff, the social upper class consists of at most .5 percent of the population, and the power elite is the institutional leadership that serves as the "operating arm" of the ruling class. Domhoff thus claims to have brought together institutional leadership and class-rule analyses. A central component of this linkage between the upper social class and the institutional ruling elite, for Domhoff as for Mills before him, is a shared ideology.

"Nowhere in America," wrote Mills in 1956, "is there as great a 'class consciousness' as among the elite; nowhere is it organized as effectively as among the power elite." Mills went on to note that despite factions and conflicts within the power elite, "more powerful than these divisions are the internal discipline and the community of interests that bind the power elite together." Mills argued that the similarities in points of view among members of the elite are grounded in "the structural coincidence of their interests as well as the intricate, psychological facts of their origins and their education, their careers and their associations." Mills especially attends to the circulation of persons from elite positions in the military or corporate or government leadership to either or both of the other arenas.

The unity revealed by the interchangeability of top roles rests upon the parallel development of the top jobs in each of the big three domains. The interchange occurs most frequently at the points of the coinciding interest, as between regulatory agency and the regulated industry; contracting agency and the contractor.[28]

Mills's observations, made thirty years ago, are especially interesting in light of Brownstein and Easton's recent work, in which they find that twenty-three of Reagan's top 100 appointees came from the industries they were then appointed to regulate or oversee. Additionally, thirty-two "key staff and advisory positions," including that of Secretary of State George Schultz, were filled by members of the Committee on the Present Danger, a private group created in 1976 to "trumpet a call to arms" against the Soviet Union and to increase military spending.[29]

Such institutional allegiances reflect the agreement among elites summarized by Ralph Nader in his "Introduction" to *Reagan's Ruling Class*:

Our studies and interviews of the officials in the book demonstrate a remarkable sameness among them—of attitudes, ideologies, and even styles of thinking and explaining. It was difficult to find a maverick, apart from a few to the extreme right of Mr. Reagan.[30]

This is an especially significant observation in light of the great number of Administration officials who came from corporate and military life. This "sameness . . . of attitudes" serves to limit any competition among these elite groups to a narrow, ideologically compatible, set of policy alternatives.

A fundamental linkage between the three main branches of the power elite is suggested in Eisenhower's term, "military-industrial complex." Production of military goods is good for the gross national product, as the Vietnam-era economic boom and the Reagan Administration have demonstrated by increasing military spending dramatically. The Administration has discovered nothing new, but is making use of corporate-military-government structures that have been in place since World War II. As Seymour Melman writes:

In the name of defense, and without announcement or debate, a basic alteration has been effected in the governing institutions of the United States. An industrial management has been installed in the federal government, under the Secretary of Defense, to control the nation's largest network of industrial enterprises. With the characteristic managerial propensity for expanding its power, limited only by its allocated share of the national product, the new state-management combines peak economic, political, and military decision making. Hitherto, this combination of powers in the same hands has been a feature of statist societies—communist, fascist, and others—where individual rights cannot constrain central rule.[31]

Melman's analysis tends to confirm Mills's claims about the significance of the military as a part of the power elite. The military, too, shares in the coincidence of interests Mills identified. It is in part sustained by what Nader describes as a "corporatist political ideology."[32]

The dominant ideological perspective Nader describes is conventional wisdom among the dominant elite. In part because they equate capitalism with "free enterprise," and freedom with democracy, the governmental, military, and corporate elites (who are often the same people) equate capitalism with democracy. Anticapitalist governments are therefore antidemocratic and the United States should oppose them—with military force, if necessary. Similarly, because the corporate-capitalist ideology is committed to profit as the first priority of corporations, and because "national interests" are so largely defined by corporate interests, our government must act to protect corporate interests abroad—again, with military force, if necessary. Militarism is thus seen as a major element of American-ism—an Americanism that enhances corporate interests at home through military spending and abroad through military intervention; an Americanism that justifies both military spending and power elitism by continually emphasizing the specter of foreign enemies.[33]

Ideological links between business and government can be further illustrated in a variety of ways. Such terse comments as, "The business of America is business" (President Coolidge), and "What's good for General Motors is good for America" (Charles Wilson) are more than mere slogans.[34] If Brownstein and Easton's work shows that "the bulwark and the fabric of the Reagan Administration are the major industrial and commercial corporations," this is not a new trend.[35] Even Jimmy Carter, who was portrayed by the media as a "populist" candidate, a peanut farmer from Georgia, was a former member of the Tri-Lateral Commission, an elite, private, industrial, and economic advisory body formed by David Rockefeller to coordinate economic policy with Japan and Western Europe. As Rockefeller said, "Governments don't have time to think about the broader, longer-range issues," and an elite group of "private, qualified citizens" can "identify the key issues."[36] Jimmy Carter's Vice President, Walter Mondale, and four other members of the Carter Cabinet were also from that exclusive organization. Its director, Zbigniew Brzezinski, became Carter's National Security Advisor, and a total of thirteen Tri-Lateralists were appointed to the Carter Administration.

It is often difficult for citizens to understand corporate and government ideological unity when we are so accustomed to thinking of corporations in competition with one another and in competition with government regulations. It must be remembered, however, that corporations and government set the rules within which the competition takes place, and this is why the "competing" corporations work so well with one another and with government. Competing oil companies work together in joint ventures every day to secure their collective interests, and they serve together on government advisory commissions for the same reasons.

It is common, but mistaken, to think of corporations as mini-democracies because all shareholders get to vote. However, this overlooks the fact that control over corporate policies resides in those stockholders who hold the most stock. Corporate Data Exchange claims that a group of stockholders holding 15 percent of corporate stock can control company policy. Edward Herman shows that control of even 5 percent of the stock in a company can begin to constitute minority control. While there are almost 500,000 stockholders in Exxon, for example, the top twenty shareholders control 16 percent of the voting stock, enough to control company policy. Of over 100,000 shareholders in Mobil Oil, the top twenty control 23 percent of the stock.[37]

This pattern of control, repeated throughout the corporate structure, is made even more exclusive by the fact of multiple stock ownership. For example, Chase Manhattan Bank is among the top twenty shareholders in four of the seven oil companies that account for half of all the oil refined in the United States. The same is true of Prudential Insurance. It is easy to see why "interlocking directorates" have developed, then, in which major corporations are represented in boards of directors of other major corporations. Herman shows that among the 200 largest nonfinancial corporations, 185 are interlocked with others, and 69 have as many as ten interlocks. Among the 50 largest financial corporations, 42 have at least five interlocks.[38]

The political power made possible by such corporate collaboration is perhaps best illustrated by the influential Council on Foreign Relations (CFR), an 1800-member foreign policy advisory body founded in 1921. Domhoff found that nearly a third of the Council's directors "served on the board of at least one of *Fortune*'s top 500 industrials." Fully 70 percent of the top 100 of those corporations are represented on the Council, which is more significant when one considers that those 100 corporations control over half of the total industrial assets of the nation. Of the top twenty-five industrials, 92 percent are represented on the Council. Of the top twenty-five commercial banks in the United States, which control 40 percent of the banking assets in the country (out of 13,500 banks), twenty-one have members on the Council. At the time of Domhoff's study (1982) Chase Manhattan and Morgan Guarantee Trust had thirty-one representatives between them.[39]

The CFR is most active at the policy-formation level in its discussion and study groups, "which bring together business executives, government officials, scholars, and military officers" to make recommendations on important issues in foreign affairs. Through this process, the CFR has been influential in the creation of the International Monetary Fund, the World Bank, the United Nations, United States policy in Vietnam, and a variety of other foreign policy initiatives.[40]

Through such extragovernmental policy groups, the dominant ideology of the power elite is made manifest. In response to the domestic and foreign problems of the late 1960s and early 1970s, the CFR created the Tri-Lateral Commission, which was so influential in the Carter Administration, as noted above. In 1975, the Tri-Lateral Commission published *The Crisis of Democracy*, a book that, among other things, sought to justify the powerful role of an elite few in determining American governmental policy. Representing the United States perspective, pluralist political scientist Samuel P. Huntington argues that the United States can no longer afford to heed Al Smith's recommendation that "the only cure for the evils of democracy is more democracy." Huntington went on:

Instead, some of the problems of governance in the United States today stem from an excess of democracy. . . . Needed, instead, is a greater degree of moderation in democracy. In practice, this moderation has two major areas of application. First, democracy is only one way of constituting authority, and it is not necessarily a universally applicable one. In many situations the claims of expertise, seniority, experience, and special talents may override the claims of democracy as a way of constituting authority. . . . Second, the effective operation of a democratic political system usually requires some measure of apathy and noninvolvement on the part of some individuals and groups.[41]

Both these dimensions of "moderation in democracy" were explicitly described by Schumpeter in 1943.

This emphasis on government by expertise—rather than "by the people"—is a central element of the ideology of the ruling elite. Domhoff dwells upon this at some length, and Ralph Nader was struck by it in the interviews with the top members of the Reagan Administration. Nader writes:

Their logic runs this way. They truly believe that the rich are simply more talented and skilled people. If unleashed and assisted, corporations can bring economic progress. If the U.S. is equipped with more awesome weaponry, war can be deterred. Washington lawyer Fred Dutton's description of Attorney General William French Smith's view typifies this perspective: "Smith's philosophy is that a small central establishment of a few people who have proven successful should run the rest of our lives."[42]

Further, it is an unquestioned tenet of this ideology that corporate leaders should have investment autonomy; that is, they should not have to be responsible to the wishes of the American public or even to the desires of their workers in making decisions about how to invest corporate profits. Therefore, corporations are seen as justified in investing in foreign factories, hiring foreign labor, and investing in profit-making ventures outside their own industries, if these moves will make a profit for the dominant elite who control corporate stock in this country. That these moves are devastating to the American worker and to abandoned industrial communities is considered to be the price we pay for "free enterprise."

The ideology shared by ruling elites not only precludes fundamental types of competition among them, but it also restricts the "openness" of the power elite to new individuals and groups. Prewitt and Stone noted in the 1970s that "the 'broad limits' within which policy views are acceptable effectively eliminate the far left and the far right from elite circles," which seems uncertain only in light of recent far-right successes through political action committees.[43] There is rivalry, of course, among members of the elite, but as Prewitt and Stone note, "Rivalry never extends to a challenge of the rules and ways of rulership itself," and those who challenge the rules of leadership are excluded from it. As George Orwell wrote, "A ruling group is a ruling group so long as it can nominate its successors."[44]

ACCOUNTABILITY OF ELITES

Pluralists have held that the governing elite groups are not only open and competitive; they are also consistent with democratic ideals because they are held accountable to the wishes of the electorate. If the people do not like the way military, governmental, and economic policies are conducted at the national level, they can elect new individuals, representing different policies, to national office. Prewitt and Stone write:

In short, the theory of electoral accountability replaces a commitment to participatory democracy (considered unworkable and unrealistic) with a faith in elite competition. . . . The "theory of electoral accountability" is much more than an academic notion. Rather, this ideal and the package of assumptions it incorporates is integral to the operating political beliefs of many American citizens.[45]

Prewitt and Stone's reference to "a faith in elite competition" illustrates the interdependence of the pluralist notions of competition and accountability. Just as the pluralist claims of competition among elites are highly questionable, however, so are their claims that elites are accountable to the people.

Domhoff argues that there are four major processes by which the upper social class dominates the nation's governing processes. They are: the "special interest" process, which relies on paid lobbyists; the policy-formation process, which is dominated by policy groups comprised of representatives of big business, industry, and finance; the candidate-selection process, in which candidates for elective office are championed by special interest groups with access to wealth; and the "ideology process," in which the views and values of the general population are significantly shaped by the few who control institutions such as schools, the media, and the workplace. All of these are processes that illustrate, in Domhoff's view, the degree to which the ruling elite is *not* primarily accountable to the populace, but accountable instead to the interests of the ruling social class.[46]

The power of the ruling class does not depend, however, upon its direct influence on government officials. If the description put forward by elite theorists from Mills to Cohen and Rogers is correct, then most positions in the power elite structure are not elective offices. In Dye's "top seven thousand" elite positions, for example, only 284 are governmental positions, and the others are nonelective positions in private and public life. Even among the powerful governmental positions, a great many, such as those in the military and in the President's Cabinet, for example, are not elected by the citizenry.

Even if the discussion is limited to elected elites, the pluralist position is weak. The very expression "elected by the citizenry" is somewhat misleading, especially to a nation taught to respect the legitimacy of majority rule. Our candidates for national office are not elected to office by a majority of citizens nor even by a majority of eligible voters. Rarely has the President been elected by over one-third of the eligible voters, and when Reagan defeated Carter by what the press called a "landslide" in 1980, the new President-elect garnered only 26.7 percent of the eligible votes.[47] Cohen and Rogers point out the difficulty in maintaining that such voter participation constitutes the voice of "the people," given that Reagan won a smaller portion of the eligible electorate than Wendell Willkie did in his decisive loss to Roosevelt in 1940. Nearly half the eligible electorate does not vote in presidential elections today. In nonpresidential election years, the turnout is even lower. Cohen and Rogers note that in 1982 only 35.7 percent of the electorate even voted, and no off-year election since 1970 has drawn over 40 percent of the eligible vote.[48] In 1984 only 53 percent of eligible voters voted in the presidential election, and the Reagan "mandate" was created by less than 30 percent of the electorate.

Pluralists are not necessarily disturbed by such figures, however, for they have often argued, following Schumpeter, that high voter participation is not necessary in modern democracies. In a recent article, "In Defense of Nonvoting," conservative columnist George Will accepted this position in arguing that "the reasonable assumption about electorates is: smaller is smarter." He went on to write that "in democracy, legitimacy derives from consent, but nonvoting often is a form of passive consent. It often is an expression not of alienation but of contentment." Interestingly, Will goes on to confirm, unintentionally, the elite theorists' critique of the narrow ideological range represented in elective office: "The glory of our politics, as conducted by two parties with low ideological flames, is that the stakes of our elections, as they affect the day-to-day life of the average American, are agreeably low."[49] What Will interprets as "contentment" may well be the voters' recognition of a lack of meaningful choice.

If the ruling elite largely consists of nonelective positions, and if even the elective positions are not voted upon by half or more of the eligible electorate, the pluralist accountability argument is compromised. But perhaps more compromising is the significance of wealth in the actual processes of candidate selection and of election. Political Action Committees (PACs) have come to prominence in the 1970s and 1980s mostly because of their ability to raise money for candidates, and this money buys media time, visibility, and, ultimately, votes. Illinois Congressman and former presidential candidate John Anderson notes that by 1980 PACs provided more money for candidates than did the Republican and Democratic parties combined. These PACs, which most often derive their funds from the business community that can profit by such investment, are particularly interested in supporting incumbents who have access to channels of power already. Terry Dolan, head of one of the most powerful PACs, the National Conservative Political Action Committee, claims that the single greatest factor in election is incumbency, and that 94 percent of all incumbents who run are reelected in Congressional races. He goes on to argue, perhaps overstating the case, that the only time incumbents lose is when they are outspent by the opposition—which illustrates the importance of the fund-raising effort for which PACs are so noted.[50]

The influence of PACs raises important questions about whose interests are represented by those in office. As Massachusetts Congressman Barney Frank laments, "Elected officials are the only human beings who are supposed to accept large sums of money for important purposes without giving anything in return."[51] Frank points out that elected officials have difficulty placing the interests of their constituencies ahead of the interests of the wealthy groups who put them in office. Former Supreme Court Justice Potter Stewart argues that the Court's refusal to limit the amount of money spent in the electoral process constitutes the position that "money is speech and speech is money."[52] Given the power of money to buy visibility, public relations, and advertising expertise, this equation appears not far wrong. The result, however, is not simple accountability of leaders to an electorate, but accountability first to the sources of wealth that allow one to succeed in the contemporary elective structure.

A recent example of how such accountability to wealth affects the conduct of elected officials is the tax reform bill that was intended in part to eliminate tax loopholes for big business. As the *New York Times* reported, the 1500-page bill contained "more than $5 billion of special favors that senators have been able to insert" for such "constituents" as General Mills, General Motors, Pan Am, Chrysler, Northwest Airlines, Control Data Corporation, and major steel companies.[53]

The monied classes continuously influence legislation. *Time* magazine cites a recent estimate that registered lobbyists annually spend "upwards of $1.5 billion" to influence members of Congress.[54] That amounts to an average budget of $2.7 million spent per year to influence the thinking of each member of Congress. Corporations do not spend such sums frivolously; they believe the expenditures are effective in protecting the interests of the dominant classes. The key to influence is, in the popular press's current term, "access," and wealth buys access to government officials. Domhoff cites the case of the president of the DuPont Corporation meeting with every single member of the Senate Finance Committee and the House Ways and Means Committee, an effort which resulted in a bill that saved millions of dollars for the members of the DuPont family.[55] Most often, however, such access is gained via high-salaried lobbyists, many of whom are former government officials themselves.

One major reason that the ruling elite can often ignore public opinion, writes Domhoff, is that it can shape public opinion when it is necessary to gain public support for a controversial policy. He cites

Huntington's finding that public opinion has little "determinate influence" in military and defense policies, for example. Even at the height of the Vietnam War, Huntington found, the majority of the public tended to support the President's initiatives after they were carried out, even if they had opposed them before.[56] This is consistent with the findings of John E. Mueller in *War, Presidents, and Public Opinion*, which treats public opinion in both the Korean and Vietnam Wars.[57]

Thus, if elite theorists are correct, the power elite is both well-insulated from the influence of public opinion and well-equipped to shape that opinion. The discussion thus far should also illustrate that the pluralist claims that the governing elite is open, competitive, and accountable are interdependently weak claims. The elite power structure is open only to those individuals and groups who will accept its ideology and position of dominance and work within it rather than challenging it. The "coincidence of interests" among the dominant elite groups—military, corporate, and governmental—prevents the checks and balances that would be likely if power elite groups had truly competing interests. And finally, the relatively closed and homogenous composition of the power elite is protected because it is not fundamentally accountable to the greater population.

Even though elite theory aids our understanding of contemporary economic and political institutions, it is admittedly flawed. Prewitt and Stone demonstrate an appropriate wariness:

Like any social theory there are limits to what the elite perspective can accomplish, and these limits may well preclude its usefulness in analysing many social processes. Indeed, one should be wary of any theory which seeks to explain too much.[58]

One might raise questions, for example, about just how far the power elite can go in protecting ruling class interests without incurring significant public opposition. The Vietnam War, the forcing of President Nixon from office, and the dismissal of a number of members of the Reagan Cabinet, for example, were to some degree influenced by the public. None of these cases, of course, threatened the elite power structure to any significant degree, but public opinion was not insignificant in influencing events. Testing the limits of what elite theory explains would require another paper; of more immediate interest here is how the work of elite theorists illustrates important features of the constitution of power. At the very least, elite theory

casts serious doubt on the pluralist justifications for the concentration
of power in the hands of so few.

The Educational Significance of the
Concentration of Power

In *Power and Powerlessness*, John Gaventa found that his efforts to
study the power relations in an Appalachian community required
asking "not why rebellion occurs in a 'democracy' but why, in the
face of massive inequalities, it does not."[59] One is tempted to ask
similarly of United States society in general: If power relations are as
antidemocratic as elite theorists describe, why do citizens not only
accept it, but continue to think of the social order as "democratic?"
Answering this question raises issues that are fundamentally
educational in character.

If the concentration of power has been somewhat accurately
portrayed by elite theorists, then this suggests two things about the
educational significance of such power. First, it is necessary to
miseducate a population in important ways in order for people to
perceive a nondemocratic society as democratic, thus contributing to
sustaining unequal power relations. Second, insofar as the processes of
participating in such a society are inadequately democratic, they must
be inadequately educational. Each of these points will be treated in
turn.

The literature that best contributes to our understanding of how
society miseducates in order to sustain nondemocratic power relations
is the literature on ideological hegemony theory. There is no single,
definitive account of ideological hegemony theory; it is regarded as
one of the most problematic bodies of concepts in the social sciences.
Some formulations are better than others, however, and the intent of
this section is to construct an account that is based on the available
literature. T. Jackson Lear's recent essay on cultural hegemony is a
"state of the art" discussion and parts of this account rely on his
treatment.[60]

The first thing to note about hegemony theory is that it is, like all
theories, an effort to explain selected facts. The general facts most
relevant in contemporary society are: the United States is made up of
many individuals and groups with different and often conflicting
interests; the social order benefits some groups far more than others, in
terms of health, wealth, access to positions of power, and freedom to
pursue one's interests; despite these conflicting interests and differing

benefits, the society is a very orderly one, with stable economic, governmental, and social institutions and a class structure that has not appreciably changed throughout the twentieth century; this stable social order is maintained not at gunpoint nor even mostly through threat of force, but through the cooperation of the citizenry. Hegemony theorists are particularly concerned to explain the basis of that cooperation as they explain the basis of the social world itself.

A first approximation of hegemony theorists' explanation of the contemporary social order might be expressed this way: A small minority of United States citizens exercise the predominant influence over the political and economic institutions that limit and shape the civic beliefs, values, and behavior of most of the population. This is only a first approximation, and this brief statement must be further developed in considerable detail.

It is important to note from the outset that hegemony theorists do not claim to be explaining widespread public agreement on social and political issues, for they recognize that available empirical evidence indicates both that there is a significant degree of disagreement between groups and that some groups reflect appreciable amounts of alienation and dissatisfaction. Among the studies reviewed by Michael Mann are several cases of disagreement between people from different classes. For example, routine production workers and white-collar workers showed sharp differences in attitudes toward the general belief that people in the United States have equal opportunities to "get ahead": 50 percent of the former agreed that "luck and 'pull' determines who gets ahead," while only 13 percent of polled white-collar workers agreed with this statement. And 60 percent of factory workers believed that "workers should have more control of industry" in contrast to 37 percent of white-collar workers.[61] Frequently, public opinion polls demonstrate differences of belief among different segments of the populace. A 1985 Gallup Poll was published under the headline, "Record 52 Percent Satisfied with Way Things Going in U.S."[62] Inspection of the poll results indicates that different population groups differ markedly in their views. While 56 percent of whites and 62 percent of the high-income people polled indicated satisfaction with the way things are going, only 20 percent of blacks and 34 percent of low-income people indicated satisfaction. Similarly, 80 percent of the high-income bracket indicated satisfaction with "the way democracy is working," while only 43 percent of the low-income group were satisfied. These divergent beliefs regarding basic social and economic matters suggest that not all segments of the population find pluralist justifications of the social order convincing.

While difficult to measure, there undoubtedly is an extensive amount of political alienation in the United States. In his comprehensive study of political alienation, James Wright estimates that half of the citizens are alienated from political institutions. For example, 48.8 percent of those polled in 1972 stated that they did not think public officials cared much about what the people believe. And only 47.1 percent of the respondents indicated that they trusted public officials most of the time; 44.8 percent said they trusted their representatives only some of the time.[63]

Wright's estimates of alienation help explain the widespread voter apathy noted earlier. A poll taken among nonvoters in the 1976 election found that 58 percent agreed with the statement, "The country needs more radical change than is possible through the ballot box." In addition, 41 percent of those voting also agreed that more radical change was required.[64] Such figures reflect widespread disgruntlement with present political institutions and demonstrate a definite lack of consensus regarding the status quo.

In contrast to a position that holds that the social order is accountable to the consensual wishes of the people and is therefore democratic, the theory of ideological hegemony argues that the social, political, and economic institutions of this society serve a relatively small group at the expense of the majority of citizens. Hegemony theory can be summarized in four general propositions, each of which requires further development.

1. Institutional elites, significantly unified by the shared economic and political interests of the upper classes, control the dominant political and economic institutions of the United States.

2. These institutional elites share a common world-view or ideology which reflects and justifies the organization of these dominant institutions, and thus their ideas are the ruling ideas of the social order.

3. Through such political and economic institutions as the government, the workplace, the schools, and the mass media, the ruling ideas of society are established as the standard—or dominant—explanation and justification of the social order.

4. Although this standard explanation and justification—or dominant ideology—does not equally reflect the experience of all social classes, it serves to limit discussion and debate across all social

classes in ways that prevent the formation of alternative understandings of society and thus contributes to a general acceptance of the *status quo*.

This four-step formulation relies upon the elite theorist perspective outlined in steps one and two. In addition, it elaborates upon what Domhoff called the "ideology formation" process, mentioned earlier. Hegemony theorists have gone beyond elite theorists to provide an account of the miseducative dimensions of a hegemonic society.

It is not possible here to document all the ways in which various social institutions structure experience to legitimize the dominant ideology, but particular attention is warranted for two institutions that have concerned hegemony theorists: the popular media and the schools. These two institutions are taken to be particularly significant by ideological hegemony theorists because they explicitly formulate ideological perspectives to the general population. It is valuable in this regard to recall Jefferson's high regard for both newspapers and the schools as pillars of a democratic society. Jefferson's faith in the efforts of a free marketplace of ideas led him to claim that newsapers were even more important to democracy than government. Cultural hegemony theorists argue that we now have reason to doubt the effectiveness of both the news media and the schools for preserving democratic understandings and forms of life.

While it is true that the news media do report a great many negatives about American society, these criticisms nearly always stay within rather clearly describable bounds of what is and is not acceptable criticism. For example, criticisms often address problems faced by American institutions but they do not address problems in that underlying structure itself, or the media may criticize how the game is being played but fail to question the rules of the game itself. A few examples can illustrate this point.

Reports on the domestic economy of the United States often point out unemployment, job layoffs, welfare cuts, and the flight of corporations to the Third World. This is presented as "bad news," but the American public is given no way of understanding how this bad news is an inevitable outcome of the structure of corporate capitalism itself. A structural critique would examine how unemployment is built into our capitalist system and how it benefits capitalists by keeping workers in competition with one another for scarce jobs. Such a critique could show how the satisfaction of the interests of capitalists is a necessary but not sufficient condition for the satisfaction of the interests of workers, and that the satisfaction of the interests of corporate owners makes it rational for them to act against the interests of the workers—for example, by investing their profits in the work force of foreign countries rather than in industries that would benefit workers in the United States.

Similarly, with respect to foreign policy, Americans are often treated to the "bad news" that developing countries are turning to socialism and communism, that this is a threat to the national security of the United States, and that the United States must intervene in the affairs of these nations with military force if necessary. What the public does not hear is what constitutes our "national interest" in these developing nations. History has shown that we can tolerate deep differences in ideology between the United States and its business partners in the Third World, and we have come under much international criticism for our support of tyrannical and violent regimes that practice human rights violations as an ongoing part of their domestic policy. Ideological differences threaten our "national interest" primarily when developing nations will not allow United States corporations a free reign in developing the natural resources and labor markets of those nations for the profit of United States corporations. Given our present economic structure, the interests of labor are dependent upon the interests of capitalists, and the interests of capitalists are best met, as they themselves proclaim, by developing Third World labor markets. Thus, our "national interests" are determined by the interests of corporate directors who readily abandon the American worker for cheap labor abroad and who determine a foreign policy that ultimately relies upon the American worker to die in foreign battles to protect the interests of capitalists. This perspective, which has been developed by a number of scholars in the United States and abroad—most recently by Cohen and Rogers in *On Democracy*—is not made available to the American public through our news media. News corporations in America are, after all, capitalist institutions whose interests would be threatened by alienating the advertisers who depend upon current American foreign policy for their profits. Further, representatives of United States multinational corporations serve as directors of major United States news corporations.

Ben Bagdikian writes in *The Media Monopoly*, "In 1979, sitting on the board of directors of RCA, owner of NBC, were people who simultaneously were directors of Cities Service, Atlantic Richfield, and the American Petroleum Institute (the leading gas and oil lobby)."[65] One would likely wait in vain for NBC to produce material deeply critical of the oil industry and its power.

In many cases, the control over media is more direct than interlocking directorates. Many major media companies are not independent but are owned by industrial corporations. Bagdikian writes:

Media subsidiaries owned by these ruling American industrial corporations include seven of the twenty largest newspaper chains, eight of the leading twenty magazine companies, seven of the ten largest radio operators, all three dominant television networks, seven of the eleven leading book publishers, and three of the four leading movie studios.[66]

Hence, the news media have good reason to protect the interests of major corporations. And the close relation that has developed between the government and the mainstream press ensures that major news agencies will not cast too critical an eye upon the domestic and foreign policies of the United States.

The government—and especially the executive branch—provides the vast majority of information regarding international affairs and a large share of information concerning domestic conditions. By depending upon government sources, journalists are ensured a plentiful supply of information, and more importantly, are in part exempted from the responsibility for the truth of their reporting—the government, not the reporter, is considered responsible for the message. The alleged "openness" of the new Soviet regime under Mikhail Gorbachev was recently criticized by the *New York Times* because that openness is in reality an increase in government press conferences: a policy of information control learned from the United States.[67]

Still another obstacle to critical reporting of government policies is described by John Rothchild, associate editor of *Monthly Review*, in "Stories Reporters Don't Write."[68] Rothchild shows that government officials can take action against reporters—and their newspapers—for writing all they know by denying them access to government press functions and to officials themselves. Conversely, "Government agencies can also reward loyalists with official leaks and early breaks on stories." The result is that the reporter becomes "the prisoner of the source." If he wants news, he must not offend the source of that news by being too critical, because the reporter will lose that source, and sources are vital to his continued employment. Critical analyses are not rewarded or encouraged, says Rothchild, because Henry

Kissinger, for example, "is a news figure" and the reporter "is a messenger boy," so that Kissinger's actions, not the reporter's critical assessments, are what count as news.

The policy of not writing all that reporters know is doubly protective of the established elite, because official actions are "staged" for the media. Dye writes:

The principal source of distortion in the news is not caused by the need for drama, action, and confrontation to hold audience attention. NBC news executive, Reven Frank, advised his producers in a memorandum: "The higher power of television journalism is not in the transmission of information but in the transmission of experience—joy, sorrow, shock, fear—these are the stuff of news."[69]

If Frank is correct about the "higher power of television journalism," serious critical reporting is difficult to accomplish.

Distortions of truth found in the mass media often reflect the editorial policies of news agencies, rather than any explicit effort by representatives to deceive the public. A remarkable congruence between government policies and information presented to citizens dependably results from the daily policies governing news agencies. The anticommunistic rhetoric articulated by presidents of the United States has been faithfully echoed by the press. Mainstream media reliably avoid sympathetic coverage of the countries currently considered enemies of the Administration: the U.S.S.R., Cuba, Nicaragua, Libya. The *New York Times* coverage of the Nicaraguan and El Salvadorean elections in 1984 provides a good example of editorial policies explicitly favorable to forces supported by the United States government, while simultaneously unsympathetic to powers opposed by government policies. In El Salvador, the Reagan Administration is aiding the present government in its war against rebels, while in Nicaragua, United States money flows to the rebels fighting the established Sandanista Government. Edward Herman has shown that in covering the Nicaraguan elections the United States press relied heavily on reports from rebels, and predictably, in El Salvador rebels were neglected and government officials provided the sources of information for United States press coverage.[70]

As Chomsky points out, reporters could adhere to their policies of objectivity while producing a message clearly biased in favor of government policies. By concentrating its reporting on United States sources, the press can ignore such issues—and the foreign press's reporting of them—as in the case of the United States refusal to abide by the International Court of Justice rulings on United States violations of international law in Nicaragua. The American public has little access to the rest of the world's knowledge of a campaign supported by the United States that includes rape, torture, and other atrocities that are a part of the day-by-day attempt to overthrow the Nicaraguan government. For years neither the United States government nor the press communicated to United States citizens what former CIA Director Stansfield Turner reports is "what we've been trying to do all along . . . All along, there's only been one objective—to overthrow the government of Nicaragua." The United States press, however, continues to report that our objective is primarily to stem the flow of arms from Nicaragua to other Latin American nations, a story that Turner says is "persiflage."[71]

Reporters themselves tend to operate in a closed circle that ignores ideological perspectives that would enable them to understand the hegemony process itself. A recent Gallup Poll shows that print and broadcast journalists receive the bulk of their information on domestic and foreign policy from other journalists in mainstream liberal and conservative news media that represent the dominant corporate-government ideology. While from 60 to 90 percent of them read *Newsweek, Time,* and local daily papers, and the *Wall Street Journal,* only 3 percent of broadcast journalists and 7 percent of print journalists read the reputable leftist weekly, *The Nation.* It is notable that of the twenty-eight publications listed by the journalists as their media sources of information, only *The Nation* can be considered leftist in orientation, unless one considers *The Rolling Stone* leftist.[72]

There is much more that could be written—and has been written—about the ways in which the communications media have institutionalized violations of the principles of a free marketplace of ideas. The news media are only a part of that picture. The entertainment media are perhaps an even greater part, and Todd Gitlin is one among several who have written about the ways in which television programming reinforces rather than questions the dominant ideology.[73] But space is limited, and it is necessary to turn to the role of the schools in hegemony theorists' analysis.

A number of researchers have investigated ways in which the school's organization and conceptual content contribute toward student acceptance of a hierarchical, authoritarian, and unequal social order in a society which claims allegiance to freedom and equality. So examined, the school can be seen as an institution that contributes to the legitimation of the social order by building in young people expectations, dispositions, and ideological commitments that will foster cooperation with the social order without their understanding it. Ideological hegemony theory suggests that it is not consent, but instead compliance, that is fostered in the schools, and that this fostering comes about through both the organization and the conceptual content of what is taught in schools.

Jean Anyon has provided perhaps the most concise accounts of these hegemonic processes in schooling.[74] Three examples of the schools' organizational structures and processes that are relevant here are the hierarchical distribution of power in the schools, the nature of work for students, and the social stratification and grouping that is part of the school structure.

Students quickly learn that the school is an institution in which unequal power relations prevail. They must obey not only the authority of the teacher's knowledge, but the institutionalized authority of the school rules as well. The teacher has authority over students because of the rules of the school. In turn, the teacher herself must obey the rules of the school and the authority of the principal, who in the students' eyes is the root authority, the court of final jurisdiction that governs both the teacher's and the student's behavior. Teachers frequently admit to students that they themselves do not approve of a certain rule, but that they must enforce it because of the requirements of the institution. The grading of students is an example of this. Teachers often tell students that they dislike having to grade them, that it does more harm than good, but that they have no choice in the matter. The message delivered to students is that the hierarchical authority of the institution cannot be questioned, but must be obeyed. This contributes to their perception of the near absolute authority of institutions and a disposition to obey that authority—to comply with the social order of the school—even if they have deep dissatisfaction and disagreements with it. It is just the way things are, and "we all have to live with it." It is not value consent that is being fostered here, but compliance despite dissent, so that compliance becomes a value itself.

Second, the nature of work becomes defined by the structures and processes of school. Work—and only work—is compulsory. One works not because it is intrinsically interesting and satisfying, but because it is assigned. We learn to take for granted that while play may be cooperative (indeed the idea of teamwork is emphasized in sports and extracurricular activities of all kinds), work is individualistic and competitive. It is against the rules to help another person with assigned work, for the nature of the institution is that one person's successful work is in part defined by another person's failure. There are scarce rewards available, and the nature of work is to compete for those scarce rewards. Further, we learn in schools that our successes and failures are due to our individual talents and achievements, not to faults in the institutional structure itself. Winners are credited with their successes, losers are blamed for their failures. The oft-cited personalization of failure fostered by these processes results in such findings as the following. Anyon cites a study in which 102 lower-track fifth-grade students were asked why they were in the low track, and two-thirds of them replied "(because) I am too dumb," or "I can't think good," or other such replies that located their failures in their own talents and efforts.[75] Such a personalization of failure has been cited by such social analysts as Sennett and Cobb as important in legitimizing the unequal distribution of goods in contemporary society. Inequalities of reward are understood in terms of one's own failures or successes in school and the workplace, not in terms of a structure that guarantees—like a grading curve—winners and losers.[76]

This issue of grouping students raises a third of Anyon's examples of organization structures in schooling: the stratification of students. First, students are grouped in a variety of ways in addition to the skill-level grouping already mentioned: they are grouped by teacher, by IQ score, by age, and by classroom behavior, for example. Students receive different kinds of education and, after being grouped very early in their careers, are provided very different opportunities for success. Students come to take these inequalities as natural. Different income groups and different races occupy different tracks, and this, too, is taken for granted, rather than questioned. That blacks, Hispanics, and the children of poor whites should occupy the bottom of the social order does not seem surprising to people who have long ago come to accept this in their institutional experience in schools. There is no consensus that this is a desirable state of affairs, but neither students nor teachers are given an alternative explanation to the view that people deserve what they get on account of their performance levels in the competitive school system. An acceptance of institutionalized inequality in schools becomes an acceptance of institutionalized inequality in the workplace and in society in general: it may not be good, but "it is the way things are."

In addition to the effects of the school's structures and processes, the cognitive content of school curriculum materials must also be considered in an understanding of how hegemonic processes apply to schooling. Students are socialized to the political-economic order not just by practicing it in schools, but by having it portrayed in their texts as desirable and legitimate. This occurs in two general ways: one by inclusion of statements praising our economic and political system and/or disparaging other systems; and the other by exclusion of negative statements about our system and the similar exclusion of statements favorable to competing systems. The first kind of political socialization is sometimes referred to by hegemony theorists as positive inculcation, the second as selective omission. These can be illustrated by examples from social studies textbooks.

An example of positive inculcation is the praise of the free market system that appears in social studies textbooks, the corresponding claim that the United States free market economy is democratic, and the delegitimation of alternative political-economic systems. A Ginn and Co. social studies textbook informs high-school students that "Communes are a failure. . . . There is good reason to believe that the average Chinese is not getting enough food to keep healthy, and in many cases to stay alive."[77] All of these claims are in some measure misleading: there is no free market economy in the United States, and if there were it would not necessarily be democratic. Some of the most antidemocratic abuses of slaves, immigrants, women, and children occurred in a historical period when our country was much less regulated by government than it now is. Similarly, the Chinese communes are a tremendous success when compared to the pervasive starvation, poverty, and death that prevailed in the dynasty these communes replaced. There is a greater incidence of low birthweight infants in the United States today, for example, than in China.[78]

It is not merely beliefs based on mistaken facts that schools inculcate, however; it is general attitudes of patriotism and reverence for authority, no matter how antidemocratic that authority might be. After the Watergate episode raised questions about the presidency in 1972 and 1973, one of the nation's most widely used government texts proclaimed:

> The Presidency is more than executive responsibility. It is an inspiring symbol of all that is highest in American ideals and purposes. No one could think of it except in terms of solemn consecration.[79]

While our system of capitalist democracy and its founders are praised, a number of important details of American social history are selectively omitted. One of these is the role of conflict in producing progressive social change. Anyon's study of high school social studies texts reveals that positive social changes in civil rights, in ending the Vietnam War, in labor unions, and in the women's movement are viewed as triumphs of the legal system and of processes of discussion and bargaining, rather than as results of disruptive protests that often involved violent repression by the police and military. The message explicitly communicated in these texts is that consensus, rather than power or conflict, is what makes history and leads to progress. The effectiveness of protest and militant collective action is selectively omitted.

A related example is omission from history texts of the success of the socialist party early in the twentieth century. If portrayed at all, it is most often portrayed negatively, as an insignificant movement of an irresponsible few.[80]

As Michael Apple points out, a fundamental linkage exists between the overt or implicit messages in school texts and the economics of textbook publishing itself. Some states regulate the political content of their texts, and publishers cannot afford to ignore those guidelines if they want to sell books in those lucrative markets.[81] Texas, for example, is the second largest textbook market in the nation, spending upwards of $50 million a year on schoolbooks. Any textbook used in Texas schools must "promote citizenship and the understanding of the free enterprise system, emphasize patriotism and respect for recognized authority," according to the State Board of Education guidelines. A commission of private citizens oversees the Texas purchase each year to make sure that the guidelines are rigidly observed, and textbook publishers have tailored the content of the books they sell throughout the nation in order not to offend Texan sensibilities. Other states, too, have approved lists of texts that publishers ignore only at risk of market failure.[82]

Given such ideological and economic constraints, it is not surprising to find gross misrepresentations of reality in school texts. In a recent and popular middle-school social studies text, *American Neighbors*, the bulk of the relations between the United States and Latin America are described in entirely friendly terms, dwelling mainly on economic aid to our southern neighbors. When conflict is addressed, it is flatly misrepresented, as in the following passage:

Several times, when some of the Latin American governments were too weak to keep order at home, the U.S. sent armed troops into the countries.

Sometimes the troops went in to collect debts that one nation owed to other nations. At other times they went in to bring order and keep the peace.

Then . . . the U.S. began to realize that it should be more friendly to its southern neighbors. It sent no more troops into their countries, and it began to show respect for their governments.[83]

The truth, of course, is that the United States has successfully carried out a policy of destabilization among left-leaning Latin American nations throughout the past forty years.[84] Our current, admitted policy of trying to overthrow the Nicaraguan government is nothing new. Young people—or their parents, for that matter—trying to understand that policy would have a very difficult time resolving the contradictions between what they are taught in schools and what is taking place in Latin America today. As long as the press remains friendly to administration efforts, the contradictions scarcely arise. But still, signs of a less than virtuous foreign policy surface, for example, in brief accounts of the condemnation of United States policy by the World Court. The content of school texts simply does not equip citizens to make sense of such a news story.

Just as the hegemonic effects of the school can be understood in terms of both school processes and academic content, so can the hegemonic effects of society as a whole be understood in terms of both content and process. By looking at the ideas put forward as correct and legitimate by the schools and the media, for example, and by looking at the alternative ideas omitted, we can get a partial picture of the conceptual content of the dominant ideology. It is important also, however, to look at the ways in which social institutions structure experience in accord with that ideology and with the prevailing power inequalities in contemporary society. When one examines the decision-making processes of the great majority of workplaces, for example, one finds authoritarian, hierarchical structures in which workers do not participate in major decisions that affect their working lives.[85] On the one hand, this hierarchy is legitimized by claims of talent and training on the part of superiors and by the need for efficiency in decision making. On the other hand, the resulting forms of work life are decidedly nondemocratic. This nonparticipatory experience in the workplace—like the citizen's experiencing of decisions determining the nation's foreign and domestic policies— contrasts markedly with the prevailing political rhetoric that United States society is democratic—a rhetoric that is taught authoritatively from the citizen's early school experiences and on throughout an adulthood of media celebrations of the United States as a protector of democracy in the free world. This conflict between the nondemocratic practical relations of daily experience and the culture's proclamations of democracy are rarely analyzed and evaluated in popular discourse. Instead, people live with the contradictions, generally not recognizing them as such. Antonio Gramsci argued this position some fifty years ago, saying that the working person in a capitalist society that claims to be democratic tends to have:

two theoretical consciousnesses (or one contradictory consciousness): one which is implicit in his activity and which in reality unites him with all his fellow-workers in the practical transformation of the real world: and one, superficially explicit or verbal, which he has inherited from the past and uncritically absorbed. But this verbal conception is not without consequences. It holds together a specific social group, it influences moral conduct and the direction of will, with varying efficacity but often powerfully enough to produce a situation in which the contradictory state of consciousness does not permit of any action, any decision or any choice, and produces a condition of moral and political passivity.[86]

Gramsci's account, perhaps, goes a long way toward answering Gaventa's question cited earlier: "Not why rebellion occurs in a 'democracy' but why, in the face of massive inequalities, it does not."

If it is correct, the hegemony theorists' analysis suggests many implications for education. Two of these are fundamental. First, it appears that society is educating in deeply contradictory ways. On the one hand, citizens are taught in the schools and through the media that they live in a democractic society. On the other hand, they are taught through daily experience not to expect participation in fundamental decisions affecting their lives. And, finally, they are not educated by school *or* society to examine and question such contradictions between rhetoric and reality. Instead, citizens learn from an early age to tolerate the contradictions if they see them at all. It requires nothing less than some form of indoctrination to convince people in a hegemonic, nondemocratic society that democracy is working well. Jacques Ellul's classic *Propaganda* argues that we should not be surprised that the most literate classes are the most convinced.[87]

Nowhere, save perhaps through the labor unions to which fewer than a fifth of workers belong, do ordinary citizens have a sustained opportunity to examine the contradictions between democratic slogans and lived experience. With regard to the interests and responsibilities of citizens in a democratic society, the miseducation of the population is thorough and pervasive.

A second dimension of the popular miseducation inherent in cultural hegemony is less obvious, however. This is the dimension that is inherent in what Bachrach calls the "developmental" view of democracy: that democratic forms of life place upon citizens demands and responsibilities that are themselves uniquely educative. As Benne's chapter earlier in this volume notes, Pateman, too, dwells upon this educative function of democracy and locates it in classical democratic theorists such as Rousseau and J. S. Mill. In this view, there is no democratic justification for decisions affecting the many to be made systematically by the few, no matter what the credentials and expertise of the few. On Pateman's account, a democracy stripped of significant, systematic participation by people in the fundamental decisions affecting their lives is not democracy at all. In such an arrangement, the decision makers continue to learn about the world around them in order to make their decisions; they learn from the consequences of their decisions and go on. Those who do not participate in the decision-making process are not required to learn, and they learn little from policies they themselves have had no part in making. The already large educational gap between the powerful and powerless grows greater.

In mid-1983, during a heightened period of publicity over war-torn El Salvador and at a time when United States involvement in Nicaragua was heating up, the *New York Times* and CBS conducted a scientific sampling of citizens' understanding of government policy. The result: "Despite months of controversy over United States policies on Central America . . . only 25 percent of those surveyed knew that the Administration supports the government in El Salvador, only 13 percent knew that it sides with the insurgents in Nicaragua, and only 8 percent knew both alignments."[88]

Involvement in Central America continues to be one of our most important foreign policy and military initiatives in the world, and the power elite has poured scores of millions of dollars into intervention in El Salvador and Nicaragua in the past three years. The American people had a very good reason for not understanding whom we have been supporting, for in the conduct of national affairs, there is no *need* for them to understand. If elite and hegemony theorists are correct, America's version of "democracy" works quite well when the people remain in the dark.

FOOTNOTES

1. Robert A. Dahl, *Who Governs?* (New Haven, Conn.: Yale University Press, 1961). President Eisenhower's address is found in Seymour Melman, *Pentagon Capitalism: The Political Economy of War* (New York: McGraw-Hill, 1970), pp. 235-39.

2. Robert J. Havighurst, "Social Class Influences on American Education," in *Social Forces Influencing American Education*, Sixtieth Yearbook of the National Society for the Study of Education, Part 1, ed. Nelson B. Henry (Chicago: University of Chicago Press, 1961), pp. 120-43.

3. Eisenhower, in Melman, *Pentagon Capitalism*, pp. 237-38.

4. C. Wright Mills, *The Power Elite* (New York: Oxford University Press, 1956).

5. Theodore J. Lowi, "Foreword," in Kenneth Prewitt and Alan Stone, *The Ruling Elites: Elite Theory, Power, and American Democracy* (New York: Harper and Row, 1973), p. xii.

6. A representative sampling of important works in the pluralist tradition include: Robert A. Dahl, *Preface to Democratic Theory* (Chicago: University of Chicago Press, 1956); Samuel P. Huntington, "The United States," in Michael J. Crozier, Samuel P. Huntington, and Joji Watanuki, *The Crisis of Democracy* (New York: New York University Press, 1975), pp. 59-118; William Kornhauser, " 'Power Elite' or 'Veto Groups'?" in Marvin E. Olsen, *Power in Societies* (New York: Macmillan Company, 1970), pp. 282-94; David Riesman, *The Lonely Crowd* (New York: Doubleday Anchor Books, 1953); Joseph A. Schumpeter, *Capitalism, Socialism, and Democracy* (London: George Allen and Unwin, 1943); Sidney Verba and Gary R. Orren, *Equality in America: The View from the Top* (Cambridge, Mass.: Harvard University Press, 1985). Representative elite theory treatments will be noted as they arise in the text.

7. See, for example, Nicholas C. Burbules, "A Theory of Power in Education," *Educational Theory* 36 (Spring 1986): 95-114. See also, David Nyberg, *Power over Power* (Ithaca, N..Y.: Cornell University Press, 1981).

8. G. William Domhoff, *Who Rules America Now? A View for the '80s* (Englewood Cliffs, N.J.: Prentice-Hall, 1983), p. 9.

9. Mills, *The Power Elite*, p. 9; Verba and Orren, *Equality in America*, pp. 180, 182.

10. Domhoff, *Who Rules America Now?*, p. 9; Thomas R. Dye, *Who's Running America? The Reagan Years* (Englewood Cliffs, N.J.: Prentice-Hall, 1983), p. 6.

11. Peter Bachrach, *The Theory of Democratic Elitism: A Critique* (Boston: Little, Brown, and Co., 1967), p. 4.

12. Carole Pateman, *Participation and Democratic Theory* (London and Cambridge: Cambridge University Press, 1970), p. 13.

13. Bachrach, *The Theory of Democratic Elitism*, pp. 7-8.

14. Clarence J. Karier, "Liberalism and the Quest for Orderly Change," in *Roots of Crisis*, ed. Clarence J. Karier, Paul C. Violas, and Joel Spring (Chicago: Rand McNally, 1973), pp. 84-107; Gabriel Kolko, *The Triumph of Conservatism* (New York: Free Press, 1963).

15. Verba and Orren, *Equality in America*, p. 184.

16. Ibid., p. 183.

17. Thomas R. Dye, *Who's Running America?* (Englewood Cliffs, N.J.: Prentice-Hall, 1976), p. 6.

18. Mills, *The Power Elite*, p. 9.

19. Ibid.

20. Prewitt and Stone, *The Ruling Elites*, p. 132.

21. Data in these two paragraphs are from Dye, *Who's Running America? The Reagan Years*, pp. 11-20.

22. Prewitt and Stone, *The Ruling Elites*, p. 135.

23. Federal Bureau of Investigation, *Crime in the United States, 1984*, cited in "Murder Is Closer Than You Think," *Parade Magazine*, 28 September 1986, p. 20.

24. Caroline Hodges Persell and Peter W. Cookson, Jr., *Preparing for Power: America's Elite Boarding Schools* (New York: Basic Books, 1985).

25. Prewitt and Stone, *The Ruling Elites*, p. 144.

26. G. William Domhoff, *The Powers That Be* (New York: Random House, 1978), p. xiv.

27. Ibid.

28. Mills, *The Power Elite*, 283, 288.

29. Ronald Brownstein and Nina Easton, *Reagan's Ruling Class: Portraits of the President's Top 100 Officials* (Washington, D.C.: Presidential Accountability Group, 1982), pp. 532-33.

30. Ralph Nader, "Introduction," in Brownstein and Easton, *Reagan's Ruling Class*, p. vii.

31. Melman, *Pentagon Capitalism*, p. 1.

32. Nader, "Introduction," p. viii.

33. See the analysis in Prewitt and Stone, *The Ruling Elites*, pp. 97-103. See also, Noam Chomsky, *Turning the Tide: U.S. Intervention in Central America and the Struggle for Peace* (Boston: South End Press, 1985), chapter 1; and Joshua Cohen and Joel Rogers, *On Democracy: Toward a Transformation of American Society* (New York: Penguin Books, 1983), pp. 76-81.

34. Prewitt and Stone, *The Ruling Elites*, p. 53.

35. Nader, "Introduction," p. xii.

36. Dye, *Who's Running America: The Reagan Years*, p. 247.

37. Corporate Data Exchange, *Stock Ownership Directory* (New York: Corporate Data Exchange, 1980), pp. 73-74, 89, 108-9, 153, 159-62,170; Edward S. Herman, *Corporate Control, Corporate Power* (New York: Cambridge University Press, 1981), pp. 24, 63.

38. Herman, *Corporate Control, Corporate Power*, p. 201.

39. Domhoff, *Who Rules America Now?*, p. 86.

40. Ibid., p. 87.

41. Huntington, "The United States," pp. 113-14.

42. Nader, "Introduction," p. xi.

43. Prewitt and Stone, *The Ruling Elites*, p. 149.

44. George Orwell, as quoted in Prewitt and Stone, *The Ruling Elites*, p. 158.

45. Prewitt and Stone, *The Ruling Elites*, p. 201.

46. Domhoff, *The Powers That Be*, p. 10. See also chapters 2 through 5.

47. Cohen and Rogers, *On Democracy*, p. 33.

48. Ibid.

49. George Will, "In Defense of Nonvoting," *Newsweek*, 10 October 1983, p. 96.

50. "The Constitution: That Delicate Balance" (Televised documentary by the Media and Society Seminar, School of Journalism, Columbia University, New York, 1985):

51. Ibid.

52. Ibid.

53. Gary Klott, "Senators Won Many Exceptions in Bill to Aid Specific Taxpayers," *New York Times*, 6 June 1986, pp. 1, 26.

54. Evan Thomas, "Peddling Influence," *Time*, 3 March 1986.

55. Domhoff, *The Powers That Be*, pp. 27-28.

56. Ibid., p. 178.

57. John E. Mueller, *War, Presidents, and Public Opinion* (New York: John Wiley and Sons, 1973).

58. Prewitt and Stone, *The Ruling Elites*, p. 237.

59. John Gaventa, *Power and Powerlessness* (Urbana, Ill.: University of Illinois Press, 1980), p. vi.   •

60. T. Jackson Lear, "The Concept of Cultural Hegemony: Problems and Possibilities," *American Historical Review* 90 (June 1985): 567-93.

61. Michael Mann, "The Social Cohesion of Liberal Democracy," *American Sociological Review* 35 (June 1970): 427-28.

62. George Gallup, Jr., *Champaign-Urbana News Gazette*, 27 January 1985.

63. James D. Wright, *The Dissent of the Governed* (New York: Academic Press, 1976), pp. 129, 140-41.

64. Ibid., pp. 140-41.

65. Ben H. Bagdikian, *The Media Monopoly* (Boston: Beacon Press, 1983), p. 63.

66. Ibid., p. 21.

67. Philip Taubman, "The Perils of Reporting from Moscow," *New York Times Magazine*, 21 September 1986.

68. John Rothchild, "Stories Reporters Don't Write," in *Inside the System*, ed. Charles Peters and James Fallows (New York: Praeger, 1976), pp. 295-305.

69. Dye, *Who's Running America*, p. 85.

70. Edward Herman, *Covert Action Information Bulletin* (Spring 1984): 140.

71. Chomsky, *Turning the Tide*, p. 94.

72. "The Media's Media," *Harper's Magazine* 268 (April 1984): 28.

73. Todd Gitlin, "Television Screens: Hegemony in Transition," in *Cultural and Economic Reproduction in Education*, ed. Michael W. Apple (London: Routledge and Kegan Paul, 1982), pp. 202-246.

74. Jean Anyon, "Ideology and U.S. History Textbooks," *Harvard Educational Review* 49 (August 1979): 361-84; idem, "Schools as Agencies of Social Legitimation," *Journal of Curriculum Theorizing* 3 (Summer 1981): 86-103; idem, "Social Class and Social Knowledge," *Curriculum Inquiry* 11, no. 1 (1981): 3-42.

75. Anyon, "Schools as Agencies of Social Legitimation," p. 90.

76. Richard Sennett and Jonathan Cobb, *The Hidden Injuries of Class* (New York: Random House, 1972).

77. Anyon, "Schools as Agencies of Social Legitimation," p. 95.

78. David Wallechinsky, "We're Number One," *Parade Magazine*, 21 September 1986, p. 5.

79. Anyon, "Schools as Agencies of Social Legitimation," p. 94.

80. Anyon, "Ideology and U.S. History Textbooks," pp. 369-70.

81. Michael Apple, "The Political Economy of Textbook Publishing," *Educational Theory* 34 (Fall 1984): 307-20.

82. John H. Faulk, "Texas Texts," *The Nation*, 2 October 1982, p. 292.

83. Prudence Cutright and Loyal Durand, Jr., *American Neighbors* (New York: Macmillan and Co., 1980), p. 446.

84. Chomsky, *Turning the Tide*, pp. 58-84.

85. This well-established theme in social science research was recently treated in Martin Carnoy and Henry M. Levin, *Schooling and Work in the Democratic State* (Stanford, Calif.: Stanford University Press, 1985). See also Arthur Wirth's chapter in this volume.

86. Lear, "The Concept of Cultural Hegemony," p. 569.

87. Jacques Ellul, *Propaganda: The Formation of Men's Attitudes* (New York: Vintage Books, 1963), p. 11.

88. Adam Clymer, "Poll Finds Americans Don't Know U.S. Positions on Central America," *New York Times*, 1 July 1983, p. 1.

Part Three
SCHOOL AND SOCIETY

CHAPTER VIII

Changing Perspectives on Schools
and Schooling

MAXINE GREENE AND MARY ANNE RAYWID

Previous chapters have dealt with changing social institutions and social conditions, and with their educative and miseducative effects on people of all ages. The authors of those chapters have not dealt with the changed institutions of public schooling. While society educates through many channels, schools remain important agencies of education, and their changing status in the minds of the public requires examination. We seek and expect different things from schools than did parents of earlier times. We value them differently and ascribe different roles to them in our lives.

To speak of changes in public schools must be to take into account the ways in which the people who pay their cost and provide their clients perceive the enterprise of schooling and what it signifies for their children and their future lives. We generally agree today that the "reality" of schools, like that of social reality in general, is a constructed reality. Members of any given culture structure their experiences with the aid of common symbol systems; they learn and share a range of prejudgments that inform what they perceive and what they believe; and, for these reasons, they inhabit a common world. There are variations, however, that make a difference over time. Personal biographies make a difference, as do group memberships, whether of race, religion, nationality, sex, or social class. It would appear that the wants, hopes, and expectations of persons with regard to education need to be taken into account if we are to grasp the ways in which the schools have transacted and now transact with the world around them.

What parents have wanted for their children has always had a significant impact on the part played by schools in the communally lived lives of their publics. Expressions of what they have wanted (and hoped for, and expected) do not always tally with what education officials have said was needed; nor has the discourse of parents always been consonant with that of professional educators. But if we are to understand how schooling is perceived today, it may be useful to examine the ways in which perceptions have changed over time. Our approach in this chapter is to highlight paradigmatic parent voices, each speaking at a different moment in the twentieth century—in 1900, in 1935, and in 1985. We charge our spokespersons with conveying their own sense of what life is about, as influenced by varying sets of social and historical circumstances and different personal and social backgrounds. It is out of their sense of what life can and should be that come their hopes for the futures of their own children. And it is these hopes that in turn shape what parents seek and expect from schools.

We realize how seldom such voices have been heard. Social scientific discourse and administrative discourse have more often than not been relied upon to describe and explain "grass roots" attitudes or parental demands. It is only lately, with the growing interest in ethnography and qualitative research, that educators have begun paying heed to the perspectives of those most directly affected by what happens in classrooms and other educative situations. In this chapter we have, as it were, drawn on a diverse literature for the sake of creating three voices we hope will be evocative.[1] Like Mrs. Loman in Arthur Miller's *Death of a Salesman*, we believe that attention must be paid "to individuals," in this case to the hopes of parents for their children and the expectations of schooling which ensue.

It is evident enough that what people seek for their children and what they expect of the schools are functions of their perspectives on the social world and on their own situations within that world. Much depends as well on how they interpret messages having to do with upward mobility, the uses of literacy, the "right" to the pursuit of happiness. The concreteness of the lived present as well as past experiences and stored memories influence their responses. So does the way in which individuals hear and mediate the metaphors and modes of sense-making that are current in their communities. Surely, talk of "equal opportunity" is heard in one manner by an immigrant from a Polish *shtetl*, in another by a black migrant from the rural South. It will mean one thing to someone intent on pursuing success through his or her own efforts and another to someone so deprived as to feel helpless in a confusing world. The very notion of "book-learning" will mean (and has meant) something different to rural people than to urban people. The fact of heterogeneity in our country has to be held in mind whenever wants and expectations are identified. The "common school," the "schoolhouse," the homogeneous school, the centralized school, and lately the magnet or alternative school—all these mean variously to publics in different parts of the country and at different moments in history. As importantly, each holds a distinctive promise and arouses a distinctive expectation, depending on how it is understood.

Class membership, even if unacknowledged, has also affected what parents want or expect for their children. We are familiar with working-class families whose sons (and later, daughters) fully expected to follow their fathers into mills, factories, and mines—and into the unions that sustained many over time. Working conditions were often difficult, but in spite of exploitation and alienation there was also pride associated with skilled, socially useful work, along with the attraction of brotherhood and sisterhood in work situations. We have only to note the passionate responses to plant closings and relocations today to acknowledge the connections between expectations and perceived futures for the young. For many, it is true, the schools have been expected to make upward mobility possible; but for others, they have been expected to teach the kinds of skills and values that would insure an intergenerational continuity in work lives seen to be worthwhile.

We are becoming increasingly familiar, too, with so-called "welfare families," whose members seem (often for good reason) to have found little hope in schooling, no matter what has been proposed in the way of literacy and useful skills. And we have always been aware of the Scarsdales and Newtons and Pasadenas, those places where parents have expected and still expect the best in the way of challenge and stimulation from their schools, and where they generally receive the best.

Religious, ethnic, and national traditions have played significant parts as well. Different priority systems have been evident where education (and books and literacy and work values) are concerned. Different weights have been placed on group loyalty and cultural membership. One of the more dramatic changes we find is in the expectations of fundamentalist Christians, who once took for granted the overlap between their own beliefs and nonsectarian curricula (or "the civic religion"), and who now make charges of "secular humanism" against contemporary schooling and express wants unfulfillable by ordinary public schools. Lately, in part fueled by the upsurge in immigration from the Far East, we are finding sophisticated pragmatic (usually technical) demands made upon schools by parents deliberately rearing their young for disciplined pursuit of vocational and personal success.

For all the particularities of perspective, for all the class and cultural diversities, the core of shared experience in the United States has been sufficient to insure a willing clientele, if not what John Dewey called an "articulate public,"[2] for the public schools. Obviously, one of the major changes has been the growing influence of television and its imposition of what might be called a common curriculum, including information, values, attitudes, and even what are registered as needs. Entangled with that (and other agencies within the culture in addition to schools) is an effort to transmit a particular, though differentially expressed, "way of life." For each of the special interests and diversities in the United States, this effort is what underlies and informs the nation's commitment to socialization and enculturation of younger generations.

Whether we see the process as a process of normalization or domination or mystification or simple adaptation, our society (like most others) identifies through its educational representatives certain patterns of behavior, clusters of skills, belief systems, and ways of knowing that are to be learned (that must be learned) by anyone expecting to participate, to provide for his or her own subsistence, to "make it" in any way at all. Schooling becomes, in consequence, one of the areas in which the requirements of cultural continuity (or reproduction, or renewal) mesh with what are perceived to be the needs of individuals and families, whether those needs are natural or artificial. What we are attempting to do in these pages is to provide some indications of how persons themselves, parents in particular, have experienced and articulated those needs.

We believe it possible to display shifts in the fabric of want, hope, and expectation by singling out certain individual voices, even if no one can be said to be representative of all there are. For all our differences, every voice speaks to a degree out of something that is shared in America, out of a common taken-for-grantedness, a commonsense reality. We have selected for our first parent voice that of a Jewish immigrant woman at the turn of the century. She offers a view of the new world and its possibilities, and of the school's role in realizing

them, that has been important in shaping the nature of our society and
its schools. The immigrant Jewish voice of the early century is
idiosyncratic in the sense that a long tradition of literacy and
cosmopolitanism lies behind it, even if the particular individual was
not in any ordinary sense an intellectual. It should be noted also that
many of the values inherent in that tradition were closely identified
with those in the Judeo-Christian mainstream of American thought. It
is not of incidental importance that the early Puritans, who left an
indelible stamp on the schools, also saw themselves as the "chosen
people," spoke in the language of the Old Testament, and forged a
work ethic and commitment to universal literacy certainly
recognizable, in its latter-day cultural embodiment, by newly arrived
Jews.

It might be said as well that the wants and expectations of the first
speaker here may have been functions of a recognition that Jewish
families had the potential for success in an urbanized, industrial
culture. They were cosmopolitan; they were also "survivors." They
had proved to themselves that they could undergo dislocation,
suffering, and discrimination in the effort to find security, if not
success. We have only to think back to the lives they had lived in
Poland and Russia, to the difficulties involved in escaping those lives,
to the culture shocks and strains experienced in trying to maintain
their traditions and at once adjust to a not always hospitable New
World. In addition, various Holocaust studies have made us realize
that millions remained behind in Eastern Europe by choice and for a
range of reasons. A number of scholars have concluded that those who
uprooted themselves often were the risk-takers, the stubbornly
hopeful ones, those who demanded more of life than the survival of
the "People." Perhaps it is this sort of quality among those who came
that accounts for the optimism and high hopes of this mother.

1900

You ask what I want for my children and what I expect them to find in this
new world. The biggest thing is chance and opportunity. Here, everybody
has a chance. In the old country, laws limited what our people could do, and
where we could live, and who could go to school. And although our lives are
not so easy now, our children will change that for themselves and their
children. I want them to have more of the good things than we have had, and
I'm sure they will. There are jobs here and many opportunities to make a
good living. So many new things are coming here all the time. There are
horseless carriages and people say there will soon be a lot more. And electric
lights and telephones in some people's houses. Americans don't seem afraid of

changes, so new things happen all the time and there are new businesses and factories and opportunities.

But for now, while they are young, there is the opportunity for my children to learn and to know. It's not like the old country where only the fortunate could enjoy books. Here, there are schools, even colleges, and libraries that are free. It is a family celebration as one by one our children become old enough for their own library cards. They take advantage of them, too, and read a lot.

We have not found streets paved with gold here, but when things seem hard, I remember the old country. Here, there will never be cossacks at the door and my sons will not disappear into the czar's army forever. We don't have to fear that our home will be destroyed and our things taken by the police. And on top of that, there is the chance for so much more for our children—to know more and be more and do more than has been ours.

I hope for my children that theirs will be happy homes. They must choose wisely the partner with whom to share a life. It should be someone who will keep the sabbath and not forget the old ways or the faith of our fathers. For finally we have found a place where we can pursue those ways without interference.

I want my children to love their new country and to remember all their lives their debt to it. They must be willing to preserve its freedoms. Its flag is precious. We are Americans now, and I want us all to be good Americans, and good Jews too.

My children should take seriously the responsibility to use their lives wisely and to make something of themselves. We try to make them understand how much school will help them. We tell them to study hard and do what the teachers tell them to. That is the way to learn and to get ahead and to be a good citizen. School is the gateway. I want my children to become the kind of people who can recognize the opportunities open to them and who will have the knowledge and discipline to make good on such opportunities.

For this woman, hope and promise are dominant themes. The fears which had to be borne in the old life have receded, and she envisions chances for her children that go far beyond the opportunities the old world afforded even to the fortunate. For this one is a world where growth and novelty are so visible that new possibilities continue to open. Such a sense, we have since had cause to learn, is uniquely tied to periods of economic expansion; but it is a sense that can dominate the outlooks of those who live at such a point in history. It is linked with the deeply embedded belief that growth means progress, and the two undergirded the widespread expectation that life would be better for their children than for those who immigrated here. Our immigrant mother's enthusiasm explicitly extends to the new nation, and she wants her children to embrace it and to recognize its uniqueness. Indeed, some of the patriotic fervency of the immigrants was so intense as later to make their children uncomfortable at its display.

Literacy itself is also a central commitment for this parent. So school becomes valuable in itself—not only for its instrumental value in opening the doors to success, but intrinsically valuable in opening the world of books. The young are privileged to receive such a precious gift as schooling, and it is their obligation to make good use of it.

Yet at the same time as this turn-of-the-century mother wants her children to learn about the new nation and to become a part of its economic and civic life, she expects them to keep the old ways intact in their private lives. Within their homes, they are to retain and pursue the faith and culture of the fathers. It would be some years before the difficulties of simultaneously pursuing these two objectives, and of coping with their incongruities, became more fully evident and tempered some of the early enthusiasm.

Is our parent voice truly representative of others of the time? It surely articulates one version of the "American Dream": the sense of promise and opportunity, and the strong belief that things will be better for one's children, the next generation. It is this conviction that enabled many living under very adverse conditions to identify with the promise of the future rather than with the squalor of their own lives. The belief in upward mobility was strong, as was at least for many the belief that education is the means to realizing that goal. Finally, there is the bond, the strong identification with the new nation—and the desire to be an active part of it.

Like other immigrant groups, Eastern European Jews were unique in many ways. It seems clear, however, that in the early years of the century virtually all immigrant groups were responding to the promise inscribed on the Statue of Liberty. An overwhelming percentage of those who came emerged from "huddled masses yearning to breathe free," whether they came from Russian cities, from peasant villages in southern Italy, from rural Ireland, or from the mountains in troubled Greece. Our picture of the feelings and aspirations of the turn-of-the-century parent derives largely from the experience of the Eastern European Jewish immigrant, as rendered in existing accounts of life in urban ghettos at the beginning of the century.

Overcrowded buildings must be envisaged, along with crowds of strangers on the thronging streets. It was a time when little but private philanthropic social support was available. Garment workers, it is true, had their unions. There were synagogue and church groups; there were political bosses and ward heelers. Many children worked and lived on the streets; they were newsboys, errand boys, ragpickers. The schools, often, were community schools, neighborhood schools in the true sense; children attended with children from surrounding streets, sometimes (although not always) of the same nationality. For people intent on relying on their own strength and their own skills, the public school was expected to open the way. For many, it did precisely that: it taught the children to speak English; it acquainted them with the heterogeneity of those who call themselves American; it taught fundamental literacies. Perhaps because a vital home life, synagogue life, and even a cafe life persisted in the cities, the schools may be said to have met such expectations as those articulated above.

The commitment to family, the hope for happiness, the perception of opportunity: these would characterize the articulated experience of most members of all of the immigrant groups of the period. But there were significant differences among them. Leonard Covello has written of the Italian peasant's disinterest in extended schooling, his view that the survival skills could best be taught in the family. Among the interferences by the Italian government in their lives, compulsory education had been among the most painful; and Covello said that southern Italians "considered it more of a burden than a blessing."[3] According to reports, truancy was encouraged by Italian families, who believed the young would learn more at work than at school. Also, there tended to be a suspicion of books and a conviction that chance had more to do with success than schooling. Thus, as James Sanders has said, we cannot assume "that all Americans shared the same attitudes toward mobility."[4]

But the turn-of-the-century period was an age of political progressivism; and the reformist hopes and confidence marking many intellectuals and well-meaning members of the White, Anglo-Saxon, Protestant (WASP) middle class could not but have fed the expectations of immigrant newcomers. The very existence of settlement houses in New York and Chicago promoted a consciousness of open doors and educational possibilities. The fresh air of what sometimes felt like a resurgent Jeffersonian liberalism touched even the slum-bound uprooted, homesick for their own countries very often, yet yearning for better lives for their children in the new world. Recent research has led many educators to recognize tracking or controlling mechanisms that long went unidentified in public schools;

and the excesses of early "Americanization" have by now been made clear.[5] It was in 1900 that a New Orleans Normal School principal wrote that the teacher was obligated to bring different nationalities "to the Anglo-Saxon (WASP) standard, train them to self-control that means freedom, the love of country that foreshadows the brotherhood of man. . . ." As he saw it, this required a teacher's knowledge of "the mazes of inherited tendencies" and the "shackles of ancestral bondage."[6] But in their eagerness to become part of the new world, none of this could fully eradicate immigrant hopes or the gratitude our chosen spokesperson expressed.

It must be held in mind that the early-century period was one of industrial expansion as well as of expanded opportunities to launch small shops and business establishments. At the very least, the schools offered what were viewed as the essential tools of language and of literacy. Many simply assumed without questioning that cultural loyalties could be maintained while those skills were being mastered. The point was to become literate enough to pursue independence and success in a country where, as it turned out, the streets were not paved with gold. There were no Czarists here, no Cossacks, relatively few marauders riding down from the hills. Schools might cramp children, might impose an alien way. But they offered young people power to open doors, to choose their own roads in what still looked like an open world. It must be added that none of this describes the lot of most black Americans of the period, whose world was circumscribed by Jim Crow laws and separatist norms. The resulting caste system closed off the American Dream to all but the physically hardiest and the stubbornest. It was not until many decades later that blacks could reasonably take on such aspirations. Many would say that time has not even yet arrived for most.

The First World War brought with it a restiveness with regard to old pieties and beliefs, even the belief in the "promise" of America. It was followed by varying bouts of internecine difficulties, by fears of radicalism and dissent, by campaigns against "foreign" ideologies and those who espoused them, by the halting of immigration from many European countries. It is difficult now to assess the full impact of the newly invented test and measurement devices on public expectations of the schools or on parent hopes when it came to the promise of the schools for the young. We do not know the particular effect of the emphasis on "manual training" for some and on their future jobs. We do realize, however, how many people turned toward the schools as symbols of hope, rather than to trade union or revolutionary action, when economic depression shattered complacencies and eroded hopes. The social order might have needed changing if children's futures were to be secured; but there seemed to be a widespread consensus that education was to be preferred over class struggle and battling over ownership in the streets as a way of change.

* * *

In the New Deal period, the federal government put far more stress on extraeducational agencies than it did on schools in its efforts to counter economic crisis. But it did promote the Civilian Conservation Corps, the National Youth Administration to help poor young people through college, and adult education through the Works Progress Administration. And members of the public maintained a stubborn confidence in education as a motor of change. The essential conservatism and nostalgia characteristic of many (particularly in small and medium-sized towns) can be seen in our second speaker's hopes for his children in the middle of an unprecedented economic depression, even though the need for sizable changes was not absent from his thoughts. In the large cities there was outspoken rage against "bankers," "business men," and those Franklin Roosevelt called "economic Tories"—certainly enough to justify George Counts in making the demand that the schools concern themselves with deliberately changing the social order.[7] Reading Counts, reading *The Social Frontier* (a journal published in New York City in the 1930s), we cannot be sure how much the public (even in Manhattan) shared the deep restiveness Counts felt and expressed. The policy statement of *The Social Frontier* reported "the death of laissez-faire individualism and the concomitant rise of collective planning and control." It also spoke of education's role "in advancing the welfare and interests of the great masses of the people who do the work of society—those who labor on farms and ships and in the mines, shops, and factories of the world."[8]

It is doubtful, however, that most people in the small towns and school districts of America saw things in such terms. There remained a desperate fidelity to traditional values, including the value of traditional schooling. In the Lynds' study of "Middletown" (Muncie, Indiana) in the late 1920s, resistance to educational "progressivism" was evident. For all their increasingly practical emphasis, the schools still mirrored the factories in their regimentation. When the Lynds returned for a reassessment of Middletown ten years later, and published *Middletown in Transition* in 1937, the schools had become still more bureaucratized and more "efficient" in managing a larger, less selected student body. The published "philosophy of education," as the Lynds themselves pointed out, expressed the professional educators' view in stressing the development of each child's individual powers through engagement "in useful and lifelike activities."9 It seems unlikely that, in the middle of the depression, most parents would have expressed themselves or their expectations in such liberal terms. And yet, doubts about the adequacy of our economic system began to occur in minds all over the country. Our second spokesperson is a midwestern workman.

1935

What do I want for my children? After the last six years of depression, I'm tempted to say, "Jobs!" But that's certainly not the whole answer. Yet without a job with pay to support himself and his family, a man's a nothing in our country. I worked on a WPA job for a while and most people didn't think it was a real job—more like I was on the dole—and oddly enough I felt much the same way, though, at the same time, I'm proud of the park we built.

They tell me the company I worked for before I was laid off is putting in automatic machinery. So my old job is being washed out. I'll have to learn some new one all over again when things start moving—unless I want to pump gas the rest of my life. I've wondered more than once whether my Dad made a mistake in moving into town. At least on the farm we didn't have to worry about the next meal. Things have got to get better soon though. Maybe the government in Washington can set things right. But people are beginning to say there's nothing that can really stop depressions. Maybe a country's like a person who feels good one day and rotten the next, and you've just got to wait for things to heal.

I've been thinking a lot about the wise sayings I learned as a kid and wondering if some of them are so wise. Any man, my folks taught me, can get ahead in America if he works hard, is thrifty, and spends his spare time improving himself. But I sure haven't got ahead the past few years and I'm not sure where I've been foolish either. I did fairly well in grade school, and even started high school. Sometimes I wonder if the man who doesn't have money to start with really can make it by himself. I can't understand how what's been happening to me really is "my just deserts," as Dad used to say.

My wife tells me that sometimes I sound like a radical. I'm not and she knows it. I believe President Roosevelt when he says things are going to be good again and for all of us, too. And when they are, I want my kids to be better prepared for the world than I was when we moved to town from the farm. Boy, was I green! I want my kids to grow up as good, honest, God-fearing people, with a firm hold on what life's all about. But they also need to be well-trained for a job that's likely to last and pay better than mine ever did. A man owes it to himself and his family—even to his country—to succeed.

They don't have to be rich, but when they reach my age, I want my children to have something to show for it.

I don't know just how they're going to get there. But I'm still sure that a good education will be part of it. School is their best way to get ahead. I never finished high school, but tough as things are, I want to be sure my kids do. Maybe even go beyond. The more schooling the better. It pays off. With all the setbacks, I may never be able to make much of myself, but I want my kids to. Going to school is the best way around the school of hard knocks.

For those who can remember the Great Depression of the 1930s, its mention almost unfailingly rouses feelings of compassion—for the era and those who lived it. Our father-spokesperson reflects the uneasy mix of hope and pessimism with which so many lived for a decade. His belief in the future sometimes becomes so tenuous as to suggest desperation (things will get better because they've simply *got* to . . .) and he is not entirely sure that even governments can cope. Yet despite it all, he retains the traditional belief that the individual makes his or her *own* way—and that dedication and pursuit of the traditional values can enable us each to rise to our own earned level. By and large, life values remain clearer for this worker-father than the means for realizing them. He expresses many doubts; but his faith in traditional values and virtues remains extensively intact. Despite his own predicament, and the threat of unemployment, he rejects solutions that would entail radical departures from the past. Whatever doubts he may harbor, they have not lessened this parent's belief in education. School, he seems to suggest, will enable his children to escape their father's predicament. Education remains the key to a more successful life, and at least something of a safety net against adversity.

For this midwestern working man, then, and for many like him, the American Dream survived the strains of the Great Depression. Surely the optimism of our early century immigrant mother is gone, and this worker father is beginning to expose some of the tensions and contradictions in The Dream: where did he go wrong to bring about his own misfortunes—or did he? Some dawning doubts are beginning to appear about the old verities, and questions about such fundamental institutions as government and business are not far from surfacing. But the faith in education remains unshaken. In fact, schooling may be even more essential in a world that's simply not going according to traditional expectations.

Numbers of desperate people at that time, anxiously clinging to old hopes and old dreams, were as unaware of the inattention of large taxpayers to education as they were of the school's increasing professionalization, reliance on expertise, and rejection of lay control. And, certainly, the average citizen of Muncie, Indiana, say, would not be likely to express unease at the burgeoning inequalities among and within the schools. It may be that most of the public were given no significant alternatives to public schooling in its traditional forms. As our speaker-father made clear, even a general fatalism and an inability to comprehend what was happening to ordinary people did not extinguish the old educational faith. And this was at the moment before the Second World War when no serious student of American society was sure whether the private economic system could ever again provide for the needy, the half-skilled, the newcomer.

* * *

The world of today appears quite a different one from that of 1935, yielding a consciousness of profoundly altered expectations, and a bewildering awareness of unsolved problems with respect to the purposes of American public schools. At once, we experience a great contradiction between the generalized prescriptions inherent in the various so-called school "reform" reports and the multiple realities of cultural life today.

Official stress is laid on testing, merit pay, common learnings, higher standards, rigor, mastery, vouchers, and school prayers, all ostensibly in the interests of restoration of the work ethic, of national defense, and of technological and military primacy in the world. Society at large, increasingly divided between the extraordinarily wealthy and the abysmally poor, is racked by the consequences of a widely heralded budget deficit used to justify an erosion of social spending and social utilities, while military spending rises year by year. Specters of homelessness and child hunger haunt the streets and television screens; and the population generally, ineffective and powerless, takes refuge in private enclaves. The clamor of official and "cost-benefit" talk silences people more and more; the hope of an "articulate public" recedes. On the one hand, the public's expectations of the schools are fed by promises of opportunity in the advancing "high technological" age; on the other, the number of high school dropouts increases annually, grim testimony to underprivileged young people's loss of faith in schools. In the middle class, there are hopes that the school will prepare young people for the "safe" and lucrative professions; among the working class, deprived of hope for the sort of work life of the older generation, people are urged to expect some moderate status in what are called the "service industries."

Whether intended or not, the ends of schooling have become explicitly vocational. Education and the economy are the watchwords, not education and personal growth, not education and the informed citizen.

Still, there are cultural memories; there are openings made in the past that cannot be overlooked. Images of the 1950s: the earlier onslaught against the schools because of their "softness," slackness, relativism, neglect of "essentials," avoidance of "discipline." There are recollections of the Soviet satellite, Sputnik, in many senses the herald of a new space age (reaching a lurid apotheosis in the crash of Challenger II). It is not difficult to recall the reactive outcry about the way the United States was falling behind in science and engineering education (in an earlier "rising tide of mediocrity"); nor is it difficult to recall the talent searches, the merit prizes, the curriculum reform movements that engaged university scholars almost for the first time in reconstructing what was to be taught in schools. Piagetianism, the Woods Hole Conference, Jerome Bruner's emphasis on "discovery," the "New Math," the "teacher-proof" curricula, the institutes, the grants, the beginnings of a federal role in education: for a moment it seemed that the middle-class public, at least, would be brought to support cognitive learning, disciplinary learning.

But a sea change in society was on its way. The "invisible" poor, and the ethnics, suddenly became visible—or were rendered visible— following the election of John F. Kennedy, our first Roman Catholic, our first non-WASP President. The Civil Rights Movement, reaching a high tide with the March on Washington in 1963, turned national attention away from talent searches and science and technical education toward the long excluded, the discriminated against, the deprived. The larger implications of the Supreme Court decision (*Brown vs. Board of Education of Topeka*, 1954) against school segregation became clear. A national obligation to compensate for the years of inequality and injustice suffered by blacks seemed, for a moment, to be recognized. Literature began appearing—James Baldwin's *The Fire Next Time*, Claude Brown's *Manchild in the Promised Land*, *The Autobiography of Malcolm X*, Jonathan Kozol's *Death at an Early Age*—and suddenly members of the educational community, along with others, became imaginatively engaged with lived lives they had never known before. It is at least conceivable that, for a few years in the 1960s, the "eclipse of the public" was overcome; and people were beginning to expect that the schools, in compensating for and remedying the effects of injustice, would realize some of the nation's fundamental values and bring into becoming a truly democratic pluralist community. But the conservative backlash was only delayed.

We recall the Elementary and Secondary Education Act, the efforts made to draw attention to injustices done to girls and women over the years, to the handicapped, to foreign language speakers, to a variety of other minorities as well as blacks. Surely, these enactments and innovations altered public expectations and, for a while, enhanced public faith in what education could achieve. The confidence (which should still be remembered, even if it cannot be maintained) was short-lived. There was the Coleman Report on educational inequality, making the appalling point that the crucial variable, after all, was the family and prior preparation for schooling. Testing was made central; the only viable remedy offered was to increase the number of middle-class children where black children went to school. By then we were deeply involved in the Vietnam War, and the fearful chain of assassinations began to constrict our hopes and ideals. A kind of malaise was widely felt with respect to what could be done to make equality possible by means of education. No one was entirely surprised by the book by Christopher Jencks et al., *Inequality: A Reassessment of Family and Schooling in America* which appeared in 1972.[10] The schools were marginal when it came to effecting economic equality, wrote Jencks; success in society was due, as much as anything else, to contingency or luck. Since, in the face of structural inequities and economic injustices, the schools could do so little, they might as well be "satisfying places to be."

The so-called "radical" or "revisionist" criticism of the schools, ranging from the libertarian-anarchist to the Marxist, exposed economic, structural, and ideological issues never confronted before in our educational literature. The so-called "myth" of public education was exposed: in a pecuniary or capitalist society, the schools could neither equalize nor liberate. Their object rather was to impose a way of life, to reproduce an insufficient culture, to domesticate individuals, to fix them on predefined steps in a hierarchy. All of this was sustained by the bureaucratic organization of the schools and by the ways in which schools met the requirements of a stratified society. The hope lay in abandonment of the structures, in the creation of "free schools," or in resistance—either through the formation of revolutionary cadres or "reflective communities" within the schools themselves. There were those who called for more parental authority, more student control. There were others who called on teachers to recognize their own "proletarianization" and, in association with fellow workers throughout society, to reform the schools. And then there were those who argued for community control through local boards and authorities, in the hope that a restoration of local community control might bring the schools closer to the expressed needs of the people, even as it provided opportunities for people to discover and articulate their needs.

It is difficult to know whether or not the public at large resonated to these political and intraprofessional arguments, since what was most visible as the 1970s wore on turned out to be struggles over busing, neighborhood schools, "white flight," and the rest. Efforts to integrate, efforts to overcome the age-long racial separations sometimes (given time) enriched the idea of the "common" when it came to schools. As often, it made the idea of "common" increasingly problematic, even as it made the idea of "public" questionable. Professional educators met the various attacks, not by a reaffirmation of the values long associated with the American public school, but by proposals for a focus on "competencies," measurable performance, basic skills. Assuming that the public, with all its doubts, wanted assurances that the "output" of the schools matched the financial "input" and wanted the kind of "quality control" typical of industry, school leaders responded with accountability plans, new modes of testing, proffered guarantees. Wrongly or rightly, many took for granted that public expectations stemmed from acquaintance with industrial achievement, industrial calculations. And it is clear enough that, as uncertainty increased and the economy began changing, the public seemed to want a focus on the basics and whatever could be done to help their children meet "market demand."

All this helped validate renewed preoccupations with assessment and evaluation, for all the occasional questions raised with respect to testing in general. As social concern eroded on the federal level, as a not so "benign" indifference replaced active interest in human rights, human needs, public housing, public health, affirmative action, equity proceedings, and the rest, people's expectations narrowed and focused further where education was concerned. Privatism, narcissism, dreary fears about the future of the children somehow merged into a desire for measurable achievement, if nothing else. Presenting themselves more and more frequently in terms of professional expertise and technicalization, schools as institutions seemed more and more remote from immediate parental concerns.

Our third spokesperson bespeaks many of these events and disappointments insofar as the middle-class individual is representative in a conservative, privatized, disenchanted America. What he or she says about what he or she wants for the children somehow deepens the silence among the threatened farmers in the midwest, the dislocated workers in the south and the northeast, the Hispanic immigrants, the hopeless ghetto adolescents, the single parent families, the mothers of teenage mothers, the thousands of would-be computer programmers, the opponents of abortion, the supporters of evangelist preachers, the homeless, the young families in declining milltowns, those living on back roads. But what this last spokesperson has to say must be heeded as a challenge to anyone who takes responsibility today for policymaking or for administering or for teaching in the public schools.

1985

What do I want for my kids? Of course I want them to be happy, but I'm not too sure what that takes. And I'm not sure the world can sustain much happiness for long. Maybe. It's hard to tell.

My folks seemed so sure about what life is and how it should be lived. What's happened to us that so many of my generation aren't at all sure about such matters? President Reagan speaks for those who think that if we try hard enough we can become what our parents and grandparents were. I almost wish we could but I'm not sure. Somehow the world seems so much different. It's not just the people who have changed, it's everything.

I know my kids sometimes worry about whether they'll grow up at all, or whether The Bomb will drop first. I can't believe anybody would be stupid enough to press that button, but with all the kooks and crazies in the world, who knows. Just because you're in power doesn't mean you're sane; and governments can be as crazy as individuals. In fact, when you watch the evening news, it sometimes seems the whole world's gone crazy.

It's hard to know how to steer kids under such conditions. My folks brought me up to expect and go after a better life than theirs. But the world seems to be going backwards in that respect. Jobs that lead to high incomes and good futures just aren't there unless you're born into a rich family or happen to be a football star. And that stuff about job commitment and satisfaction, forget it! In my thirteen years since college, I've not had a job interesting enough to get excited over—and I guess the chances are it wouldn't last even if I had. They're saying now that people will probably have to change vocations six or seven different times during a lifetime. So there's no sense teaching kids to care too much about what they're going to do for a living.

On the other hand, you may not be doing them much of a favor by getting them to care too much about their families either. I used to think you could count on families. But since neither my "ex" nor I came from large families, my kids don't even have aunts and uncles and cousins. My folks think our marriage might have lasted if only one of us had been working. But we couldn't have bought a house without two salaries and we both wanted that.

So what do you teach your kids to value most, if you can't count on much permanence in families or vocations? It's hard to tell them to look beyond themselves and those they know. President Kennedy's ringing "Ask what you can do for your country" sounds about as out-of-it-all as the dinosaurs. Public institutions including governments are just too out of control, if not out-and-out corrupt, to send kids into. It doesn't even pay to vote, much less to spend real time and effort on improving things.

So do you try to bring up your kids to be honest, open, trusting people? But if so, with whom? That's certainly not such sound advice for city kids. And the number of country kids gets smaller and smaller. It seems that there are more and more people to be feared these days, not met with honesty and openness. Besides, most of the people we see today don't enter our lives as individuals but as employees of one outfit or another. We don't know them because they're Sally Jones or Bill Brown. We know them since they're the travel agent or the gas company representative. So when we deal with Sally and Bill we're really dealing with one corporation or another. Do we owe them the same kind of honesty we owe individuals? And do we get honesty from them?

Maybe it's just as well that getting kids to listen is hard. It's not so clear what we ought to be telling them! Do we urge them to become as educated as possible? Why? We've certainly learned that knowledge can become the enemy as well as the friend of human beings. And we seem to be nearing the end of the road of education as a job advantage. My college degree hasn't helped me much in my work; and it didn't even help me much in getting a job in the first place. Crazy, isn't it?

I realize that this must all sound very cynical. I don't think of myself that way though, and I'm certainly not bitter. But trying to put together what you hope for your children seems to turn up quite a lot of question marks. Certainly I want my kids to feel they belong somewhere, but I'm not sure where. I want them to be able to earn an adequate living, but it's no longer clear what kind of education will do that for them, if any. Certainly they must finish high school, but does college really pay? After all, school is not the real world and maybe kids ought to experience that earlier than we did.

Like everything else, school has become large and impersonal, and I'm not convinced it always has each and every kid's interests at heart. My mother used to say that if she as a student got in trouble with a teacher, her mother always considered it Mom's fault. That's not a sound assumption now, and I'm afraid I've more than once had to step in to get a fair shake from the school for my youngsters. Don't get me wrong: I'm not one of those people who are down on schools and teachers. But they operate like any other big outfit; and individuals—especially the helpless ones—can get trampled on.

The kids don't seem to like school much. Maybe it would be better to say they don't really seem to notice it very much, except to complain about the work. TV is so much more fun and demands nothing of them. I wonder if school has to be so dull. If it were more interesting, maybe the kids would cooperate more willingly and it wouldn't be such a struggle getting them to do school work. Maybe all the hype about excellence will help. It looks like at least it will sort the sheep from the goats so that only the willing are still in school. I just hope my kids are among them! Schools no longer guarantee a decent living, but it's clear enough that not graduating promises a poor one.

If one were seeking a capsule rendering of this report, it might be that "the bloom is off the rose." Certainly, as compared to the parent voices of earlier eras, this one speaks with far less confidence, clarity, certainty. There is a profound sense of instability and rootlessness and confusion about the directions which might lead to better circumstances. Our spokesperson seems convinced only that we can't turn back the clock by reinstating earlier solutions, as some are attempting. This parent explicitly challenges the relevance of old values and verities to contemporary life. We see evidence that doubts and instabilities are considerable, in the individual's private world as well as in the relation to the public sphere. And, unfortunately, in an era when individuals' private worlds sometimes yield so little assurance and support, it must sometimes appear that the public world is undergoing a parallel kind of disintegration. Our contemporary spokesperson bespeaks little faith in institutions—neither in corporations nor in governments nor in schools.

Gone is the American Dream with its bright vision of tomorrow. A sense of opportunity and promise are hard to find as this parent wrestles with the challenge of "What do you want for your children?" Gone is the expectation of upward mobility, the promise that life will be better for the next generation; and gone is the conviction that work and striving will earn one a better life. In fact, effort seems to have no place in this parent's statement. One gets no sense that education is held to be of intrinsic value. The school is acknowledged as a probable condition of employment, but only its gatekeeping functions merit mention. Gone is the conviction so strong in our turn-of-the-century parent that learning and knowing are goals important in themselves. And gone is the sense of the school as beneficent enabler—as facilitator and provider of efficacy and empowerment for its charges.

The resulting challenge to schools and education runs deep. It is not clear that even the most effective of school improvements would solve the problem of our third speaker. Institutional changes would doubtless be welcomed, but the hesitations and perplexities appear fundamental. Our parent of today lacks certainty about the nature of the social world—and whether and how it might be salvaged and what objects and values are worth seeking within it. All these questions appear antecedent to forming any but the most amorphous hopes for children. For one must possess one's own picture or "map" of the world before one can muster much confidence on how to educate, why, or what to educate for. Somehow, we must simultaneously sort out both our social world, *and* the kind of education that will best equip our children for entering and participating in it as adults.

Can schools help with this particular predicament? Or must we now look elsewhere for what earlier generations sought from schools? Or should we be seeking the same things? These are the perplexities to be confronted. Only occasionally does it appear that we can revive the American Dream which for so long articulated a widely shared set of beliefs and values about life and living. For many, education was a central value in the Dream, and school thus a pivotal institution. It remains to be seen what kind of image will take its place and what sort of role education will assume within it. And yet, as we try to confront the challenges of the era and to consider which of the old verities still holds true, we are struck with the enduring wisdom of two thinkers who continue to evoke significant responses: we must still, as Hannah Arendt stressed, strive to maintain and renew a common world.[11] And we must at the same time, as John Dewey insisted, empower the young to become persons in their own right, willing and able to cope with novelty and change.

FOOTNOTES

1. In addition to references cited in the following footnotes, other key sources for our composite voices are: Stephen Birmingham, *The Rest of Us: The Rise of America's Eastern European Jews* (Boston: Little, Brown and Co., 1984); Ingrid Canright, "The Education of Ingrid Canright," *Antioch Review* (Fall 1985): 428-33; Peter Collier and David Horowitz, *The Kennedys: An American Drama* (New York: Summit Books, 1984), chapter 1; Irving Howe and Kenneth Libo, *How We Lived: A Documentary History of Immigrant Jews in America, 1880-1930* (New York: Richard Marek, 1979); Mark Sullivan, *Our Times: The United States, 1900-1925*, vol. 1, *The Turn of the Century* (New York: Charles Scribner's Sons, 1928); "The New-Collar Class," *U.S. News and World Report*, 16 September 1985, pp. 59-63.

2. John Dewey, *The Public and Its Problems* (Athens, Ohio: Swallow Press, 1954), p. 123.

3. Leonard Covello, *The Heart Is the Teacher* (New York: McGraw-Hill, 1958), p. 288.

4. James Sanders, "Education and the City: Urban Community Study," in *Historical Inquiry in Education: A Research Agenda*, ed. John Hardin Best (Washington, D.C.: American Educational Research Association, 1973), p. 223.

5. Clarence J. Karier, *Shaping the American Educational State* (New York: Free Press, 1975), pp. 254-74.

6. Ibid., p. 255.

7. George S. Counts, *Dare the School Build a New Social Order?* (New York: John Day, 1932).

8. "Orientation" (an editorial), *The Social Frontier* 1 (October 1934): 5.

9. Robert S. Lynd and Helen Merrell Lynd, *Middletown in Transition: A Study of Cultural Conflicts* (New York: Harcourt, Brace and Co., 1937), p. 221.

10. Christopher Jencks et al., *Inequality: A Reassessment of the Effect of Family and Schooling in America* (New York: Basic Books, 1972).

11. Hannah Arendt, *Between Past and Future* (New York: Meridian Books, 1954).

CHAPTER IX

Becoming Educated in Contemporary Society

H. S. BROUDY

"School and society" has been a familiar theme on the American educational scene for more than half a century. Courses bearing that name have been fixtures in teacher education programs, while in the public schools "social studies" have been part of the general education curriculum, or "hovered" over it. The reasons for the persistence of these studies and their current uncertain status are fairly obvious. On the positive side is the stark fact that school children will have to live in and with social institutions. It would be foolhardy not to instruct each generation in the ways of these institutions. Equally obvious is the fact that these institutions and their cultural reverberations change rapidly—in some respects, every decade. The foregoing chapters of this Yearbook provide ample evidence for the extent and rate of this change. How, then, is the citizen to become educated in this state of affairs?

Social institutions are organizational embodiments of the basic functions of a society. The family, the community, the professions, industry, the military establishments are parts of a social order. Each has a unique function for which it has special responsibility, but is related to all the others by ancillary functions. Thus hospitals have the special function of ministering to the sick, and ancillary relations with relief agencies and insurance companies. Schools also have a primary function—instruction—and ancillary involvements with health, industry, family life, and the general requirements of citizenship. Chief of these ancillary functions are its surrogate roles, namely to stand *in loco parentis*, *in loco communitatis*, and *in loco humanitatis*. Presumably schools are expected to (a) represent the values of the family, the community, and the race, and (b) communicate them to the young.

What happens when the school becomes unsure of its surrogate roles? When it is no longer clear about the household arrangement, the mores of the community, the quality of life of the nation it is to

247

represent, what is the school to teach? What is the school to teach and represent when such basic ideas as democracy, freedom, justice, civil rights are construed differently by various segments of the population? What is the school to teach about these ideas when they are in continual litigation in the courts and under constant debate in legislatures? And what is the school to teach and represent when technology blurs the borders of nations and continents? Where is the public school to find its public?

These are some of the questions that have to be the themes of the social studies at every level of schooling. The task would be formidable if the answers to these questions were clear and unequivocal. What if the questions themselves are the subjects of political, economic, and philosophical controversy?

If one were to take the questions seriously, what would it mean to become educated in a modern society? Table 1 may serve as an outline of the task.

TABLE 1

VALUE DOMAINS AND THEIR INTERACTIONS

Value Domains / Value Domains	Economic	Health	Recreation	Affectional	Civic	Intellectual	Aesthetic	Moral	Religious
Economic		X	X	X	X	X	X	X	X
Health	X		X	X	X	X	X	X	X
Recreation	X	X		X	X	X	X	X	X
Affectional	X	X	X		X	X	X	X	X
Civic	X	X	X	X		X	X	X	X
Intellectual	X	X	X	X	X		X	X	X
Aesthetic	X	X	X	X	X	X		X	X
Moral	X	X	X	X	X	X	X		X
Religious	X	X	X	X	X	X	X	X	

The horizontal and vertical categories in the table represent selected value domains. Taken by itself, each category in the table also represents a type of experience with a distinctive character and fairly well-defined types of activity. Thus economic values represent the activities involved in production of goods and services, employment, savings, and so forth. Read across, the table maps the relations of each type of value to the others, for example, the relations of economic activities to those of health and recreation. Vertically, each entry represents a distinctive cluster of ideas, acts, feelings, images. These vary in both range and sensitivity. Horizontally, each entry explores the interaction of the several value domains to each other.

Being able to interpret the diagram in all its cells comes close to answering the question of what it means to become educated in a modern society. The diagram could serve as a checklist, not only for curricula in social studies, but for the curriculum of general education.

Each cell represents a body of literature by scholars from which curriculum material is to be culled and adapted to grade levels. There is no inherent impossibility of constructing a curriculum in the schools from K-12 that would educate successive generations in the nature of societies in general and ours in particular. What, then, are the obstacles?

A technical obstacle is the task of selecting from the vast volume of material represented in the table. Perhaps the most troublesome obstacle is the defense of the curriculum against those portions of the citizenry who object to the selection of such materials on one ground or another. The situation is exacerbated in a society that has proclaimed its citizens free to express their preferences and animadversions at the ballot box. This raises an important question, namely, whether there is a nonpolitical criterion for curriculum selection. As will be noted below, this takes us into the nature of authority in general and that of the school in particular.

Furthermore, we live in a society that has also publicly proclaimed its hospitality to immigrants, regardless of political, ethnic, and economic status. The result has been a society in which variety is king and unity a rhetorical phantom.[1] And yet our aim and goal, nationally and repeatedly avowed, is unity in variety, a society in which individuals enjoy the maximum of freedom within agreed upon bounds. It is the nature and extent of the bounds that challenge both theoreticians and politicians in a democracy.

In light of these circumstances, it is not difficult to understand why in the public school immersed in so many swirling currents the social studies are tempted to tread water, shift into neutral, to avoid conflict.

In proclaiming itself to be a "free" society, the United States ruled out autocratic determination of ideology. Industrial revolutions, technological progress, immigration all have conspired to make realization of *e pluribus unum* more and more difficult. Unity has never caught up with social and cultural change. Advances in technology have made the one-world society an impending reality, but the unifying effect of technology has not produced the social unity needed to take full advantage of it.

On the contrary, technology, as the preceding chapters by Wirth, Waks and Roy, and Carnoy tell us, has its own dialectic. While it unifies communication, travel, and industry, it exacerbates differentiation in work roles, gender roles, and political constituencies. While it demands a high order of theoretical and technical ability to create the new technology, it dispenses with the need for the user to understand it. The argument that technology will call for and produce a better educated public is on dubious ground, for the glory of technology is precisely that the user of it need not know how or why it works. The average American household is replete with refrigerators, television sets, microwave ovens, and telephonic gadgets that the inhabitants can neither understand nor repair. To paraphrase Winston Churchill in a somewhat different context, "Never have so many lived so well on the brains of so few."

If to become educated in contemporary society means becoming sophisticated in technology and its artifacts, very few of the citizens will become educated. The same conclusion would follow if the citizenry is expected to become technically or professionally knowledgeable in the other cells of our value table.

The remedy is to formulate a principle or mechanism for unifying diversity without destroying its benefits. The principle, therefore, has to meet the requirements of unity in variety. The arts have struggled with this requirement and have used a number of devices. Repetition of elements, theme and variation, hierarchy, balance are devices used to produce unity. Philosophers have been busy for centuries formulating solutions to the unity-variety problem, an enterprise guaranteed to provide perpetual employment. Religion has also proclaimed norms that unify a society. Metaphysics has postulated superempirical entities to keep the diverse elements in a society on track. Common interests, common values, a common cause (such as war) have all been means for unification. Whether they are successful depends on their acceptance willingly or not by the members of that society. All attempts at unification, therefore, sooner or later are translated into methods for determining the will of the people. Authoritarian societies tend to rely on military power; free societies gauge that will by plebiscites of one sort or another.

Among the numerous factors motivating and directing the will of the people are the diverse commitments to ideologies, and the diversity is as extensive as the table of values itself. Nevertheless, they can be roughly sorted into three requirements for the good society. These are freedom for achievement, justice to keep the competition fair, and compassion for those who end up in misery despite opportunity to achieve and despite justice.

The triple criteria of a good society are themselves heterogeneous. A society that maximizes opportunities for personal achievement will promote progress and be attractive to those with the energy and ability to compete successfully. Chronic losers lose their enthusiasm for the game. If achievement is not evenly distributed, the fairness issue arises. The question whether the superachievers have not taken unfair advantage is raised. History does not lack for instances in which the winners of the race in one generation see to it that their offspring do not have to start the race from scratch. It was this realization that persuaded the Hebrews to institute the Jubilee so that at the end of every fifty years all lands reverted to their original owners and all Hebrew slaves were to be set free.

Why fairness or justice, which promises legally organized fairness, is so fundamental a factor in the notion of good and right is puzzling. The notion has no standing in the subhuman world of plants and animals. Natural selection presumably is indifferent to all but the preservation of the species. Perhaps the notion has its origin in the biological and subsequently the aesthetic demands for formal balance. Balance is required for aesthetic pleasure, but it is also a vector in "rightness" at the same time. Bodies, buildings, activities of all sorts depend on balance for "right" functioning. A disturbed balance needs to be righted, hence the most familiar symbol of justice is a scale in the hands of a blindfolded woman.

For those who argue that power is distributed unequally and not according to merit,[2] equality is a doctrinal sham. They would contend, therefore, that without *egalité* of power, *liberté* and *fraternité* are illusions. Their remedy would have government control the distribution of power so that it will be most just, that is, more fair. That "legal," "just," and "fair" are not synonymous goes without saying.

The drive to achievement need not be incompatible with other than merely selfish ends. It may be the desire to increase knowledge or to serve one's fellows. Justice becomes mixed up with national security and compassion, which may tip the scales more than strict requirements of fairness would dictate. Compassion, too, is more than simple pity when it becomes involved with social costs. Questions as to whether compassion is deserved become intertwined with justice. Conceivably, a score card by which these three criteria are being met by a given society, might be devised, and perhaps even now is on the drawing boards of sociological supercomputers.

Nevertheless, compassion sounds a somewhat discordant note in the trilogy. It has a spontaneous, almost visceral source that is independent of logic. Pity is a response to actual misery and suffering or to reports of them. To enjoy another's misery or to approve it or even ignore it borders on callousness, however much it may be "justified." Some religions make the relief of suffering a duty. In our country sympathy for suffering, when translated into a financial contribution, qualifies for a tax deduction.

Democracy as a Unifying Principle

In free societies democracy is the most frequently cited principle of providing unity in diversity. But the principle itself is subject to a wide variety of interpretations, as this volume demonstrates. The honorific connotations of the term have led Marxists, anti-Marxists, sundry groups of revolutionaries, and bands of terrorists, as well as a wide variety of conservatives, to invoke it.

THE DEWEY CONCEPT OF DEMOCRACY

John Dewey's concept of democracy as a way of communal life and a design for education has had a powerful effect on both education and political theory. To become educated in contemporary society certainly presupposes the willingness and ability to reason with others about social problems in accordance with the rules of Dewey's analysis of the complete act of thought (CAT) as set forth in his *How We Think*.[3] This process not only is supposed to issue in testable hypotheses and convincing conclusions, but agreement on action as well. The method could be used to negotiate value differences, provided the personal dynamics of the participants, that is, differences in motivation and social orientation, were taken into account.[4] However, taking them into account and managing the discussion of them will tax the ingenuity not only of psychologists, but of shrewd group leaders as well. How well-equipped public schools are to do this on a regular basis is problematic. Even if the school could be equipped to do so, should it undertake the functions of promoting social integration? This comes down to the role of the school in society. If one holds that social institutions have a primary function and an ancillary one that relate them to the work of other institutions, then the school should abjure the responsibility for such integration, albeit its primary function (formal instruction in the arts and sciences) might contribute to such a result. If, on the contrary, one's theory of social organization grants to every institution the same agglomerate of functions, then it makes no sense to try to identify the distinctive role of the school. Uncoerced agreement on social problems conducted by the rules of scientific inquiry is a promising formula for rational unification of diversity.

The method presupposes, however, that the participants will not be grossly unequal in wealth, power, and ability to understand the relevant factors in community problems. The free yeomen of Britain and the farmers, artisans, and independent business men of a small New England town were ideal participants in such a process. These conditions are difficult to satisfy in a modern society, especially in urban enclaves. Scientific surveys of the "facts" involved in societal strife rarely eliminate that strife, especially when the disagreement is about fundamental values, which are held independently of the empirical evidence for them.[5]

Nevertheless, it is difficult to envision becoming educated in a modern society without competence in the use of the CAT. For this reason no curriculum can omit some direct experience with molar problem solving in the classroom. Practice in shaping a predicament into a problem (for predicaments do not become problems until they are trussed up for theoretical inquiry), searching for and evaluating relevant hypotheses, devising methods of testing the promising hypothesis are the basic gambits in the inquiry game. There are those who would have the entire curriculum take this form, but whether or not one agrees with this view it is hardly debatable that a strand of any curriculum in general education should be devoted to it.

THE AMERICAN CREED

Another version of the potential of democracy for unification was developed by Gunnar Myrdal, a Swedish economist, in a study of racial problems in the United States.[6] He was impressed by the strange amalgam of ideas and attitudes in the writings of the Founding Fathers and the defenders of the American experiment. He called it the American Creed, a mixture of ingredients drawn from the English common law, certain principles of Christianity, and political philosophies of the Enlightenment.[7] Myrdal regarded the American Creed as embodied in the Declaration of Independence and the Constitution as the most explicit set of ideals a modern society has ever had.

Myrdal noted that rich and poor, conservatives and liberals, invoked it and all the heroes in American history have been reformers in the name of the American Creed. In its name, high-level evaluations (liberty, equality, and what the French later called fraternity) were enunciated. As slogans these norms were so emotionally conditioned as not to be arguable. However, particular policies and legislation were arguable indeed, especially as to their conformity to the Creed. There was also room for disagreement when beliefs about the social reality did not accord with the facts, such as some of the beliefs about race, gender, and economic conditions. When legislation was enacted that was not consistent with the high-level valuations of the Creed, Myrdal argued, a strain toward consistency was set up. It was to this strain that he looked for a steady and reliable pressure for social reform.

However, long ago consistency was branded as the hobgoblin of little minds. Inconsistency in personal behavior is nowadays regarded as evidence of a free, unfettered mind, of a creative personality. Economic conservatives, as interpreted by the editorial board of the *Wall Street Journal*, complain about the "tedious moralism" of the liberals, that is, their insistence on high-level evaluations. It is only on issues such as illicit drugs that high evaluations energize policies and legislation.

The Nature of Self as Unifier

Can the nature of the human self supply the unifying principle? That depends on a shared respect for selfhood, on what it means to be a self. On what grounds can a society demand that citizens respect each other because they are selves? Two relationships between selves might furnish such grounds. One is empathy, by which one self can imagine the feelings of another and thus engender sympathy. A second is respect for selfhood because of its divine origin or because selves are regarded as the loci of moral autonomy. However, sympathy is limited to a small circle; as the circle is enlarged to include persons and conditions remote in space, the range of sympathy required outdistances its capacity for empathy. It may, perversely, expand the targets of antipathy.

The second principle grounds an absolute respect for persons in their ability to subject the will to a moral law. Without such a presupposition, Kant argued, morality as independent of mere inclination would be impossible. From this it follows that selves have an inherent dignity because they become legislators of the moral law, for they are willing that the maxims of their choices become universalized for everyone in similar situations.[8]

This principle would unify a society if such a respect for persons as ends in themselves were accepted by actual societies. It runs counter to theories that define the common good as that which would yield the greatest pleasure to the greatest number or which perfectly rational citizens would judge to be the common good or just in an "original position of equality," that is, before differences in power, status, and the like had developed.[9] Persons as ends in themselves, never to be used as means merely, as Kant would have it, somehow do not figure prominently in theories of society.

Among other principles of unification might be listed the unity of common ancestry, a divine destiny or mission, and not least, a common enemy.

War is a potent force for social unification—if it does not last too long and ends with a victory. Given a "just war," unity is tantamount to duty; lack of it may be fatal. Perhaps it is the power of war to equalize sacrifice that endows it with a moral dimension. Even inequality of sacrifice, under certain circumstances, is justified by the overarching need for victory. A common enemy poses an unambiguous threat; the common good is an abstraction. The common good is subject to diverse interpretations; once the justice of the war is opened to debate, it loses its unifying potency. To use war to suspend debate and unify the populace is a familiar political ploy.

These melancholy conclusions as to the search for unity in variety do not discourage social reformers from seeking legislation to achieve the good society, one that maximizes opportunity for achievement, justice, and compassion. The tensions between formulas for the good society and diverse interpretations of them have to be taken as givens. To become educated in a contemporary society includes the ability to develop understanding both of the formulas and their difficulties.

Schooling for Education in Contemporary Society

As long as diversity on all dimensions of social policy persists, becoming educated in a contemporary society will also propagate a diversity of theories and schemes to accommodate them in the curriculum of the public school. As to content, the problem is the selection from vast amounts of material in the sciences, philosophy, and political theory. What criteria for such a selection can the school defend against political and ideological pressures, especially those that deny the validity of any common required curriculum? If the content is determined, who shall have the responsibility for instructional design, taking into account age, grade, social, and individual differences? This task is worthy of the best cooperative efforts of the academic and educational establishments. Does such cooperation exist?

Unlike the basic physical sciences, the social sciences do not agree on a set of basic concepts or canonical texts. To incorporate sociology, economics, political science, ethics, history, and social psychology as separate courses into an already crowded curriculum of the public school is virtually impossible. Formulating a curriculum design to meet these limitations is the first task. Providing regular exercises in dealing with societal problems in the classroom is the second. One attempt to fashion such a curricular design includes the following strands: symbolics of information; basic concepts of physics, mathematics, chemistry, and biology; developmental strands (of the cosmos, institutions, and cultures); molar social problems; and value exemplars.[10]

This curriculum and dozens of others should be matched against the cells of the value table. Does the curriculum touch on the disciplines that deal with the concerns of each cell? Is it compact enough to meet the time constraints of the school? Is the content such as could reasonably be required of all students, that is, does it qualify as general education?

The latter question touches on the meaning of "general" as used to designate general education. "General" can mean that which is useful to all pupils in a wide variety of tasks. Thus it would be useful for all pupils to be able to repair a leaking roof or faucet or a balky automobile, just as it would be generally useful to be familiar with such institutions as banks, hospitals, and the police, and to be able to read, write, and compute. Curricula have been designed to meet this criterion of generality, and it is a criterion that has strong support. Another meaning of "general" contrasts it with "particular." It denotes abstraction from the particular instances to class characteristics. The difference between the two conceptions is crucial in three ways. First, it affects the theoretical level of the contents of instruction and their putative uses. Usefulness in a variety of tasks promises development of the associative and interpretive uses. Second, the difference in the meanings of general have implications for the role of the school, that is, as a distinctive institution performing a unique function or as an institution that shares its function with other institutions. Third, the meaning of general education leads directly to the issue of validation. The authority to shape the curriculum is claimed by religious, economic, and political groups. In a democracy such groups have the right to try to make their wishes effective through the ballot. This is a form of political authority, *vox populi, vox dei*. Are there and can there be nonpolitical criteria for validating what is to be taught in a public school?

As long as the school was recognized as a surrogate of the family, the community mores, and the values of the general culture, there was little occasion for challenging its authority to fashion instruction. In today's society the challenge is real and in many instances potent. Challenges to textbooks, to books assigned in courses, to books in the school library, and to topics of instruction are frequent. The courts are busy with suits occasioned by these challenges. The controversies over sex education and the teaching of evolution and creationism are typical. Clearly, the citizenry in objecting to this or that item in the curriculum believe they are exercising their right to determine what their taxes should or should not support. It is a political right and ultimately a plebiscite of some sort registers the will of the majority, which, in turn, brings about the desired change in the curriculum or a change of the school board and the superintendent of the schools. On what grounds can the school challenge this authority?

One such nonpolitical authority resides in the consensus of the learned, the scholars who produce and evaluate the content and methods of a particular discipline. Good history, good physics, chemistry, sociology, at any given time, are what scholars in these fields say they are. The disciplinary guilds are the custodians of the criteria for adequacy of theory and modes of inquiry. They are in charge of inducting new scholars into the guild. The elaborate system of degrees, examinations, publications, and debates are all controlled by the consensus of the learned, which has been institutionalized in colleges and universities. The whole apparatus at one time or another has received the imprimatur of the state in the form of charters and legislation.

This does not mean that within the disciplines there is no disagreement, but it does mean that the disagreement must be carried on by the rules of scholarship. That Professor A disagrees with the theories of Professor B does not give to every registered voter the right to disagree with the professors. However, if enough registered voters are determined to get rid of both professors and their institutions, they can do so.

Intellectual authority is in essence not political, although a doctrine may acquire political influence by indoctrination. Adam Smith's theory of economics rests on an intellectual base, which many have accepted on nonintellectual grounds. The so-called Puritan ethic favors the free market philosophy for quasi-religious reasons. Hence it acquired political power among the Puritans. Conversely, free market economics is not popular with those who have religious scruples about usury.[11]

In every value domain, therefore, the intellectual authority rests with the consensus of the learned. The guilds of scientists are the authorities in their special fields; theologians are the arbiters of standards in the study of religious doctrine, and art historians and critics represent a consensus of the learned on the nature and merits of art.

This does not mean that we can teach only what is already known beyond reasonable doubt. In every discipline the consensus of the learned does not abolish doubt and disagreement. Every discipline has its schools of thought, but they do not disagree on the canons of inquiry and scholarship. Indeed, there is more agreement on the methods of inquiry than on its results, and these methods generate the authority of the expert. Those who wish to engage students themselves in inquiry must respect the criteria and methods approved in the respective discipline.

Those who argue that the school has the duty to alert the pupils to understand issues that penetrate their lives are on solid ground, but systematic study of the arts and sciences should demonstrate that such issues exist, and how they should be studied. This does not mean, however, that the public school curriculum should be organized around these issues, or determined by what has been referred to as "creative bargaining" among varying outlooks and perspectives.

The school, when faced with the controversy over evolution and creationism, has to distinguish between the authority of science and that of religion. In the ideal school curriculum the pupil would learn about various types of authority, but not in the same course. Creationism would be encountered in the materials taught in developmental studies, especially the development of institutions and the culture, but not in the biology class. These are subtle but crucial distinctions. If the school does not claim the authority to make them, it loses control of the curriculum and surrenders it to the will of the electorate.

This line of reasoning does not convince those who do not believe that a common school and a common curriculum is defensible in the current state of society. There have been movements to promote alternative schools to meet a variety of needs and preferences. There is a persistent push for vouchers that would allow parents to tender them as tuition in various types of schools. The rationales for these movements differ, but they all have the effect of diluting the meaning of public education by means of common schools. Although excellence and equality as slogans are shared by all schemes for educational reform, the goal of excellence without snobs and equality without slobs has yet to be realized.

To become educated in the contemporary world, finally, will entail attendance at schools in a system conducted by teachers and administrators who can make genuine claims to professional status rather than conventional ones. It will require staffs who have achieved the same understandings and resources deemed essential for the pupil populations. In addition, it will demand professional competence in the various aspects of instruction. There is general agreement that two million or more classroom teachers will not be paid salaries to warrant the time and cognitive strain required to reach genuine professional status. We are discovering that those who are willing to invest their time in doing so can find more lucrative rewards in fields other than teaching. However, it is possible and it may become imperative that between 10 and 15 percent of the classroom teaching personnel be paid sufficiently to become professional rather than to remain in the status of paraprofessional with a bachelors degree. To become educated in contemporary society will require attendance at schools where the materials, instruction, and administration are determined by a consensus of the learned—in education.

Uses of Schooling in Contemporary Society

What does becoming educated mean in terms of schooling? One can learn in places other than the school and by means other than formal instruction. Learning from experience is highly regarded. Learning on the job is the mark of good apprenticeship.

Even in schooling there are different types of learning. Vocational education, for example, is designed to produce specific skills. Skill training involves becoming familiar with the predicaments encountered by the plumber, carpenter, electrician, auto repairer, secretary, and so forth, and the standard methods of coping with them. The skilled worker recognizes the predicament as belonging to a class of similar difficulties and applies the remedy that has been prescribed for that class. Such workers use their training pretty much as learned. It replicates the learning. We all use considerable doses of schooling replicatively: language and computational skills, the multiplication tables, certain facts in history and geography, among others.

Professional education differs from trade training in that it concentrates on the theoretical principles from which the practice of the profession is derived. The professional is expected not only to know how, but why. Professional practice illustrates the applicative use of schooling. The testee is asked to replicate some of what has been studied and to apply it in paradigmatic situations, usually in the form of case studies.

Although public schools, depending on their size and location, do offer vocational programs, their primary responsibility is for general studies. The subject matter for such studies is selected from the arts and sciences and claims to broaden understandings and refine appreciations. The general studies curriculum also contains the tool subjects necessary for decoding the languages in which these arts and sciences are expressed. How are general studies used in postschool life?

General studies are sometimes called liberal studies, but these are not equivalent terms. General, as has been noted, can connote a wide range of usefulness or a level of abstraction. Some subjects, such as mathematics, are general in both senses of the term. Astrophysics may not be. The meaning of "liberal" has more to do with abstraction level than wide application to a variety of tasks commonly encountered in daily life. True to its etymology, liberal connotes freedom, but freedom from what? Aristotle thought it was the education appropriate for those who were free from the obligations to make a living and serve the state. This freedom would insure time and energy to cultivate virtue, that is, the excellence peculiar to man as a human being. Clearly, a very small portion of the population would be free enough to undertake this cultivation of virtue, but then it probably never occurred to Plato or Aristotle that a large portion should be. When we prescribe general education for all the people, do we seriously expect them to cultivate excellence? Was this what democratic education was intended to provide for all the youth of the nation? Does some such expectation account for the general or liberal studies requirements in undergraduate curricula in most colleges? Probably not, for college education is not compulsory and is not regarded as the right of every youth. The college preparatory curriculum is not the only one available. The liberal studies, therefore, retain their somewhat special status. The notion that they should be required of the total secondary school population, therefore, would be unusual, to say the least.

On Aristotle's criterion, namely, that liberal education is for those "free" to undertake it, only college-bound adolescents or the well-to-do retirees qualify. How many of the well-to-do retirees take advantage of their freedom to undertake liberal studies remains to be seen. The adolescent population, especially that portion of it enrolled in college for bachelors degrees, has doubts about devoting their early adulthood to the cultivation of virtue. This is clear from statistics on enrollments in bachelor degree programs in the last decade. As indicated in table 2, there is a trend away from programs in education, English, foreign languages, mathematics, library and archival sciences, psychology, and the social sciences. The increases have been in those

TABLE 2

BACHELOR'S DEGREES CONFERRED BY
INSTITUTIONS OF HIGHER EDUCATION

PROGRAM AREAS	1973-74	1983-84	PERCENT CHANGE*
Business and Management	131,766	230,031	75
Communications	16,250	38,586	137
Computer and Information Sciences	4,756	32,172	576
Education	185,225	92,382	−50
Engineering	42,840	75,732	77
Foreign Languages	18,840	9,479	−50
Health Sciences	41,394	64,338	55
English	55,469	33,739	−39
Library and Archival Sciences	1,164	255	−78
Life Sciences	48,340	38,640	−20
Mathematics	21,635	13,211	−39
Philosophy and Religion	9,444	6,435	−32
Physical Sciences	21,178	23,671	12
Psychology	51,821	39,872	−23
Social Sciences	150,298	93,212	−38

*Minus sign indicates declines.

Source: National Center for Education Statistics, U.S. Department of Education.

bachelor programs that stress business and management, computer sciences, engineering, and life sciences, with the most dramatic increases in computer and information sciences.

Furthermore, in a relatively short time after graduation from high school or college, course content in general studies fades from memory, unless one becomes a teacher of these subjects. The opportunities for applying course work in literature or astronomy to the problems of life are infrequent and irregular, unless one's profession consists in making such applications. Ten years after graduation few college graduates who passed examinations in their courses would care to take these examinations again. Was taking the work in the first place worth the effort? If general studies are to be justified as necessary to becoming educated in contemporary society, it must be on uses other than the replicative and applicative ones.

At least two other uses can be identified: the associative and the interpretive. The associative use calls up ideas, images, feelings from all sorts of experience, including those in school, that give significance to a situation. The interpretive use translates a situation into the concepts of a discipline. It *sites* the situation on a map of conceptual structures. The associative and interpretive resources constitute the individual's allusionary base. Education furnishes that base with resources that function even when the content of school courses can neither be recollected in detail or applied.[12]

On what grounds, however, can one argue for the existence of these unfamiliar uses of schooling? One is the theory of tacit knowing developed by Michael Polanyi; another is the difference between the educated and uneducated response to tasks of interpretation.

Reading comprehension depends on the associative store for meaning. Those who have never studied Latin will not bring to the word "conspiracy" images of breathing together. Foreigners ignorant of English, even with the help of a dictionary, may not be able to construe the locution, "We worked around the clock." It may become mysterious even to English speakers, if digital watches replace the conventional sort altogether. The reading of literary materials, especially poetry, would lose just about all significance were the associative resources inadequate. Hence, at least one meaning of "becoming educated" refers to the breadth and depth of the allusionary base. The items in that store come from ordinary experience, fairy stories, schooling, movies, television, and from the transactions of everyday life. What a stimulus will elicit is explained roughly by the laws of association. When that store contains the ideas and images of the exemplars of the arts and sciences the response is clearly distinguishable from that of the uneducated one.

The difference is even more marked in the interpretive use of schooling. Scholarly disciplines may be likened to stencils that impose their structure on the object. Place the chemistry stencil on a strange disease and it will be translated into the concepts of chemistry such as molecules, atoms, elements, ions. Place the biology stencil on the same disease and a different set of concepts interpret the symptoms and the probable causes. The ability to use the relevant stencils with some facility marks the educated mind.

The notion of knowing with, in contrast to knowing that and knowing how, is closely related to what Michael Polanyi called "tacit knowing." Tacit thinking occurs when mental resources that are not at the focus of attention affect the perception of what is at the focus. One of Polanyi's examples of such cognition is the use of a stereopticon. Two images of an object, taken from slightly different positions, are put into an apparatus that allows the images on the two retinas to merge into one. Polanyi notes that if we concentrate on the two-ness of the picture, the unification will not take place; if we concentrate at the object at focus, we do not sense the doubleness. One or the other becomes focal, while the other becomes subsidiary. Subsidiary contributions are precisely what the images and concepts, including those acquired in school, contribute to the perception and understanding of the object at the focus of our attention. Polanyi argued that focal knowing alone cannot explain the thought processes of scientists like Copernicus or Galileo. He held that the subsidiary resources, which were not explicit, gave intimations of importance that led these great minds to pursue problems that stimulated their discoveries.[13] This is not the occasion for a discussion of Polanyi's theory of knowledge, but it does help to make sense of the ambiguous attitude toward general studies, namely, that they are very valuable yet highly postponable. If we accept the associative and interpretive uses of knowledge as being tacit or serving subsidiarily to understanding what is at the focus of our attention, we are closer to understanding this anomaly. It explains why materials studied in schools are not recollected as learned and yet continue to function in important ways.

Despite the arguments and praise for general education, is it plausible for a person to say, "I don't choose to be an educated person. I can do quite well with the associative resources and interpretive mechanisms of the untutored mind. Commonsense science will do, as will the value systems of the group in which I live. As for the arts, the mass media provide a plentitude of them for little expenditure of mind or money. If, as you say, this education will not provide vocational skills and a better standard of living, why should I exert the effort and time to become educated? Furthermore, as you have already argued, 'never have so many lived so well on the brains of so few.' "

In the contemporary society such an argument is not to be dismissed summarily. General studies cannot guarantee superior economic status, a higher level of morality or citizenship. History is replete with famous counter examples. Are we then not brought to the conclusion that enlightened thinking and cherishing must rest their case on what they *are* rather than on what they *produce*? If these values are not intrinsic, it is difficult to meet the argument of the doubters on extrinsic grounds. General education is not a necessity unless the absence of it impairs the *quality* of experience in all the value domains. However, unless in youth one has had a chance to taste the best that has been thought and said and wrought, one will never sense what the quality of life can be. The school is society's mechanism or institution responsible for seeing to it that the young do experience it.

This may be good rhetoric, but what is this quality of enlightenment that is to be regarded as an intrinsic good? The attempt to define it goes back to Western civilization to the Greeks who, according to Plato, were the discoverers of "man inside man." The means for that discovery, according to the classical tradition, were the literatures of Greece and Rome.[14]

It would be paradoxical indeed if a Yearbook that stressed in chapter after chapter the rapid change in contemporary society should end with an educational prescription that smacks of the eternal verities sought by the classicists. Here is a sample of what these chapters report:

Chapter 1 (Benne): Despite an expressed social commitment to democracy, there is no social consensus on what democracy means, in theory or practice.

Chapter 2 (Waks, Roy): Technology is increasing more rapidly than the citizen's capacity for understanding it and perhaps more rapidly than the experts can control.

Chapter 3 (Wirth): The workplace is at once inconsistent with democratic ideals, inimical to intellectual challenge and growth for most people, and diminishing in its ability to promise employment *at all* for many people in the future.

Chapter 4 (Carnoy): The impact of high technology on the workplace is to exacerbate differences in work status, reward, and gender and racial discrimination.

Chapter 5 (Boulding): Traditional conceptions of the family now apply to only a small minority of households, and men and women are trying to define gender roles for themselves and their children in unexplored territory—what it is to be a man or a woman is not clear in contemporary society.

Chapter 6 (Pratte): In the absence of a "melting pot" in U.S. society, ethnic and religious groups have had to vie for respect without becoming fully "Americanized," a process which often results in sustained oppression and caste-like status for some. Neither *pluribus* nor *unum* benefits from such a hierarchy of values, values which change slowly under challenge from various groups.

Chapter 7 (Tozer): The hierarchy of power in the U.S. arguably is *not* consistent with democratic ideals, and the stability of this condition rests, in part, upon the power of ideology over critical thought; this is in part sustained by media and schools that consistently miseducate the populace with regard to its own interests.

Chapter 8 (Greene, Raywid): Neither the schools nor other educative institutions in society hold promise of social mobility nor personal fulfillment, and it is not clear where else to place hope for one's self and one's children.

These eloquent and on the whole credible analyses of the culture with its variety of internal forces obviously have implications for the curriculum of the public schools. Where in the course of schooling will the pupil learn of this diversity in institutions and ideologies? One alternative is to study these ideologies separately. Yet analyses of society are themselves the product of scholarship in one or more of the disciplines. Should not the study of these disciplines reveal them to the pupil? As to the judgments concerning the validity of these views what recourse has the school but to those fields of study that seek the source and validation of a value and of value systems? Can the public school curriculum find ways and means of including the vast array of historical, scientific, and philosophical studies that have dealt with these issues?

General education has to find a way of including the results of these studies without demanding that they be in the form of separate courses in the curriculum. Nor is it necessary for general education to revert to the study of the literatures of Greece and Rome or the *trivium* of grammar, rhetoric, and logic. The school can supply the resources *with* which to construe the problems of value. In the curriculum described earlier, the strand called "Exemplars" is one way of exhibiting to the student the best that has been wrought and thought in a form that is amenable to formal study. They encapsulate the judgments of a generation of scholars in all the disciplines.

This brings the discussion to the most radical change of all, namely, the way in which the world and its problems are perceived by the citizen. In the small community to which Dewey's method of collective deliberation exemplified the ideal democratic society, the problems and the information relevant to them were available directly to all the participants. The "facts," so to speak, were known to all concerned, or if challenged, could be verified by direct observation.

In today's society very few so-called "facts" are open to direct inspection. It requires elaborate commissions with expensive staffs and months of meetings to determine the facts, which almost routinely are challenged in the courts. The facts cited by the Surgeon General on the effect of cigarette smoking are stoutly challenged by the scientists employed by the tobacco industry. The facts on the dangers of the sale of guns to the citizenry are countered by the Rifle Association's dictum that people, not guns, kill people. The complexity of information matches the complexity of events. Ascertaining the facts becomes more and more a specialized, professional activity. The citizen, however well educated, is dependent on the media reports and interpretation of this plethora of specialized studies.

But what does the citizen bring to these reports? What associative materials and what categories of interpretation are processing what is being heard or read in the media? When economists cannot agree on the nation's future, when experts differ on the meaning of every international incident, what is the citizen to make of the flow of opinion and information coming from the media?

The dependence on media affords a method of testing the distinctions among the several uses of knowledge and schooling. Reading a modern metropolitan newspaper or a general magazine will quickly help to identify areas in which formal schooling was inadequate or lacking altogether. Case studies of college graduates with baccalaureate degrees in different areas showed clearly that in areas where formal coursework was not taken, interpretation of selections taken from a metropolitan newspaper differed markedly from those in which the relevant courses had been taken. Yet there was little to indicate that the successful interpreters were using their formal studies replicatively or applicatively.[15]

A more systematic test would ask the subjects to interpret the relevance of what is read about a subject to all the other cells in the table of values. For example, an article reporting the balance of trade has relevance not only to economic judgments, but to events that have occurred or may occur in matters of health, recreation, and all sorts of interpersonal relationships. If events have national and international reverberations, so have the reports and interpretations of those events by the media. The entertainment media also reflect developments in the various domains. Indeed much of what is purveyed on news programs are items about what is happening in the field of entertainment. And entertainment has economic, political, moral, and religious relevance.

I have discussed elsewhere the citizen's dilemma as being forced to choose between warranted assertion and warranted belief.[16] The situations described in this Yearbook and the difficulty of ascertaining the facts pertaining to their significance force the citizen to rely on impressions of credibility. The citizen is forced to look for signs that warrant belief. What are such signs? Sometimes the judgment is made on appearance, the appearance of a person or an office or a residence. Despite the warnings on the fallibility of appearances, a great many of our judgments are grounded in the congruence of an appearance with an image of sincerity, reliability, status, and other qualities of character. Sometimes the judgment of credibility is made on impressions of consistency, as when there seems to be a contradiction between what a person or a party asserts and the behavior that belies it. A highly paid executive announcing to the press that his firm's work force must be drastically curtailed in order to remain competitive may be telling the truth, but it would be more credible if it were not announced amid the luxurious splendor of his office.

It is difficult to pinpoint the particular learnings that contribute to such judgments, but it is difficult to doubt that highly generalizable images of intellectual, moral, religious, and aesthetic values are involved, and that education has contributed to them.

What then does it mean to become educated in contemporary society? It means acquiring the imagic and ideational resources with which to think about, feel, and evaluate the society in which we live and the societies we shall have to live with. It means a system of schooling that provides these resources in a curriculum that relies on the consensus of the learned for its content. It means also a more systematic collaboration between academics and educators so that the realities of schooling are kept in mind. It means a faith that the search for the "man in man" will reveal a principle of unity that will not destroy the variety of a free society.

Footnotes

1. For a while in the late nineteenth and early twentieth centuries, the melting pot idea, with the help of the public schools, was expected to dissolve these differences so well described in the essay in this volume by Maxine Greene and Mary Anne Raywid. That image has given way to the ideal of ethnic individuality and pluralism, not only in folkways and mores but in language as well. See also, Richard Pratte's chapter on "Social Heterogeneity, Democracy, and Democratic Pluralism."

2. See chapter 7 in this volume, "Elite Power and Democratic Ideals," by Steven Tozer.

3. John Dewey, *How We Think* (New York: D. C. Heath and Co., 1910).

4. R. Bruce Raup, George E. Axtelle, B. Othanel Smith, and Kenneth D. Benne, *The Improvement of Practical Intelligence* (New York: Harper & Bros., 1950).

5. Arthur Wirth, in his chapter on "Contemporary Work and the Quality of Life," asks "Can there be any legitimate incorporation of democratic values within corporate capitalism?"

6. Gunnar Myrdal, *An American Dilemma* (New York: Harper & Bros., 1944).

7. Among the early immigrants to North America were dissidents of various kinds: Quakers, Puritans, Socinians, Anabaptists, as well as indentured servants and African slaves. See Bernard Bailyn, *The Peopling of British North America* (New York: Alfred A. Knopf, 1986).

8. Immanuel Kant, *Fundamental Principles of the Metaphysics of Ethics*, trans. T. K. Abbott (London: Longman's Green & Co., 1926).

9. See John Rawls, *A Theory of Justice* (Cambridge, Mass.: Belknap Press, 1971). Rawls called it the theory of justice as fairness.

10. H. S. Broudy, B. Othanel Smith, and Joe R. Burnett, *Democracy and Excellence in American Secondary Education* (Chicago: Rand McNally, 1964; Huntington, N.Y.: Robert Krieger Publishing Co., 1976).

11. The aura of authority that adheres to the scholarly guilds reflects the implicit claims of the intellectual values to pass on the truth claims of all the other value domains. The scholarly guilds were once thought to possess arcane knowledge by which the several professions were taught to minister to the special needs of the public. They were to be the intercessionaries in crises that threatened the health, liberty, or salvation of the citizen. These professionals were under oath to minister to those who needed their services regardless of the beneficiaries' ability to pay for them. This earned honor and status for the professional as well as the gratitude of the beneficiary. Scholarly and professional guilds retain this special status, but are reluctant to rely on gratuities for compensation.

12. Interpretation in this sense covers the preferred definition of interpret: "to explain the meaning of." It includes "to conceive in the light of individual belief," but is narrower in that the belief in question is drawn from the academic disciplines. It does not include "to represent by means of art" or "bring to realization by means of performance." The main force of my use of the term is to distinguish interpretation from the random collection connotated by association.

13. Cf. Michael Polanyi, *Personal Knowledge* (Chicago: University of Chicago Press, 1958), and idem, *The Tacit Dimension* (New York: Doubleday & Co., 1966).

14. Cf. Werner Jaeger, *The Greeks and the Education of Man* (Annandale-on-Hudson, N.Y.: The Bard College Papers, 1953).

15. Cf. H. S. Broudy, *Case Studies in the Uses of Knowledge* (Chicago: Spencer Foundation, 1982). Ed 224-015.

16. H. S. Broudy, *Truth and Credibility: The Citizen's Dilemma* (New York: Longman, 1981).

Name Index

269

Subject Index

INFORMATION ABOUT MEMBERSHIP IN THE SOCIETY

There are two categories of membership, Regular and Comprehensive. The Regular Membership (annual dues in 1987, $20) entitles the member to receive both volumes of the yearbook. The Comprehensive Membership (annual dues in 1987, $40) entitles the member to receive the two-volume yearbook and the two current volumes in the Series on Contemporary Educational Issues. For their first year of membership, full-time graduate students pay reduced dues in 1987 as follows: Regular, $16; Comprehensive, $36.

Membership in the Society is for the calendar year. Dues are payable on or before January 1 of each year.

New members are required to pay an entrance fee of $1, in addition to annual dues for the year in which they join.

Members of the Society include professors, researchers, graduate students, and administrators in colleges and universities; teachers, supervisors, curriculum specialists, and administrators in elementary and secondary schools; and a considerable number of persons not formally connected with educational institutions.

All members participate in the nomination and election of the six-member Board of Directors, which is responsible for managing the affairs of the Society, including the authorization of volumes to appear in the yearbook series. All members who have contributed to the publications of the Society are eligible for election to the Board of Directors.

Each year the Society arranges for meetings to be held in conjunction with the annual conferences of one or more of the major national educational organizations. All members are urged to attend these sessions. Members are also encouraged to submit proposals for future yearbooks or for volumes in the series on Contemporary Educational Issues.

Further information about the Society may be secured by writing to the Secretary-Treasurer, NSSE, 5835 Kimbark Avenue, Chicago, Ill. 60637.

RECENT PUBLICATIONS OF THE NATIONAL SOCIETY FOR THE STUDY OF EDUCATION

1. The Yearbooks

Eighty-fifth Yearbook (1986)
> Part 1. *Microcomputers and Education.* Jack A. Culbertson and Luvern L. Cunningham, editors. Cloth.
> Part 2. *The Teaching of Writing.* Anthony R. Petrosky and David Bartholomae, editors. Cloth.

Eighty-fourth Yearbook (1985)
> Part 1. *Education in School and Nonschool Settings.* Mario D. Fantini and Robert Sinclair, editors. Cloth.
> Part 2. *Learning and Teaching the Ways of Knowing.* Elliot Eisner, editor. Cloth.

Eighty-third Yearbook (1984)
> Part 1. *Becoming Readers in a Complex Society.* Alan C. Purves and Olive S. Niles, editors. Cloth.
> Part 2. *The Humanities in Precollegiate Education.* Benjamin Ladner, editor. Paper.

Eighty-second Yearbook (1983)
> Part 1. *Individual Differences and the Common Curriculum.* Gary D Fenstermacher and John I. Goodlad, editors. Paper.
> Part 2. *Staff Development.* Gary Griffin, editor. Paper.

Eighty-first Yearbook (1982)
> Part 1. *Policy Making in Education.* Ann Lieberman and Milbrey W. McLaughlin, editors. Cloth.
> Part 2. *Education and Work.* Harry F. Silberman, editor. Cloth.

Eightieth Yearbook (1981)
> Part 1. *Philosophy and Education.* Jonas P. Soltis, editor. Cloth.
> Part 2. *The Social Studies.* Howard D. Mehlinger and O. L. Davis, Jr., editors. Cloth.

Seventy-ninth Yearbook (1980)
> Part 1. *Toward Adolescence: The Middle School Years.* Mauritz Johnson, editor. Cloth.
> Part 2. *Learning a Second Language.* Frank M. Grittner, editor. Cloth.